46188

786

THE
SYNTHESIZER
&ELECTRONIC
KEYBOARD
HANDBOOK

THE
SYNTHESIZER
& ELECTRONIC
KEYBOARD
HANDBOOK

DAVID CROMBIE

PAN BOOKS · LONDON AND SYDNEY

The Synthesizer and
Electronic Keyboard
Handbook was conceived,
edited and designed by
Dorling Kindersley Limited,
9 Henrietta Street,
London WC2E 8PS

Project editor
Phil Wilkinson
Art editor
Nicholas David Harris
Designer
Julia Harris
Illustrator
Gary Marsh
Managing editor
Alan Buckingham
Art director
Stuart Jackman

This paperback edition first
published in Great Britain in
1985 by
Pan Books Limited
Cavaye Place, London SW10
9PG

Copyright © 1984 by
Dorling Kindersley Limited,
London
Text copyright © 1984 by
David Crombie

ISBN 0 330 28681 1

Printed in Italy by arrangement
with Graphicom, Vicenza

CONTENTS

FOREWORD

It was a rainy Friday afternoon, not that long ago. I was 15, and I struggled through London rush-hour traffic to catch the bus home, clutching under my arm the object of my wildest fantasies: a secondhand Micro Moog synthesizer in an old cardboard box. It cost me a good few months' savings, and only played one note at a time (usually out of tune). These days the same amount of cash would easily have bought me a portastudio, a drum box, and a simple polyphonic synthesizer, the bare essentials for an eighties songwriter. Yet when I started out, synthesizers were a comparative rarity.

In those days the big problem was affording one, whereas now the hardest thing is choosing one from the scores of different models on the market to suit your particular needs, and safeguarding your investment in an age when every month seems to bring a tide of new machines that render the previous generation totally obsolete.

If you feel at all perplexed by the incredible array of hardware in the shops, then maybe this book will put it all into perspective. It takes a long look at everything that's available, the good and bad points of each instrument and the new possibilities of expansion through home computers and the MIDI interface system now adopted by the major manufacturers. It's also a comprehensive guide to the most important keyboard players of this century and their contributions to the music scene. Today, they've practically taken over, pushing the guitar into the back seat after a reign of twenty or thirty years.

Before you spend your cash, read this book, study what it has to say, and think hard. Then pick out the machine of your dreams . . . and borrow one!

THOMAS DOLBY

INTRODUCTION

Music reflects the technology of the day. From the piano in the eighteenth century to the electronic keyboards of the seventies and eighties, musical instruments have appeared because of technological advances. They have also influenced the ways music is written and played.

So each new generation of instruments sets new challenges. This book is designed to help you face the challenges set by current electronic keyboard instruments.

How the book works

This book is divided into four main sections. The first, *Sound and electricity*, gives you basic information about how sounds are formed and how electricity works. The next section, *The instruments,* looks at the keyboards themselves. It starts with early keyboards and the acoustic piano. The piano, as well as being an important instrument in its own right, is an ideal instrument on which to learn keyboard playing. Then the section goes on to the electronic instruments themselves – from simple portable keyboards, to complex computerized synthesizers. The third section, *Playing technique*, tells you about music – from basic musical notation to playing quite complex chords. The last main section looks at the techniques of *Amplification and recording.*

The history of keyboard playing

The next few pages chart the course of keyboard playing through the twentieth century, to show how earlier styles have led to those of today's players. Most of the musicians included in this introduction are more than just piano players, organists, or electro-pop stars – they are people who have influenced our whole approach to keyboard music and how it is played.

We start with ragtime, from which so much pop music stems, and go on to the various styles of jazz piano, before looking at rock and roll. The worlds of rock and jazz-rock are covered next, followed by electronic music, and the synth-pop sound of current bands.

◁ **Herbie Hancock** From his acoustic days in Big Band Jazz, to his more recent electronic ventures, Herbie Hancock's musical abilities have led him through most forms of modern music.

◁ **Thompson Twins** One of the first "Art School Bands" of the eighties, the Thompson Twins (far left) have had remarkable successes with their refreshingly clean rock sound.

▽ **Ultravox** Their unique electronically produced timbres, used within strong rock and ballad themes, have made Ultravox a pioneering musical unit.

◁ **Vince Clark**
After becoming famous with Yazoo, Clark has consolidated his position as a first-rate keyboard artist.

△ **Thomas Dolby**
Much of Dolby's success comes from very intelligent use of electronic keyboards to create atmosphere.

Ragtime and boogie woogie

At the beginning of this century there were really only two popular piano-playing styles. On the whole, the more sophisticated musicians in more elegant venues played ragtime, while boogie woogie was the music of clubs and saloons.

Both styles were created by black musicians in the US – many of whom were professionally trained and some of whom became classical concert artists and teachers. In contrast to popular opinion, their music was not crude and primitive. Ragtime is a sophisticated style. It consists of an early form of "stride" left hand, with a highly syncopated melodic right hand.

Ragtime pianist **Scott Joplin** (1868-1917) was one of the trained musicians. His compositions are skilfully constructed and, unlike much later jazz, intended to be played as written. "Maple Leaf Rag" was his best known composition until the film *The Sting* (released in 1973) popularized more of his music.

Boogie woogie was a cruder style, typified by a hard-driving left-hand based on repeated chords or figures, with a florid right-hand part that was also often repetitive. The style gave the player a powerful rhythm, which, in the days before electric amplification, could be heard above the noise in the bars where it was played.

Early jazz pianists

Most early jazz was improvised, so we know it only from recordings made on the paper rolls used for player pianos, and from disks made later, in the twenties. Many of the most successful early jazz pianists used the left-hand playing style that is called stride.

Probably the best known of these early pianists is **Ferdinand "Jelly Roll" Morton** (1885-

◁ **Master of ragtime** Both pianist and composer, Scott Joplin was the leading musician of the ragtime style. Ragtime, unlike most jazz, was not improvised music. But the practice of improvising on ragtime themes started early and ragtime became one of the most influential styles of the early twentieth century.

1941). In his early days he played in the brothels of New Orleans' famous Storyville district, and later in Memphis, St Louis, and Kansas City.

The increasing use of the gramophone in the twenties coincided with the spread of jazz. Two of the most outstanding pianists of this time were **Thomas "Fats" Waller** (1904-43) and **Earl Hines** (1905-83). Waller, who developed the stride style, became one of the world's most popular performers, because of his extrovert singing and his many successful compositions, like "Honeysuckle Rose" and "Ain't Misbehavin'".

Earl Hines is one of the supreme technicians of piano jazz and one of the most inventive improvisers. He began playing in clubs while still at school and had his own big band by the time he was 23, though later he worked with smaller groups. His playing style is extremely fluent, with the two hands often working independently. He had

a vast number of followers and in the early thirties was probably the most highly regarded of all jazz pianists.

In terms of sheer skill Hines was second only to **Art Tatum** (1910-57), whose dexterity was such that even the greatest classical pianists were daunted by his technique. But dexterity alone is not enough; Tatum was a superb musician whose recordings are among the most expressive to be found anywhere in any type of music.

A pianist who was even more influential than Tatum was **Teddy Wilson** (born 1912). After playing with local bands in Detroit, he joined Benny Carter in New York, where he made records that brought him international fame. He went on to play in the Benny Goodman trio with Gene Krupa in 1935.

His distinctive playing style was – and still is – apparently very simple. It is economical, swinging, and inventive, and has little technical complexity. Because of this seeming simplicity, his style was imitated widely by thousands of pianists in the thirties and forties.

Other styles

Although the stride left-hand dominated piano playing in the thirties, there was one outstanding player who did not depend on it – **William "Count" Basie** (1904-84). The characteristic Basie sound consists of deceptively simple, apparently casual solo passages inserted into the music of his own big band. It's a style that is difficult to describe but easy to recognize.

With the rise of the double bass, increasingly used with amplification to give a rhythmic pulse, it was not so necessary to use the piano as a rhythm instrument. This led players to try different left-hand styles, such as Basie's technique, and the

repeated guitar-like chords of **Erroll Garner** (1921-77). At the same time, improvisation became more and more adventurous, producing the style known as *bebop*.

Bebop pianists improvised much more freely than before. They departed quite radically from the chord structures of their original themes, in pursuit of striking effects. The most important innovators in this style were **Bud Powell** (1924-66), **Horace Silver** (born 1928), and **Thelonious Monk** (1920-83).

Monk became well known only in the fifties. While most jazz players tend to discard the melody and improvise on the chords alone, Monk rarely loses touch with the melody but often modifies the harmony radically. Many consider him to be one of the most important pianists in

modern jazz, although some people find his rather angular style hard to enjoy.

Jazz individualists

In any jazz hall of fame one pianist has a special place. Canadian **Oscar Peterson** (born 1925) is probably the jazz pianist most widely known to the general public. After a performance at the Carnegie Hall in 1949 his fame spread rapidly, and he has since appeared all over the world. His style has many sources – a single Peterson concert can include stride playing, boogie woogie, bop, and other styles, but he transforms them all into a type of music that is uniquely his own.

Another player who does not fit easily into categories is British pianist **George Shearing** (born 1919). He has developed a distinctive playing technique that is known as "locked hands". This consists of playing the melody with close harmony with the right hand, and doubling it an octave below with the left. The basic pulse is left almost entirely to the double bass and the guitar.

The style of **Dave Brubeck** (born 1929) owes a lot to Art Tatum. Brubeck and his octet were outrageous in their use of rhythm and harmony, and for this reason they weren't really accepted in the jazz world. But the later Dave Brubeck Quartet won international fame, especially with the album "Time Out". This contained two of Brubeck's best known works, "Take Five" and "Blue Rondo". Brubeck's mastery of the keyboard is based on his use of chord clusters. This makes his sound unique and the voicings are so good that the clusters never sound muddy. More recently, Brubeck has been playing with his sons. The freshness of their approach has influenced Brubeck's music.

▷ **Popular jazzman** Dave Brubeck's "Time Out" was the first jazz album to sell a million copies. It broke many of the jazz rules, featuring all-original compositions and using oblique time signatures, but this originality probably made it more, rather than less, successful. Brubeck made this album with the Dave Brubeck Quartet. He now plays with his three sons in the New Brubeck Quartet.

Rock and roll

In the fifties, the real problem that faced piano players was their immobility on stage. Guitarists could leap around the stage at will, but the piano and its player were rooted to the spot. Rock and roll changed all this. Pianists who once sat quietly behind their keyboards jumped on to their instruments and even danced on the lid. Anarchy had arrived.

Jerry Lee Lewis (born 1935) was one of the no-nonsense rock pianists of the fifties. He realized that to be noticed you have to be a showman. He taught himself to play, and his technique was limited. But the important thing is the emotion he conveys when he is playing.

· Lewis' gospel background is clear from his early recordings. His break came when he met Sam Phillips of Sun Records, who realized that Lewis could pro-vide exactly the quality missing from the Sun sound. Lewis' solid, rhythmic style is best heard in his solos on "Hound Dog" and "Jail House Rock".

His most successful record was probably "Great Balls of Fire", which got to No. 2 in the US and to No. 1 in Britain. He made film appearances in *Disk Jockey Jamboree* and *High School Confidential*, and these spread his fame still further. But in 1958 his career was almost destroyed by the bad publicity he received when he married his thirteen-year-old cousin.

Little Richard (born 1935) also has a gospel background. On his first recordings he was primarily a rhythm and blues vocalist. But he played piano on some tracks, including the classic "Tutti Frutti", which featured his typical "high-speed" technique. He followed this with other well known tracks, such as "Good Golly Miss Molly", "Tru Fine Mama", and "Long Tall Sally".

▽ ▷ **Rock and roll showman** Jerry Lee Lewis (below) is famous for his rhythmical style and on-stage acrobatics. Rhythm was also important for Little Richard (right). Sometimes he would keep punching out the same chord for as long as 30 seconds.

In the studio, Richard's voice often turned out to be too strong – his voice simply drowned out the piano. To overcome this problem, he had to use stand-in pianists. But his style was so widely copied that there was no difficulty in finding substitutes.

By the end of the fifties piano style had changed. There was more emphasis on right-hand melodic playing. Danny and the Juniors' "At the Hop" (1957) is a good example. **Walter Gates,** the pianist on this recording, "opened up" rock piano style.

The Hammond organists

It was only in the early sixties that rock players began to see the full potential of the Hammond organ. **Brian Auger** (born 1939) was at the forefront in promoting the organ in the guitar-based rock world. He moved from piano to organ in the same year as he formed Brian Auger's Trinity. Vocalist Long John Baldry and Rod Stewart worked with the Trinity and Julie Driscoll later joined the outfit, which was renamed Steampacket. The band released several albums between 1964 and 1966, primarily featuring Auger's jazz-based rhythm and blues sound.

Auger continued to work with Julie Driscoll, and in 1968 they released Dylan's "This Wheel's on Fire", one of the first recordings to use the studio effect of "phasing". It enjoyed international success, and hallmarked Auger's organ sound.

A popular organist at this time was **Manfred Mann,** though he originally started as a pianist. Mann's style was strongly influenced by such players as Dave Brubeck and George Shearing (see p. 9). His style sustained the band through many of their 15 hit singles, but when rhythm and blues became less dominant, Mann himself withdrew from the front line.

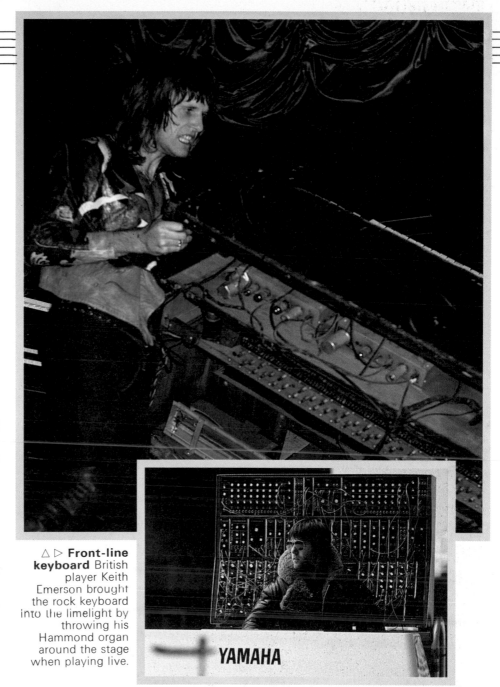

△ ▷ **Front-line keyboard** British player Keith Emerson brought the rock keyboard into the limelight by throwing his Hammond organ around the stage when playing live.

The rock keyboard players

The sixties and seventies saw the evolution of a vast new musical culture – rock. This period was also to see the dawn of the most dramatic change in musical technology. Of all types of instrument, the keyboard was changed most by this. For players, the challenge was both to master the new idiom of rock and to come to terms with the technology.

Among rock keyboard players, two British names dominate the period – Keith Emerson and Rick Wakeman. With Patrick Moraz, these players set the pace for over a decade.

Keith Emerson

It was Keith Emerson who did most to promote the keyboard as a rock instrument. He arrived on the scene at the right time, displayed an amazing talent, and had an element of bravado gleaned from the rock and roll pianists of the fifties.

Like many aspiring musicians keen to form his own group, Emerson soon put together his own three-man jazz-pop outfit (the Keith Emerson Trio). But he was dogged with the problem of most piano players. He couldn't tour with his own instrument, and had to rely on the piano and amplification system at each venue. So he decided to invest in an electric organ, and bought a Hammond L100.

Electric organ players were still rare, and this fact helped Emerson get an invitation to join the T-Bones, a rhythm and blues band with lead singer Gary Farr. It was at this time that Emerson began to evolve his dominating stage presentation, using the Hammond as a musical instrument, a sound-effects generator, and a vaulting horse. This earned him a reputation, but his keyboard talent was such that he could not simply be condemned for frivolity.

Hitherto, the keyboard had never been a true front-line instrument like the guitar – the keyboard player was always rooted to his instrument. Emerson changed this by throwing the Hammond round the stage.

Emerson's next band was the Nice, and with them he really moved center-stage. The histrionics and gymnastics were stepped up to dizzier heights. He would use knives to sustain notes on the keyboard, then, while riding the L100 across the stage as if it were a horse, he would bury knives in the speaker cabinets. He would pour lighter fuel over the organ and set fire to it, and play it from behind, inside, or even with it lying on top of him. Yet, unbelievably, he seemed to maintain control over the final sound.

Emerson next joined forces with Carl Palmer and Greg Lake to form another keyboard-based trio called Emerson Lake and Palmer. Emerson now started to make full use of electronics. He had a Moog modular synthesizer and was determined to take advantage of the vast range of timbres and sounds it offered. In some cases the instrumenta-

tion actually dictated the themes of the songs. Emerson was also the first to take a Moog modular system on tour – a risky thing considering the delicacy and instability of the early models. Despite the complexity, he was able to control all the synthesizer's parameters while still playing live on stage.

The album "Tarkus" (1971) was perhaps the most original rock album of the seventies. Not only did it use electronic voicings never heard before, but it contained chord sequences and rhythmic patterns of a complexity and originality that defeated all would-be imitators.

Emerson's output with ELP was more mature than with the Nice. He showed that he had ability as both performer and arranger, the synthesizer allowing him to construct music more accurately. But he was drawn to the use of an orchestra to augment the ELP sound still further. This proved a financial burden and eventually led to the group disbanding.

Rick Wakeman
Originally set on becoming a concert pianist, Rick Wakeman went to London's Royal College of Music when he was 16. But he was soon attracted to the world

of club and pub playing, and from this started to do a lot of session work.

Over the following two years he did over 3000 sessions, featuring on such recordings as Cat Stevens' "Morning Has Broken" and David Bowie's "Space Oddity". He left the studio circuit to join first the Strawbs and then Yes.

But Wakeman's strength was working on his own and in 1973 he recorded his first solo work, "The Six Wives of Henry VIII". This was followed by an album based on Jules Verne's book *Journey to the Center of the Earth,* and another concept album, "The Myths and Legends of King Arthur". The live premiere of the latter took place in London's Empire Pool in 1975 and was performed on ice. The work used choirs and an orchestra with 45 players. It was a financial disaster, and it took Wakeman a long time to overcome the ridicule that the music press made of the project.

At this time Wakeman started to make use of the new-technology keyboard instruments. He added Moog synthesizers and instruments such as a Mellotron to his musical arsenal. To recreate the studio sound he found he had to take fourteen keyboards on

◁ **Rock soloist**
After working with Yes Rick Wakeman followed a solo career. Among his more recent solo albums have been "Rhapsodies" and "1984".

tour, making him one of the first multi-keyboard players.

Wakeman has continued to produce solo albums, and also rejoined Yes in 1977 to make "Going for the One".

Patrick Moraz

Swiss-born Patrick Moraz came on to the scene a little later than Emerson and Wakeman, and today he is still a major force in the music world. He replaced Emerson in the Nice at the beginning of the seventies, and later took Wakeman's place in Yes.

During his time with Yes he recorded an unusual solo work, "The Story of i", based on his own short story. Moraz had previously worked with a Brazilian singer and had been on tour with the Brazilian ballet. He had become fascinated by the South American approach to rhythm and tone color. The "i" album used Latin and rock rhythms in a unique fusion.

But Moraz's true talent shows itself on "Future Memories". This was designed as an experiment in instant composition. His keyboard rig was set up in front of a Swiss television crew, and Moraz performed live for 25 minutes in front of both cameramen and recording engineers. The album was released with no overdubs yet the depth and complexity Moraz achieves puts most studio artists to shame.

Moraz later joined the reformed Moody Blues. Although their first album together was not a great success, Moraz proved himself to a be master all-rounder on "Long Distance Voyager", a No. 1 album in 1981 in the US.

Geoff Downes

Currently heading the "super-group" Asia, Geoff Downes is a multi-keyboard player of the old school – "techno-flash" was the word used to describe his style in the seventies. He certainly

◁ **Technique and technology** Multi-keyboard player Geoff Downes (left) has always displayed an impressive mastery of hardware. He is also one of the few keyboard players of recent years who owe a lot to a producing background. Patrick Moraz (below left) is another impressive musician who, like Downes and Rick Wakeman, has played with the band Yes.

lives the part when on stage with Asia, using as many as 20 different keyboards.

In the days before programmable instruments, players had to take a large number of keyboards on stage, simply because there wasn't enough time to reset sounds. But with modern programmable synthesizers is such extravagance really necessary? Downes has certainly received some criticism for his stage ensemble. He justifies the arrangement by reference to the multi-layered "wall of sound" he uses with Asia.

Geoff Downes' musical career started with production work in London with fellow producer Trevor Horn. Having worked to-

gether for several years, they released an album of their own, "The Age of Plastic", under the name "The Buggles". The hit single "Video Killed the Radio Star" was a massive international success for them.

In an unlikely move, Horn and Downes replaced Jon Anderson and Rick Wakeman in Yes, as vocalist and keyboard player respectively. They can be heard on the band's "Drama" album. Downes brought the Yes sound back full circle, with powerful organ chords used as a rhythmic device. But the association with Yes was not to last, and when the opportunity came to form Asia with Steve Howe (who had played with Yes in the past), John Wetton, and Carl Palmer, Downes made the move.

Elton John

Electronics may have replaced acoustic instruments in many forms of popular music, but the acoustic piano still has unique qualities of expressiveness. One artist to make full use of the traditional acoustic piano in rock music is Elton John.

Elton John first started to show interest in the piano at the age of four. By the time he was sixteen he was working as a pub pianist as well as playing with his first band, Bluesology. The band was reasonably successful as a backing group to visiting American soul singers and in 1966 was signed up to back blues singer Long John Baldry.

This partnership did not last long and John joined Liberty records, where he was teamed up with lyricist Bernie Taupin. By the time they produced their third album, ''Tumbleweed Connection'' (1979), John and Taupin had perfected their style. They also had the services of producer Gus Dudgeon, together with Dee Murray on bass and Nigel Olsson on drums. It was this combination that proved successful and ''Tumbleweed Connection'' marked the big breakthrough for Elton John, especially in the US.

Albums and chart successes have followed continuously ever since. John has an outstanding talent for simplicity. ''Song for Guy'' demonstrates this: it features only John on piano and string synthesizer, backed by a rather average drum machine. But there is such emotion in his playing that you don't notice the flat, repetitive rhythm track unless you listen for it.

Elton John's live performances were outrageous. His costumes became increasingly glamorous, but it was his eyeglasses that became his trademark – they got larger and larger. His appearance as the ex-pinball wizard in Ken Russell's film production of

Pop pianist What Keith Emerson did for rock keyboards, Elton John (right above and center) did for pop piano. His glamor is unsurpassed and his style unique.

▷ **Complete musician** Singer, keyboard player, songwriter, and composer, Stevie Wonder (right) has probably achieved more than any other solo performer in rock and pop music.

Tommy took this image to its farthest extreme.

Stevie Wonder

From a poor, black family, Stevie Wonder was blind from birth. But, in spite of these apparent handicaps, he has set about creating his own brand of music and was a top recording star by the age of thirteen.

By the age of 21 he had sold over 30 million records, and his 1972 tour of the US with the Rolling Stones was to give him a wider audience still. It was at this time that he started to take complete control over the composition, arrangement, and production of his entire output.

Although he is considered primarily as a singer-composer, the keyboard plays an important part in Stevie Wonder's sound. A hallmark of his earlier works was his rhythmic use of the Clavinet – he has probably done more than any other player to promote the use of this instrument. More recently he has been experimenting with computer musical instruments.

Jazz-rock keyboard players

The world of jazz-rock keyboard playing has been dominated for some years by five Americans – Joe Zawinul, George Duke, Herbie Hancock, Jan Hammer, and Chick Corea. All five have made use of the latest technology without forsaking completely the acoustic piano. They have done a lot to promote keyboard instruments and have shown that electronics are completely valid in music – they can be just as expressive as conventional instruments, and often more so.

Herbie Hancock

In "Headhunters" (1973), Herbie Hancock produced one of the most popular jazz-rock albums ever. But he had been a jazz musician for years before this.

He worked with legendary jazz trumpeter Donald Byrd, who helped persuade the record company Blue Note to let Hancock record his own album. This album featured the classic track "Watermelon Man", which established Herbie Hancock's musical reputation.

In the sixties, Hancock discovered the new wave of electronic instruments, and quickly became one of the country's leading multi-keyboard players. He was also an established session player, playing in many memorable advertising jingles, as well as writing the score for Antonioni's film *Blow Up*.

Recently, he has enjoyed yet more success in the charts. He is now experimenting with computer systems such as the alphaSyntauri and Fairlight CMI.

△ **Jazz-rock master** Herbie Hancock is one of the most versatile keyboard players. The styles he has used range from acoustic jazz to electric funk and electro-pop. The many musicians he has worked with include Freddie Hubbard, Eric Dolphy, and Miles Davis.

Joe Zawinul

As keyboard player with the jazz-rock group Weather Report, Joe Zawinul has been responsible for some remarkable original work. He was one of the first players to use a synthesizer and one of his most impressive skills lies in getting it to sound like other instruments. He is especially good at producing faithful string sounds.

Zawinul has made some comments about imitating other instruments: "I think that everyone plays what they hear. I know what I want to hear and I know I can duplicate that sound. There's a certain way you have to play those sounds. I was a violin player, so I know the nature of how to play it. There's a certain way of playing a violin; with the right hand there's the gravity factor, and with the left hand you have vibrato. That's what I'm thinking about when I record a string line."

Technically, Zawinul is a master keyboard player. He also likes experimenting. He once inverted the keyboard of his synthesizer, so that the top notes played the low frequencies and the bottom notes played the high ones. He then used this "mirrored" keyboard to improvise and from this he evolved the song "Black Market" from the album of the same name.

George Duke
Duke Ellington was the player who first interested George Duke in the piano. His love of jazz stayed with him when he studied at San Francisco conservatory and led him to work with Dizzy Gillespie and Bobby Hutcherson.

Since then, Duke has probably cut more tracks than any other keyboard player of his generation. He has worked with almost every jazz-rock artist. He is a true multi-keyboard player; his work with synthesizers is particularly impressive. He makes full use of both the rhythmic and the melodic qualities of the instrument.

Duke was the first keyboard player to "go mobile" by using the keyboard controller called the Clavitar. This enables him to wear a keyboard on a strap exactly like a guitar.

Jan Hammer
The "Jan Hammer synthesized guitar sound" is famous for its incredible accuracy. Hammer has studied the synthesizer deeply and his style and understanding of voicing on this instrument is second to none.

Hammer was born in Czechoslovakia, but emigrated to the US, where he started by playing in strip joints and clubs, before getting a job as pianist for Sarah Vaughan and then in 1972 joining John McLaughlin's Mahivishnu Orchestra. It was here that he made his mark, developing his stage persona and his playing technique.

Many people think of Hammer as a frustrated guitarist. He spends much of his time imitating guitar licks and, like George Duke, plays a synthesizer keyboard suspended from a strap around his neck. Ten percent of the secret of his sound comes from the fact that he uses a Minimoog together with an Oberheim expander module and employs a lot of distortion. But the other ninety percent derives from sheer technique. In particular he uses the synthesizer performance controls brilliantly.

Chick Corea
The last of this group of players, Chick Corea found his way into jazz via bepop and, unlikely as it may seem, through classical music. He served an "apprenticeship" with Miles Davis in the sixties and also worked with Stan Getz and Herbie Mann.

Corea made a successful solo album called "Return to Forever" in 1972. Following this, he formed a band of the same name.

Chick Corea's style has many facets – one night he will be performing chamber music, the next playing with an electronic jazz trio. He has also entered the world of computer music.

▷ **Keyboard controller** Since he often makes guitar-like sounds with his synthesizers, George Duke's use of the Clavitar controller is quite appropriate.

◁ **All-rounder**
With a background in both classical music and jazz, Chick Corea is still a very versatile performer. Recently his band Return to Forever was re-formed, and the magic created by Corea and Al diMeola on guitar was still there for all to hear and see.

The electronic soloists and arrangers

Some of the most influential players have made their reputations as soloists and arrangers. These include Walter Carlos and Tomita, famous for their very different arrangements of classical music, and figures such as Vangelis and Beaver and Krause, who have produced a variety of solo albums in their own right, as well as music for various movies.

Walter Carlos

Electronic music was virtually unknown to the general public until 1968, when Walter (now Wendy) Carlos' album, "Switched-on Bach" appeared. For the first time this took electronics outside the realms of science fiction soundtracks and advertising jingles.

Carlos realized that he could use a synthesizer to play a complete musical score. He used only the best known Bach compositions, so that people were familiar with the tunes and he kept his arrangements quite faithful to the originals. But he didn't adhere to the exact timbre of every instrumental sound. He analyzed the role played by each instrument and designed sounds that would complement rather than directly imitate the acoustic sounds of the original.

The album was an enormous success, becoming the best-selling classical album ever. Together with producer Rachel Elkind, Carlos went on to make more albums of classical re-workings, original pieces, and film scores. The latter include the score for the Disney production, *Tron*.

Tomita

No one has followed Carlos and Elkind, but one musician, the Japanese Isao Tomita, has followed a parallel course. He re-arranges classical pieces, but uses completely new sounds.

He sees the synthesizer as best suited to composers like Debussy and Ravel – impressionists, who created evocative tone poems, often based on natural sounds.

Vangelis

Vangelis Papathanassiou has become one of the most celebrated electronic composers of the decade – partly because of his Oscar-winning work on the soundtrack of *Chariots of Fire*.

Born in southern Greece in 1943, Vangelis is completely self-taught. He formed his first band at the age of 18, having acquired, with some difficulty, the most coveted rock keyboard of the time – a Hammond organ. The band, Formynx, became one of the most successful in Greece.

Moving to Paris in 1968, he formed a new band, Aphrodite's Child, with fellow refugee Demis Roussos. The band was extremely successful in Europe, and their best known recording, "Rain and Tears", was a major international hit. The album "6 6 6", which dealt with the darker sides of the supernatural, was also in keeping with the times, and became a cult record.

By the end of the sixties, Vangelis' enthusiasm for rock was waning, and he realized that a more fruitful and lasting career lay in soundtrack work. His first major film score was for Frederic Roussis' French film *L'Apocalypse des Animaux* (1973). This was followed by *L'Opéra Sauvage*.

In the mid-seventies Vangelis moved to London where he set up his own music studio, "Nemo". The studio is like a temple dedicated to music, with towering columns and arches giving a strong Greek flavor.

Vangelis' first album release after his move to the UK was "Heaven and Hell", an ambitious project based on Milton's *Paradise Lost*. On the album Vangelis played virtually all the parts. "Heaven and Hell" was staged as a live show featuring choirs and dancers, and earned the unkind comment from one critic "It was Hell".

"Albedo 0.39" (a reference to the light reflectivity of the earth) is probably the best known of Vangelis' album work because many of the themes have been used as incidental music to TV documentaries.

Other more recent works of Vangelis include "Spiral", "Cosmos", "China", and, of course, the score for *Chariots of Fire*. The success of this movie led him into writing the score for *Blade Runner*, a 21st century thriller, and the score for *Missing*, a movie tracing political problems in Chile. All three are impressively different.

Beaver and Krause

Movie music has become one of the most creative outlets for keyboard musicians. In fact, the keyboard is the most obvious compositional tool. And with

▽ ▷ **Layering sounds** Jean-Michel Jarre gets his effects by layering sounds from the instruments surrounding him. When he plays live there is often not enough time to set up instruments, so he will use one keyboard for a single effect — hence the amount of hardware.

such a wide variety of keyboards available these instruments are ideal for musicians who want to work on their own. Many rock players of the sixties and seventies, in addition to Vangelis, have moved into the movie business with varying degrees of success. Emerson has done several movie soundtracks, and Wakeman has also turned his hand to movie and television scores. But Paul Beaver and Bernie Krause took the concept one stage further.

Paul Beaver was one of the pioneers of electronic music in the fifties. He worked on movies such as *The Magnetic Monster* (1953) and was an associate of Robert Moog's in the early days of his instruments. He contributed to the scores of *Catch 22*, *The Graduate*, and *Rosemary's Baby*, and when he teamed up with producer Bernie Krause they wrote much of the sound-

track for Nicholas Roeg's *Performance*. But their greatest work was the legendary "Ghandharva" (1971) which they considered to be "A soundtrack for a non-existent film". Truly majestic, it was recorded live in Grace Cathedral, San Francisco, to make use of the building's extraordinarily long reverberation time.

Beaver and Krause's approach was highly original. Though they advanced many electronic techniques, they also used traditional jazz and folk themes. For example, their 1975 recording of Scott Joplin's "A real slow drag" from his 1910 opera *Treemonisha* was the first ever made of the piece.

Jean-Michel Jarre

One of the few musicians to package electronic music in a commercially acceptable form is Frenchman Jean-Michel Jarre. Jarre was born in Lyon in 1948 to an already musical family. Maurice Jarre, his father, has composed some of the best known film scores ever, including *Lawrence of Arabia* and the Oscar-winning *Dr Zhivago*.

His father encouraged his musical education, from piano lessons at the age of five through to a degree at the Paris Conservatoire. Jarre then moved to the Paris Music Research Center and got interested in *musique concrète*. This involves using sounds from the natural world and man-made objects, as well as from musical instruments. His first major work, "The Cage" (1970), was recorded while he was still at the Research Center.

In 1972 Jarre released an electronic single recorded almost totally on an EMS synthesizer. It was called "Zig Zag Dance" and the royalties from the quarter of a million copies it sold enabled him to finance his own recording studio. At this time he worked on many jingles and TV soundtracks, as well as writing and recording songs for such major French artists as Françoise Hardy and Patrick Juvet.

But it was his 1976 recording of "Oxygene", originally released on the small independent Freyfus label, that was to break Jarre into the big time. The main "Oxygene" theme (Part IV) relies on a simple single-note riff played against a swing beat and a swirling, bubbling synthesizer background. But it is the subtle layers of timbral shading that give "Oxygene" its real and outstanding quality.

The success of "Oxygene", later released by Polydor, enabled Jarre to upgrade his eight-track studio to a sixteen-track facility and record

"Equinoxe", a more dynamic and rhythmic album. He purchased a Fairlight CMI in 1981 and used it for the album "Magnetic Fields" (1981).

Brian Eno

A founder member of Bryan Ferry's Roxy Music, Brian Eno (then known as Captain Eno) was one of the first keyboard players to use only a synthesizer, together with accompanying electronic equipment, on stage.

After leaving Roxy Music in 1973, Eno has followed a successful solo career and has worked with such musicians as Robert Fripp, John Cale, Nico, and also with Bowie on his controversial "Low" album.

Eno's strangest project was the Portsmouth Sinfonia, a group of musicians who were required to play on instruments with which they weren't familiar.

Another of Eno's ventures has been in the field of what he calls "Ambient music". This is specially composed as background music.

The electronic bands

Electronics are not only useful for the solo performer. In the late sixties and early seventies electronic bands began to appear, using new technology both live and in the studio. Germany was the first home of the electronic band, with groups such as Tangerine Dream, Kraftwerk, Can, Faust, and Amon Duul II.

Tangerine Dream

The first to succeed commercially in this field were Tangerine Dream. In 1967 they were a rock band with electronic overtones but founder member Edgar Froese wanted to explore new areas more fully. This led to the release in 1970 of the album "Electronic Meditation", which relied heavily on the manipulation of recording tape.

But it was the album "Phaedra" that was to be the band's big success. It was one of the first to make use of the sequencer as an effective rhythmic device. Tangerine Dream toured extensively to

◁ **Varied projects** Ambient music and the Portsmouth Sinfonia are two of Eno's more recent musical ventures.

△ **Electronic improvisers** In spite of an uninteresting stage presence, with band members shrouded in darkness, Tangerine Dream's brand of electronic improvisation has been successful, especially in Europe.

promote this album. Their sound was enhanced by reverberant cathedral acoustics.

Kraftwerk

Ralf Hutter and Florian Schneider were the two founder members of Kraftwerk. In 1974 they released "Autobahn", which included Wolfgang Flur playing one of the first electronic drum kits. "Autobahn" was successful both as a three-minute single and a twenty-two-minute album track, combining driving rhythms with electronic effects, and mixing *musique concrète* with "easy-listening" elements.

Kraftwerk attempted similar effects in "Trans Europe Express", but this lacked the freshness and originality of "Autobahn".

Yellow Magic Orchestra

The Japanese electronic band Yellow Magic Orchestra have built on the Kraftwerk style. Enormously popular in their native Japan and elsewhere, they have perfected the use of devices such as Roland Micro-composers and computers, and, although these are essentially studio-based instruments, they use them when playing live. YMO often use hard, computer-driven rhythms to achieve their unique electronic sound.

Recently, one member of the band, Sakamoto, both made the soundtrack of the movie *Merry Christmas, Mr Lawrence* and played a starring role. His music showed again that a soundtrack for a movie set in a certain period (in this case the 1941-45 war in Asia) doesn't demand the use of traditional instruments.

△ **Computers and clarity** From a use of electronic video devices, Kraftwerk have moved on to computer-controlled sound. The clarity of their music comes from their intelligent arrangements and deliberate understatement.

◁ **Touring synthesists** The Japanese band Yellow Magic Orchestra are one of the few who take their modular synthesizers on tour. Normally this type of equipment is used only in the studio. The band's tight, rhythmic sound makes use of electronic percussion synchronized to sequencing devices.

The pop synthesizer bands

In the fifties and sixties the electric guitar made an inroad into popular music. It was also the outlet for the punk generation of the seventies. Punk was a reaction against bands like ELP and Led Zeppelin and the music had more political than artistic content. But it was not long before punk was taken over and neutralized by the big record companies, leaving the players and the music press looking for a new style.

Electronic instruments had developed dramatically during the years of punk. Keyboards had got cheaper and more sophisticated, so that young players could buy their own instruments. As a result, young bands that used electronics to shape their whole sound started to emerge.

Gary Numan

One of the first bands to come to prominence in this way was Tubeway Army in 1977. This was the band from which Gary Numan was to emerge. Numan achieved much more on his own (with the album "The Pleasure Principle" and the single "Cars") than he did with this band. He was keen to move away from his guitar-oriented past to the world of electronic instruments. With the new polyphonic synthesizers (particularly the Polymoog) and electronic percussion Numan managed to create his own individual sound.

Ultravox

Another band of this era to use electronics commercially and successfully is Ultravox. Their epic recording "Vienna" was the turning point in a long struggle to establish themselves. With Midge Ure on vocals, guitar, and keyboards, Billie Currie on keyboards and violin, Chris Cross on synthesizer and bass, and Warren Cann on electronic percussion, the band has a strong electronic sound that owes a lot to ARP Odyssey synthesizers. Nevertheless the members of Ultravox give a surprisingly emotional air to their work. It is probably this quality that has led to their continuing success.

The Eurythmics

The Eurythmics' first album was recorded cheaply on an eight-track machine. But it was very successful. Annie Lennox adopted an asexual persona, projecting her haunting vocals over Dave Stewart's original brand of electronic keyboard playing.

Depeche Mode

Depeche Mode is another synth-pop band of the eighties, influ-

△ **"String" soloist** Gary Numan will always be associated with solo string lines over gothic rhythm tracks. His use of instrumentation and his rather nasal vocals made his work instantly recognizable.

◁ **Varied resources** Dave Stewart and Annie Lennox are the Eurythmics. Stewart, the keyboard player, recognizes that all instruments have something to offer. His sound features everything from Fairlight computer keyboards to cheap portables — it is the effect that counts.

enced by groups such as Kraftwerk and the Human League. They started by using traditional instruments, but they found that synthesizers were easy to travel with, as well as giving them a wider range of sounds.

Depeche Mode are often compared to OMD, and it's true that both bands seem keen to keep to a similar musical formula. But Depeche Mode strive to get a sound that's as clear and clean as possible, using rhythm units rather than electronic percussion and synthesizers like the PPG Wave 2.

The Human League

In 1977 a new band was formed with Philip Oakey at the controls – the Human League. Following

▷ **Depeche Mode** One of the most interesting electro-pop bands, Depeche Mode make much use of sequencers and drum machines, but their sound is not too clinical.

little commercial success the band split in the early eighties to reveal a new Human League (now with two female singers) and Heaven 17. The resulting 1981 album "Dare" was a classic thanks to Oakey, the band, and producer Martin Rushent. Rushent's production technique hinges on the use of electronics to produce the desired sound. Although Ian Burden, Jo Callis, Philip Wright, and Oakey himself all played synthesizers, it was Rushent's use of the Roland Microcomposer and the Linn Drum that made the album such an original one.

In spite of these successes, though, there are no star pop keyboard players of the kind seen in the seventies. Eighties pop relies more on production and composition than on technique and showmanship. This can sometimes lead to bland-

ness. But it also means that the field is open to originality and creativity rather than only to those whose technical ability lifts them above the mass of keyboard players.

Thomas Dolby
One of the most original contemporary keyboard players is Britisher Thomas Dolby. He worked with Bruce Woolley and the Camera Club before embarking on a solo career. His talents are diverse. Although his music has a flavor of the eighties pop synthesizer sound, he is also influenced by people such as Dave Brubeck and Thelonious Monk. His image is of the quiet eccentric – he is very English.

▷ **Human League** One of the most successful bands of the early eighties, Human League's album "Dare", made with producer Martin Rushent, marked the pinnacle of their career.

Sound and electricity

Music is the arrangement of sounds. It is therefore important that, if you play a musical instrument, you should understand what sound is and how it reaches our ears. Sound is the sensation we experience when our ears detect vibrations in the air. Our ears convert the vibrations to impulses that are transmitted through the nervous system to the brain, which translates them into what we perceive as sound.

The elements of sound

Almost every sound has three basic elements: pitch, "timbre" (or tone color), and loudness. The exceptions to this are unpitched sounds (such as the noise of wind and waves) that do not seem to feature a recognizable note. If you can specify these three elements, you can define any single sound. A complex sound source such as a choir would require different definitions for each voice.

To reproduce a particular sound we need to know how these elements change over a period of time. For example, a note played on an acoustic piano may have a virtually constant pitch, but its timbre and loudness will be constantly changing. There is a further complication because every time you play a note on a piano, three strings are struck, so we should really think of a piano note as coming from three separate sources. Because timbre and loudness are continually changing, it is often difficult to analyze a given sound. But instruments such as synthesizers can create sounds with continuously changing timbre, loudness, and even pitch. If you can accurately recreate the changes in these elements, you can simulate most naturally occuring sounds. But before we look at each element of sound in turn, we need to see exactly how sounds are created by vibrations in the air.

How sounds are created

When you pluck a guitar string, it vibrates. If you look closely you will see that when you actually pluck the string you are stretching and bending it, so that it is no longer straight. At this point there is an extra amount of tension in the string, and when you release it, the string tries to return to its original position. But it shoots past the initial position, until the tension builds up again and sends it back in the opposite direction, to repeat the cycle. This swinging between two points is known as *oscillation*. Of course, the string doesn't go on vibrating for ever – it has to overcome the resistance of the air, which reduces the movement at each "sweep". This effect is called *damped oscillation*.

Two things primarily affect the sound made by this kind of oscillation – the *rate* and the *amount*. The rate – the time each vibration takes – depends on the length of the string, its thickness, and its tension when at rest. Therefore, although the vibrations get weaker due to damping, the length and initial tension stay the same and each oscillation takes the same amount of time. But the amount the string oscillates is continually changing. It is the distance from the "straight" position to the extremities of movement that determines how loud the string will sound. The damping effect makes the volume decrease.

How vibrations produce sound

How does a vibrating object like a guitar string produce a sound that we can hear? The air surrounding the string consists of millions of microscopic particles, and it is these particles that transmit sound. As the string oscillates it disturbs the air particles around it. These particles in turn disturb other air particles until the air surrounding your ear is disturbed – causing the hearing sensors in your ears to vibrate so that you hear the sound.

When no sound is being transmitted, the air particles are distributed fairly evenly and air pressure is uniform. But if you suddenly make a noise the air particles will start to move back and forth. The density of the particles starts changing, so that waves of high-density and low-density particles spread out from the sound source, in a similar way to the ripples created when you throw a stone into a pond. Like the waves on a pond, the air particles themselves are only moving within a localized area. The wave motion keeps spreading outward, but the particles – like the pond water – stay more or less where they are.

The speed at which these sound waves travel through the air depends on the air particles themselves and is known as the *speed of sound*. This is a more or less constant figure – generally about 1,100 feet per second – although alterations in temperature and atmospheric pressure do change the exact value.

The principle of sound waves created by moving air particles is the same for all sound sources. In fact the way a drum disturbs the air particles is very similar to the action of a loudspeaker. In a speaker, the cone vibrates back and forward, increasing and decreasing the density of the air particles.

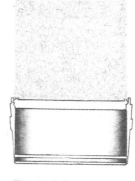

◁ **Silence** When there is no sound, air particles adopt a random pattern with fairly even overall distribution. There is the same density above and below the drum skin and air pressure is uniform.

◁ **Drum beat** As you strike the drum, a space is created just above the skin. The same number of particles is now filling a larger space, so their density is lower. This is known as rarefaction.

◁ **Upward movement** When the skin moves upward, the air particles immediately above are compressed, while those below the skin are rarefied.

◁ **Return** The skin then returns to the concave shape, so that the particles above the skin are rarefied. But the compression caused in the previous stage has produced another wave of compressed particles further away from the skin.

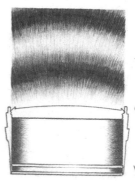

◁ **Continued vibrations** The drum goes on vibrating, continuing to produce waves of compression and rarefaction. The effect of the vibrations is less powerful at longer distances from the skin, so the more distant waves are shorter.

Pitch

The quality that makes a sound seem "high" or "low" is called *pitch*. Deep notes, like those from a bass guitar or bass drum, have a low pitch, while those from a soprano singer or a flute have a high pitch.

Sound travels at a fixed speed, but the compressions and rarefactions of the air particles can occur at any rate – they depend on the speed at which the source oscillates. If a drum is oscillating at 110 times per second, the air pressure will be constantly changing at the same rate. If you plot these pressure changes on a graph, you will produce a diagram known as a *waveform*. The waveform can be of any shape, but if the sound is to have any recognizable pitch, there must come a point where the waveform returns to its start position and repeats itself. This is called a *periodic waveform*.

When a waveform returns to its start position it has completed *one cycle*. It doesn't matter where you take the start position to be, since each cycle will have the same length.

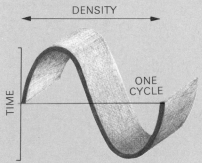

△ **A periodic waveform** This continuously repeating sine wave has to cross the center line of the graph twice before its whole cycle is completed and it can start to repeat.

Frequency and wavelength

If an instrument, such as a drum, vibrates 110 times every second, we say that it has a *frequency* of 110 cycles per second. Another way of expressing this is to say that the frequency is 110 Hertz (Hz). The pitch of the note is defined by its frequency – the more times per second the waveform oscillates, and the higher the frequency and pitch.

Our ears can detect frequencies from around 20 Hz to about 20,000 Hz (or 20 kHz). This general range of frequencies is known as the *audio spectrum*.

Wavelength

We can define the pitch of a periodic waveform using another measurement: *wavelength*. As the term implies, this is the actual distance spanned by one cycle of the waveform.

Imagine the drum, vibrating at 110 Hz, with the waveform traveling at the speed of sound, 1,100 feet per second. 110 cycles, which represent one second's worth of oscillations, must span 1,100 feet. It therefore follows that one cycle will span 10 feet.

The speed of sound is constant, so the greater the frequency, the shorter the wavelength, and vice versa. As more oscillations are crammed into a second, the physical length of each must become smaller.

All musical instruments are capable of producing a range of frequencies and there is a wide variation between the frequency ranges of different instruments.

▽ **Frequency ranges** This chart shows the frequencies of common instruments and voices, linked to staff and keyboard.

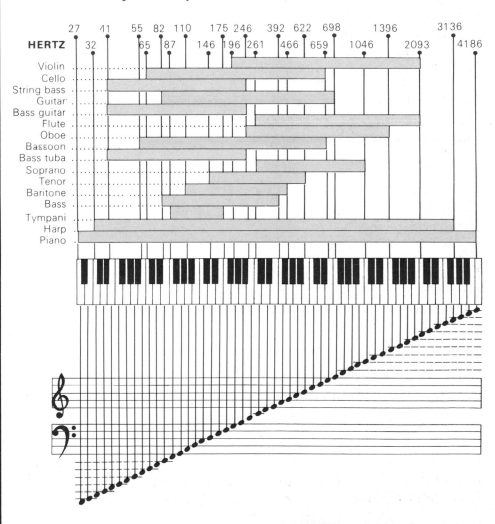

Octaves

Musicians do not usually talk about specific numbered frequencies. Instead, a system of frequency identification based on the *octave* has evolved. If you listen to a sound with a frequency of 220 Hz and compare it with one of 440 Hz there is an air of similarity between the two. They sound very much the same except that the second is pitched noticeably higher than the first.

This fact gives us the basis of our entire musical system. By doubling the frequency of a note you raise the pitch by what is known as an octave. So a tone of 110 Hz is an octave below the 220 Hz tone, and two octaves below 440 Hz. Because you have to double the frequency for each octave, the difference in frequency does not remain constant for every octave jump.

Our western musical system is based on the twelve-tone scale, so the octave is divided into twelve equal steps (see p. 89). Again, the frequency jumps between each step vary, but the frequency ratio between notes is a constant. Originally only seven different notes were used to divide up the octave, and these were identified by the letters A through G. These form the white notes of the keyboard. However, five further notes were found necessary and these were named with reference to the original seven (see p. 86). These five notes are represented by black notes on the keyboard.

On a particular keyboard instrument the actual frequency differences between the notes will depend on exactly how that instrument has been tuned. For more information on tuning, see pp. 89-91.

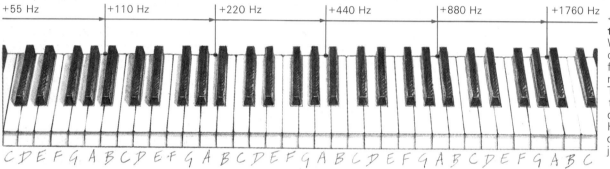

| +55 Hz | +110 Hz | +220 Hz | +440 Hz | +880 Hz | +1760 Hz |

C D E F G A B C D E F G A B C D E F G A B C D E F G A B C D E F G A B C

◁ **Octaves on the keyboard**
With each jump of an octave, the frequency of the note doubles. This means that the frequency difference in Hertz varies with different octave jumps.

Reference frequencies

The diagram above shows you the notes that make up an octave and how the octaves on a keyboard relate to each other. If the frequencies double with each octave, as shown in the diagram, then the instrument will be in tune with itself. But how do you ensure that it is in tune with other instruments, that the note C on your keyboard oscillates at the same frequency to the C on another instrument?

To solve this problem a reference pitch is used. This defines the frequency of the note A just above the middle of the piano's keyboard. In 1859 the Paris Academy set the standard tuning frequency at A-435. It remained at this level until the thirties, when A-440, almost half a semitone higher, became increasingly popular because it suited a wider range of instruments. Finally A-440 was ratified at an international conference in 1939.

It has since remained the standard and is known as *concert pitch*. Some countries use a different reference frequency but A-440 is standard for most western nations.

The tuning fork

The simplest source of a reference frequency is a tuning fork. It is also one of the most effective. It is a metal device with two accurately machined prongs. When you strike the fork on a firm surface, the prongs vibrate. You then hold the base of the fork between your thumb and forefinger and place it on a table, or on an instrument's soundboard, to help to amplify the vibrations.

If you look closely at the prongs after you have struck them, you can see them actually moving – hold the fork up to the light and they will appear blurred. They are acting just like the drum skin (see p. 24), causing compressions and rarefactions of the air particles and setting up a wave motion away from the fork.

The frequency of the fork's vibrations depends on the length and thickness of the prongs and the composition of the metal. Since these factors stay the same once the fork has been made, the frequency of the note is constant. (Very small variations in frequency are possible if you use a fork in extremes of temperature.)

The fundamental frequency

Every pitched note has a basic, or *fundamental,* frequency. This makes the A below middle C sound different from the other As on the keyboard. Most sounds are in fact compounds of several frequencies (see pp. 27-8), but if the sound as a whole has the feel of a particular pitch, this frequency is known as the fundamental.

Timbre

If you listen to a note produced by an oboe, and then the same note played on a clarinet, you will be able to detect differences in the character of the two sounds. The oboe has a thin, delicate quality, while the clarinet has a more mellow tone. We can tell the difference between the two sounds because they both have a specific *timbre* or "tone color". Unlike frequency, timbre cannot really be measured precisely. But there are ways of defining it.

Timbre and air particles

While the the speed at which the air particles move determines the pitch of a sound, the way these particles move governs the timbre. You can see this if you look at the shapes of the waveforms produced by different sounds. For example, the tuning fork produces a smooth, flowing curve called a *sine wave*. This is the basic waveform – a number of others are shown below.

◁ **Sine wave** This gentle, flowing waveform is produced by the pure tone of the tuning fork.

◁ **Triangle wave** Similar in shape to the sine wave, the sharp edges give it a brighter, crisper sound.

◁ **Square wave** With its sudden expansion and compression of the air particles, this wave has a sound like a clarinet.

◁ **Sawtooth wave** This waveform has a rich, full sound, rather like a brass instrument.

Overtones and harmonics

Most sounds contain several extra frequencies that vibrate simultaneously. These frequencies are called *overtones*. They are directly responsible for creating the timbre of the sound.

The sine wave, the simplest sound, features no overtones. But by adding together sine waves of different frequencies and different amounts it is possible to create other waveforms.

The overtones of most musical instruments have a special relationship to each other. This can be shown mathematically because their frequencies are multiples of the lowest (or fundamental) pitch. These overtones are known as *harmonics*. Each harmonic is numbered and its pitch is the corresponding multiple of the fundamental frequency. So the second harmonic is twice the frequency of the fundamental (or an octave above). If you play the notes of a natural harmonic series, you will notice how the progression sounds "right".

The influence of harmonics

By adding together harmonics from the natural harmonic series (below) you can create other waveforms. As you add more harmonics to the composite waveform it becomes more and more like a sawtooth wave. The higher the harmonic, the sharper the teeth of the wave become. This is useful when you are working with a synthesizer and designing your own waveforms.

Another result of adding harmonics is that the amplitude (see p. 29) decreases. By the time you reach, say, the 20th harmonic, the amplitude is virtually zero.

▽ **The harmonic series** The harmonics produced by a vibrating string vary. Every extra division of the vibrating string equates to a higher harmonic.

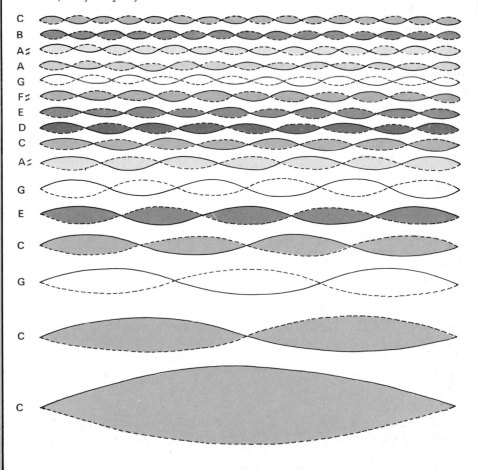

Other harmonics and overtones

Although the sounds produced by most musical instruments consist mainly of harmonics, you will also find that some instruments produce overtones that are not related mathematically to the fundamental frequency. This is most noticeable with percussive instruments. A bell is a particularly interesting example. It produces many non-harmonic overtones that contribute to its full, rich sound.

You can also hear non-harmonic overtones when a wind instrument is blown too hard. This sound is often used on acoustic organs and can be reproduced on a synthesizer.

Artificial harmonics

These occur mainly on stringed instruments, but they do help to show the way the harmonic series is constructed. Place your finger lightly at the center of a guitar string (over the 12th fret from the neck) and pluck the string. You will get a note that is twice the frequency of the open string. Now move your finger to the seventh fret, to divide the string in a 2:1 ratio. Its frequency will now be three times the fundamental frequency.

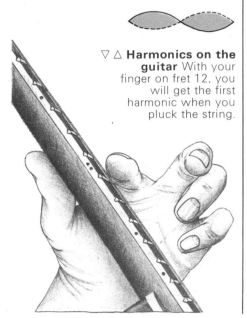

▽ △ **Harmonics on the guitar** With your finger on fret 12, you will get the first harmonic when you pluck the string.

Resonance

Any object that can vibrate has its own natural frequency. So when it is hit by another object, it will vibrate at this frequency. This phenomenon is known as *resonance*. A simple example of resonance occurs when you tap a pencil on your teeth. You will notice that the sound produced has a definite pitch. (This can be changed as you change the shape of your mouth.)

You don't have to hit an object to make it resonate – you can produce the effect in other ways. For example, try going into a small bathroom with a good echo and humming through the low pitches of a scale. You should find that one note will sound much louder than the others. This is because you've hit upon the resonant frequency of the room. By producing a sound of that frequency you have made the air particles in the room move more easily, giving a louder sound.

This principle applies to anything that oscillates – if you activate it at its resonant frequency you need less effort to get it moving.

Feedback

One form of resonance that is often unwanted is *feedback*. This can occur when you amplify an acoustic guitar. If you turn up the gain control on the amplifier too far the guitar body, excited by the sound of the speaker, starts to resonate at its natural frequency. The microphone picks up this resonance so that it is amplified and this in turn makes the air inside the guitar's soundbox resonate further. Then the whole system starts to oscillate at the resonant frequency, giving a ringing tone.

How resonance affects sound

When a sound is amplified acoustically it is altered by the material used for amplification. For example, in a violin, it is the instrument's wooden body that amplifies the strings' vibrations so that we can hear them.

All instruments, even electronic ones, rely on resonance to determine the character and timbre of their sound. You may also find that an instrument has more than one resonant frequency – in fact the human voice gets its specific character from a number of resonant frequencies.

To get the best use out of filters on a synthesizer, you should know how the resonant frequency affects the waveform of a particular sound.

The rising part of the waveform acts rather like a trigger that fires off the resonance. The effect of this is to make the wave overshoot before it tries to re-establish itself with an oscillating motion. The greater the resonance, the more the wave overshoots, until a point is reached where the wave can no longer re-establish itself and positive feedback occurs.

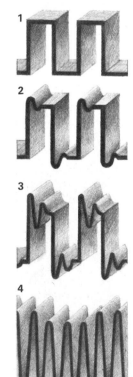

◁ **Resonance and the waveform** These four diagrams show the effect of gradually increasing the resonance of a simple square wave (**1**). With slightly increased resonance the wave starts to overshoot its original position (**2**). As you increase the resonance further, it takes longer for the waveform to settle down (**3**). Finally, the resonance takes over completely, so that the waveform becomes a sine wave (**4**).

Loudness and amplitude

When you listen to a sound it is fairly easy to tell how loud it is in relation to other sounds but it is impossible to give the loudness a precise quantity. Information about frequencies and waveforms has given us ways of specifying exactly the pitch and timbre of sounds we want to create. What we need now is a way of specifying the loudness. This is why the *amplitude* of a sound is important. Amplitude, the amount the air particles are disturbed at a given instant, can be measured precisely.

The amplitude of a musical note is not normally a simple single value, because the figure changes as the note is played. The term amplitude *envelope* is used to describe how the amplitude changes.

You can show the amplitude envelope in the form of a graph. This is known as a waveform, but it is unlike the waveforms that show pitch because it doesn't repeat itself – an envelope is a "one-shot" waveform, has no inherent pitch and exists only in theory.

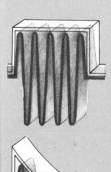

◁ **Organ envelope** The amplitude envelope of an organ starts suddenly, continues at a steady rate, and stops suddenly. This is a square envelope.

◁ **Piano envelope** The piano's amplitude envelope begins suddenly, but decays gradually, giving a ramp-like waveform.

Changes in amplitude

Alterations in the amplitude of a sound are known as *dynamics*. If you listen to a heavy-metal band you may be confronted with a wall of sound, but the overall level will remain fairly constant. So although the sound is loud it is said to have a narrow *dynamic range*. But a classical orchestra can have a far wider dynamic range, with quiet solos and full-orchestra sections.

The dynamic range of an instrument is an important feature. For example, the keyboard of an acoustic piano is highly touch-sensitive. So you can produce a very soft or very loud note depending simply on how hard you hit the key. Many of today's electronic keyboards try to imitate this feature, but they do not usually have such a wide dynamic range as their acoustic counterparts.

Measuring amplitudes

There are two principal ways of measuring amplitudes. One is to determine the changes in atmospheric pressure that result

The ear's response

When you listen to a piece of recorded music, its volume level actually affects what you hear – at lower volume levels the bass frequencies tend to disappear. So if you are involved in recording, you should always monitor your music at the levels at which you expect it to be heard.

Another result of the way we hear is that brighter sounds (those with more harmonics in the upper frequencies) will sound louder to the ear than

Spatial effects

When a musical instrument produces a sound it does not simply beam it directly to your ears (unless it is produced by an electronic instrument and you are listening to it through a pair of headphones). Sound travels

when a note is played. The other method, more common in the musical world, uses a unit called the *decibel* (dB). The decibel is a ratio, so to make any sense of the decibel measurement of a sound you need to know what the value is being compared to. A common use of a decibel rating is the signal-to-noise ratio quoted by manufacturers of amplifiers and tape recorders. A figure of −40 dB means that the amplitude of the signal is 40 decibels greater than that of the noise (the hiss and hum) produced by the system. So the decibel scale works by comparing two levels and telling you the gap between them.

Every time the amplitude doubles, the decibel value increases by 6 dB. The most useful amplitude measurement uses the threshold of hearing as the reference sound level. This is known as the sound pressure level (SPL) and decibel measurements that use this level are specified as "dB SPL". The human hearing range is from 0 to approximately 134 dB SPL.

more mellow sounds. You may have a synthesizer that can generate triangle and sawtooth waveforms. These will naturally have the same frequency (since they are from the same source). But even if they also have the same amplitude the sawtooth wave will actually sound far louder than the triangle.

In a similar way, if you listen to a triangle wave at a frequency of 110 Hz and then at 880 Hz, it will sound much louder at the higher frequency.

outward from its source in all directions. The pattern of sound waves is very similar to the pattern of ripples on a pond, except that sound waves move outward from the source in three dimensions rather than in only a single plane.

Reverberation and echo

Sound waves travel in a spherical pattern from the source. But this pattern is changed if there are obstructions such as the walls of a room. The sound waves will be reflected off the walls and will therefore have to travel further to reach the listener. The result is that the reflected waves also take longer to reach your ears, arriving slightly after the direct signal. In most rooms there will be countless reflections and they will merge together to form a *reverberation.* You hear the direct signal and then, almost instantaneously, the reflected waves arrive, blurring the sound slightly. This is why open-air concerts have a different sound: there is no reverberation.

If you are in a room with hard surfaces such as tiled walls and floors and a solid flat ceiling, a lot of sound will be reflected and the reverberations will be louder. But if you are in a room with thick curtains, soft furnishings, and a deep-pile carpet, very little sound will be reflected, drastically reducing the reverberations. In addition, a large hall will produce far more reverberations than a small room, since there will be longer time delays between the direct signal and the various reflections.

An audience can dramatically change the acoustic properties of a room or hall. A highly reverberative hall when empty can become much less so when full of people. Clothes are very good absorbers of sound and direct reflections from a flat floor will be almost completely cancelled out by an audience.

Reverberation usually enhances the sound quality of a musical instrument. For example, a church organ relies on the strong reverberations produced by the building. The effect is to reinforce the sound, and this can work especially well for the singer with a weak voice.

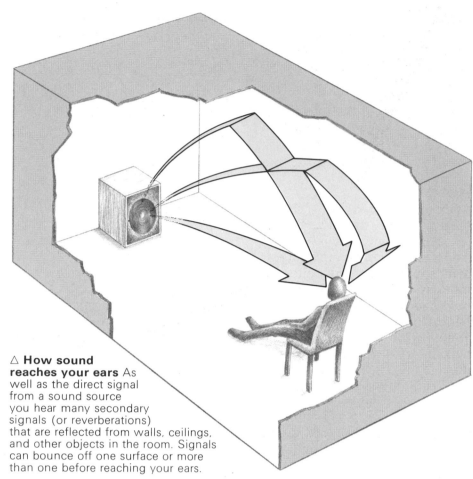

△ **How sound reaches your ears** As well as the direct signal from a sound source you hear many secondary signals (or reverberations) that are reflected from walls, ceilings, and other objects in the room. Signals can bounce off one surface or more than one before reaching your ears.

Reverberation can also improve the sound of electronic instruments. The sound from a loudspeaker can be rather flat and uninteresting, especially in a well damped room. Adding a little artificial reverberation can enhance the sound quality.

Measuring reverberation

There are two elements of reverberation that can be measured – time and amount. The reverberation *time* is how long it takes for the reverberation to halve in amplitude. The larger the space and the more reflective the surfaces, the greater the time. The *amount* of reverberation you hear in proportion to the direct signal is also important. This ratio can create an impression of depth. For example, if you are sitting near the sound source you will hear the direct signal with a small proportion of reflected sound. If you sit nearer the back of the room, away from the source, the amount of reflected sound you hear will be larger.

So the reverberation is a very important influence on the character of a sound, and you can use it to good effect by means of artificial reverb on electronic signals.

But reverberation does change the timbre of a sound and it may be something you want to reduce. To get an idea of how a direct signal sounds you have to listen to it in a room specially designed to prevent any reflection of sound waves taking place. This type of room is called an *anechoic chamber.* It consists of heavily padded walls, floor, and ceiling, often with irregular dimensions. Recording studio control rooms also have to be as free as possible from reverberation. So they are well damped with absorbent soft furnishings.

Echo

Echo and reverberation are similar effects – they are both caused by reflected sound waves. Echoes occur when you can actually distinguish the separate reflections of sound. Of course, there is still an overlap between each echo, but this doesn't stop your hearing each one as a separate sound.

Usually, for the first echo to be heard distinctly, there must be a delay of at least 0.1 sec. Because sound travels at 1,100 feet per second, the reflected sound has to travel 110 feet to be delayed by this time. So a reflective surface 55 feet away is sufficient to produce an echo. This is because the sound has to travel to the surface and back again.

In a long hall with a fairly low ceiling you may be able to hear a joint reverberation and echo effect, with the echo produced by sound reflected from the back wall. You will hear the echo after most of the reverberations have died away.

Stereo

Electronic keyboards produce a wide range of sounds across the audio spectrum but these sounds are usually all derived from a point source – a single loud-speaker. An acoustic piano makes its sounds from strings that can be several feet long, spanning the whole length of the instrument to give a "stereo" effect. So an ordinary electronic piano will never have the same "presence" as an acoustic one.

With inexpensive portable keyboards this weakness is even more obvious. These machines offer many different voice-producing sections but only have a built-in speaker.

Both reverberation and echo are stereo effects. If you are listening to a solo flute playing you may think that you are hearing a mono sound coming from a point source. But because of the reverberation produced by the room your left ear will receive a slightly different signal to your right one.

When the sound source is in a central position the signals are very similar for both ears. But if the source is moved to the right-hand side of the room, the signal will reach your right ear before your left. This means that there is a phase difference between the two, so that while the air is being compressed in one ear it may be rarefied in the other. Our ears detect the position of a sound by analyzing this phase difference.

If you are listening to a stereo signal using headphones neither ear directly receives signals from the opposite channel. You therefore get a different stereo picture from when you are using loudspeakers.

Moving sound sources

When a sound source moves toward you, the pitch rises; as it moves away the pitch falls. We've all experienced this effect (known as the doppler effect) when we hear an ambulance or fire engine go past with its siren on. As the vehicle is approaching, the siren's pitch is about a semitone higher than it would be with a stationary source, and when it passes there is a similar lowering in tone.

The rotary speaker allows you to use the doppler effect in performance. As the sound source rotates, the pitch of the sound coming from the speaker rises and falls a small amount.

This gives the sound a greater depth and, because the output is projected in all directions, the sound seems to have more "presence".

Several ways have been found to simulate the rotary speaker electronically (see p. 140). But these methods can only really imitate the shift in pitch.

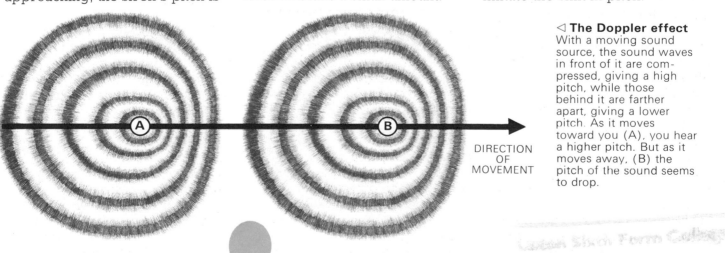

◁ **The Doppler effect**
With a moving sound source, the sound waves in front of it are compressed, giving a high pitch, while those behind it are farther apart, giving a lower pitch. As it moves toward you (A), you hear a higher pitch. But as it moves away, (B) the pitch of the sound seems to drop.

DIRECTION OF MOVEMENT

LISTENER

Electricity

To understand fully how electronic instruments work you need a basic knowledge of electricity. Electricity is an energy source that employs the flow of *electrons* through various substances. Electrons form part of a material's molecular structure.

We are all familiar with household electricity. This is a powerful source of energy that can be used for heating and lighting. But the electricity used by electronic musical instruments is used for controlling and shaping. It does not do any physical work and needs less energy.

The electrons flow through the conductor in a *circuit* – if the circuit is broken (for example, by using a switch), the electrons cannot flow. The force that drives the electrons round the circuit is called the *voltage*. When a switch is closed the circuit is completed and there is a difference in the voltage levels of the battery's two terminals. The wires are good electrical conductors, so little energy is required to drive the electrons through them. But if there is a piece of electrical equipment such as a light bulb in the circuit, it acts as a *resistance* to the flow, and work has to be done to force the electrons through the bulb's filament. The result of this work is heat and light. The resistance of the bulb is measured in units called *ohms;* the amount of electricity flowing (the *current*) is measured in *amps*.

AC and DC – the voltage standards

The voltage from a battery is a constant value, so that the current remains steady – this type of current is called *direct current* (DC). Mains current, however, works differently. Its voltage continuously oscillates between a positive and a negative value, so it is called *alternating current* (AC). If a mains supply is rated at "240 volts AC 50 Hz", the current swings between +120 and −120 volts, 50 times every second. (The human ear can detect frequencies of 50 Hz, and this pitch is produced by mains hum on some amplifiers.)

An electronic instrument may be mains powered, but its internal workings do not function with AC. So the current has to be transformed to DC.

Sound as changing voltage

Air particles vibrate in different ways to produce tones of varying timbres (see p. 27). Electrons behave in a similar way. In order to make the air particles vibrate in a sawtooth waveform, a loudspeaker must compress the air very rapidly and then more gradually reduce the density before the cycle repeats itself.

It is a changing voltage that makes the speaker cone vibrate in this way, so if the voltage varies with a sawtooth shape, then the compressions and rarefactions in the air will also have this waveform. So the changing voltage at the keyboard's output corresponds directly to the sound produced. This is a principle on which electronic music synthesis is based.

Analog and digital systems

These two terms are often used by people talking about electronic instruments. An *analog* quantity is continuously variable. A dimmer switch in a lighting circuit is an analog control – you can set the brilliance of the lighting at any level. But you could use four bulbs, each with a conventional switch, to vary the strength of the lighting (see right). This is a *digital* system.

The "on" and "off" settings in a digital system are usually represented by the figures 1 and 0, which can be combined together to form *binary numbers.* The advantage of binary numbers is that they can be read by a microprocessor – the tiny computer at the heart of modern electronic keyboards.

The control panel of your keyboard may have a number of knobs. These are analog devices that you can set at any position. For the microprocessor to understand these settings, the instrument has to translate the setting into a binary number. This is done using an analog-to-digital converter circuit.

Digital systems, increasingly popular on electronic instruments, have two main advantages over analog types. First, they are very stable. Second, they are cheaper and can perform a far wider variety of tasks.

SWITCH				TOTAL WATT-AGE
1 (200)	2 (100)	3 (50)	4 (25)	
0	0	0	0	0
0	0	0	1	25
0	0	1	0	50
0	0	1	1	75
0	1	0	0	100
0	1	0	1	125
0	1	1	0	150
0	1	1	1	175
1	0	0	0	200
1	0	0	1	225
1	0	1	0	250
1	0	1	1	275
1	1	0	0	300
1	1	0	1	325
1	1	1	0	350
1	1	1	1	375

△ **A digital system** With four bulbs of different wattages you can control the lighting level in a room using this digital system. In binary code "0" means "off" and "1" means "on".

The instruments

The range of keyboard instruments available today is wider than ever before. From a tiny portable keyboard to a sophisticated polyphonic synthesizer, from an electronic organ to an acoustic piano, they offer different features and are suited to different uses. This section of the book looks at the instruments in detail. It helps you to choose the best keyboard for your requirements, and shows how to get the best use out of the instrument that you choose.

How keyboard instruments have developed

The first instruments were acoustic – they were not designed to be used with any form of electric amplification. Acoustic instruments range from early keyboards like the harpsichord and clavichord, which have only limited use today, to the acoustic piano, which is still favored by many musicians and remains unsurpassed for many purposes.

Electric instruments, in which the sound made by vibrating components is amplified electrically, began to emerge at the beginning of this century. Some electric instruments, such as the electric piano, are still widely used.

But it is the field of electronic instruments that has seen the biggest expansion. These instruments produce sound by means of electronic circuitry. Modern electronics can produce instruments that are both compact and laden with every conceivable gadget and control. Even the portable keyboards designed to be easy to play have an array of buttons and switches that at first seems baffling. This section of the book, divided for easy reference according to different types of instruments, comes to your aid in deciphering these controls and showing you how to use them.

Early acoustic keyboards

From the sixteenth to the eighteenth century the harpsichord was as familiar as the piano is today. Two other instruments of the harpsichord family, the virginal and the spinet, were also popular at this time. These three instruments are basically harps that have been rotated into a horizontal position. Instead of playing the strings directly with your fingers, they are plucked by a series of small picks or "plectra" that you operate via a keyboard.

Another popular early keyboard was the clavichord. Like the piano, the clavichord is a *percussive* instrument – its sound is produced by small hammers *hitting* the strings. But unlike the piano, it produces an extremely soft and delicate sound. So the clavichord was used mainly in the home – it does not produce a loud enough sound for performances in large halls. For this reason, few composers wrote very much for the clavichord, but with modern amplification techniques its sound is now becoming popular again.

The harpsichord family

The mechanism of these instruments is quite simple. As you press one of the pivoted keys, a wooden "jack" rises in a see-saw motion and the pick or plectrum, which is a small piece of leather, brushes against the string and plucks it. When you release the key, the jack falls in such a way that it misses the string. Instead of being plucked again by the plectrum, the string is damped by a piece of felt, to stop any unwanted vibrations. This gives a clipped sound that you can reproduce on many electronic synthesizers.

The virginal and spinet have similar mechanisms to the harpsichord. There is little difference between the two instruments. Both have a fixed sound that is rather "twangy" in quality.

The harpsichord itself is the largest instrument in the family, and has two sets of strings, mounted parallel to the keys. The harpsichord's big advantage over the spinet and virginal is that you can vary the timbre of its sound using "stops" and pedals. These control the number of strings activated by each key, and also how the strings are plucked. Single and dual-manual harpsichords were made, and some have a volume control.

The acoustic piano

The clavichord

Clavichords have a series of strings running at right-angles to the keys. When you press a key a hammer (known as a *tangent*) covers the string, where it stays until you release the key. It divides the string into two lengths, one of which is free to vibrate, while the other is damped. The tangent is therefore both making the string vibrate and determining the length of the vibrating section and hence the pitch of the note.

The clavichord, ancestor of the modern Clavinet, can be quite an expressive instrument. You can sharpen the pitch of a note a little by pressing harder to stretch the string. And by giving alternately hard and soft pressure you can introduce vibrato.

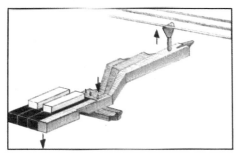

△ **The clavichord mechanism** The clavichord has a set of pivoted keys. Each key controls a hammer that strikes one of the strings from below. When you release the key, the mechanism damps the whole string. The strings themselves run at right angles to the keys.

◁ **Early keyboard** This eighteenth century English harpsichord shows the quality of craftsmanship that went into the making of these early instruments.

◁ **The harpsichord mechanism** On a harpsichord, each key is connected to a wooden component called a "jack". On each jack a plectrum or pick is mounted and this plucks the string when you press the key. The strings run parallel to the keys. The action of the spinet and virginal is similar to the harpsichord, except that, on these instruments, the strings are set at 45 degrees to the keys.

Many keyboard players use the acoustic piano – an instrument invented over 270 years ago but in many ways still unrivalled. The piano is an excellent instrument on which to learn keyboard technique (see p. 82) and its touch-sensitive keys give you control over the loudness and timbre of its sound. Most electronic instruments can imitate the piano's sound, but few have its touch-sensitivity.

An Italian harpsichord maker called Bartolomeo Cristofori is said to have produced the first piano in 1709. He realized that he could produce a totally different sound from his harpsichords if, instead of the strings being plucked, they were struck. One of the main problems with the harpsichord was that, no matter how you hit the keys, the plectra plucked the strings in more or less the same way. But if a keyboard was used to *strike* the string remotely, you could control the amplitude by using the keys.

But the harpsichord does have one advantage. It has what is called an *escapement* mechanism. This is the device that makes the plectrum fall from the string without any damping effect. It will do this even if you keep the key pressed down. Cristofori combined the hammer system of the clavichord with the harpsichord's escapement mechanism. The French manufacturer Sebastien Erard improved the mechanism further.

Developments in piano design

The early pianos of Cristofori and Erard were different from modern instruments in several ways. Erard himself extended the range of the keyboard to five and a half octaves, designed the pedal mechanisms, and strengthened his piano frames with cast iron, allowing heavier, thicker strings to be used. Early pianos, with their thin strings, had a rather weak tone – by using a thicker gauge of string a fuller, richer sound could be produced. But it was Alpheus Babcock who invented, in 1825, the first one-piece cast-iron frame – probably the most important step of all.

The piano suffered from being one of the largest musical instruments. One way to cut down on the size was to use cross-stringing, with the long bass strings running underneath the shorter treble ones. This led to the appearance of the upright piano. In this type of piano, the harp is set vertically, so that the strings run above and below the keys.

The piano took about a hundred years to evolve. Since the 1850s there have been only slight changes in design.

There are several different types of piano, from the most expensive grands, weighing up to a ton to uprights designed for use in the home. But apart from the action (see pp. 36-7), they all have three distinct sections: case, harp, and strings.

The case

This is the piano's outer shell and is probably the most widely varying of the instrument's three main elements. There are variations in both shape and size. Baby grands and concert grands have similar shapes but differ greatly in size. Among upright pianos, spinet models are usually between 36 and 38 ins (91.5 to 96.5 cm) high, consoles taller, and studio pianos taller still.

Piano cases are usually made of solid wood, although veneer is also used on more recent models. Unlike a guitar, the case has little influence on the tone.

The harp

This is made from a cast iron plate, and its purpose is to provide a solid mounting for the strings. The harp consists of the frame, soundboard, and pinblock. The forces involved are incredible – the 200 strings of a regular piano generate about 18 tons of force. Most of this has to be supported by the frame.

The soundboard is usually made from spruce. When it is installed in the piano it is under tension and this gives it a gentle curve, which is stressed by glued-in ribs. This helps to enhance the instrument's sustaining qualities. The strings' vibrations are transmitted to the soundboard via two bridges. These work in the same way as the guitar bridge, which carries the vibrations from the strings to the body of the instrument.

The pinblock is the laminated piece of wood bolted to the iron frame. It contains the tuning pins and is one of the most vital parts of the piano's construction. The piano's strings are attached to the tuning pins.

The strings

Short, thin strings produce high-pitched notes; long, fat strings give low notes. For the notes spanning the top two-thirds of the keyboard there are usually three strings, tuned in unison, for each note. The bass notes have pairs of strings. Parallel strings enhance the timbre and quality of the acoustic piano's sound. To keep the bass strings to a reasonable length, wire is wrapped around them to make them thicker and give a deeper note. Thinner, longer strings would produce a better bass sound, but would be too long.

The piano action

When you press a piano key a series of events, known as the "action train", takes place. It is this that causes the note to sound, and so a piano's action is an extremely intricate piece of engineering. Every note has its own mechanism, which must be as silent and smooth as possible. In addition, each note must have a similar feel.

The action of a piano must satisfy several other conditions. When the key is at rest the strings must be damped so they do not vibrate. When you press one of the keys, a hammer must move toward a string. The speed at which it strikes the string must be in proportion to the speed and force with which you strike the key. The hammer must hit the string only once, and then return to a "reset" position as quickly as possible. And finally, the damper must only be re-applied to the string once you have released the key.

There are three basic types of piano action: the direct action of the upright, the drop action of the spinet type, and the grand piano action.

Direct action

As you press the key, a lever mechanism, the *wippen,* is activated. The end nearest the front of the key moves up and the other end moves downward. The upward movement projects the hammer toward the string while the downward movement lifts the damper off the string. The wippen pushes the jack upward and this in turn makes the hammer move toward the string. The jack is then disconnected from the hammer butt and from this point on the hammer moves toward the string on its own. Its momentum, determined by how fast you originally hit the key, dictates the speed at which it will strike the string. So once the note has been de-

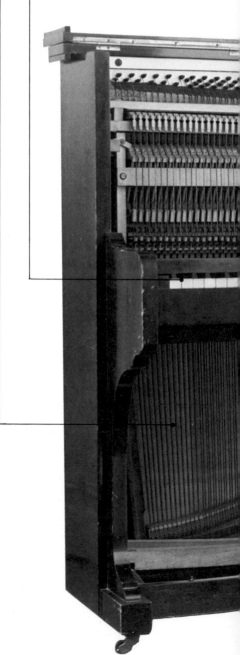

The strings Piano strings are made of steel wire in various thicknesses. To reduce their length, the bass strings also have wire wound round them.

The keys Most pianos have 88 keys, giving a range of $7\frac{1}{4}$ octaves. Because piano keyboards are touch-sensitive, you can obtain a wide range of expressive effects.

The pinblock Each string is attached to a tuning pin, which is inserted into the pinblock. This block is usually made of laminated maple wood, a material which is especially effective in stopping the pins slipping and keeping the instrument in tune.

The hammers Each key operates one hammer. Apart from striking the string, the mechanism has to make the hammer fall away from the string after use. But this is done in such a way as to allow you to repeat notes in quick succession.

The frame Made of a single piece of cast iron, the frame takes all the tension generated by the strings.

The soft pedal On an upright piano, the soft pedal moves the hammer rail closer to the strings. This means that the hammers have less momentum when they hit the strings, they move more slowly and the notes are softer.

The sustain pedal By means of a series of rods and levers, this pedal lifts all the dampers away from the strings. The strings stay undamped until you release the pedal.

pressed you have no control of the hammer's movement.

With direct action, the force of gravity is not strong enough to return the hammer to its original position, so a special mechanism, consisting of the bridle strap and hammer spring, is employed. As the key is released the front end of the wippen lowers and the jack follows. Because the jack spring is being compressed, a force is applied to the jack knuckle which makes the upper end of the jack return to its position in contact with the hammer butt. So even before the key is fully released, the mechanism is ready to trigger another note – allowing you to play repeated notes very quickly. As long as you hold the key down, the damper is kept away from the string. As soon as you release the key, the damper returns to the string, suppressing its vibrations.

Drop action

This type of action is used mainly in spinet pianos, because it allows the manufacturer to reduce the size of the instrument. The main difference between drop and direct action is that drop action pianos have an extra linkage allowing the wippen to be placed on a level below the key. This means that the hammer can also be at a lower level, so that the whole instrument can have a lower height. Because it has this extra transmission stage, many players feel that drop action is inferior to direct action.

Grand piano action

Grand pianos have a different action mechanism, although many of the parts are the same. Because its strings run horizontally, the action can make more use of gravity for restoring the hammer than the upright. Some actions are very complicated, with as many as seventy moving parts for each key.

The pipe organ

From the earliest times, pipes have been used as musical instruments. Reeds, because they are hollow, proved particularly popular, and pan pipes were in a way the first organs. They consist simply of a series of varying-length reeds. These were cut off just below a knot to form closed pipes, lashed together and played by blowing across the top. The longer the reed, the lower the note.

Later someone realized that you could produce a "whistle" version of the pipe by making a small hole in the knot, cutting a bevelled notch in the reed, and blowing through the knot. The organ, in its earliest recognizable form, used a constant source of air pressure, directed to the pipe by means of a simple keyboard, to make a sound with whistle-type organ pipes.

By the twelfth century, "mixtures" had been introduced, allowing more than one pipe to sound when you play a single key. The fifteenth century saw the organ evolve into its modern form, with two keyboards and a pedal board. In the eighteenth century an entire section of the organ was enclosed in a box with a sliding front. Known as the swell organ, this provided an effective volume control.

Other developments followed, mostly in the area of control systems, and different mechanisms for supplying air to the pipes.

The organ mechanism

The pipe organ has two basic sets of controls. The *stops* dictate which ranks of pipes are to be used, while the keyboard or keyboards determine which pipes are to sound.

Pipe organs have a reservoir of air, which is compressed to provide a "wind pressure". The compression was originally achieved using mechanical bellows, but modern organs use electric blowers.

Tracker organs have a complex mechanical linkage going directly from the keys to the pipe valves. This type of action is usually found on older instruments. It is heavy, often noisy, and prone to failure. The electric action found on modern organs is an improvement on this.

Types of organ pipe

There are four main types of organ pipe. All these types are normally available at a range of different footages (see p. 39). *Diapasons* (or principal pipes) are the main foundation when you are forming a voicing on a pipe organ. They are made of alloys of zinc, or lead and tin. The greater the tin content, the brighter and louder the sound.

Probably the first imitative organ stops to appear were the *flutes*. These have a softer, rounder sound than the flute itself, similar to a recorder. Like diapasons, these pipes are available at all the major pitches. They are usually made of wood, although a metal alloy (typically with 30 percent tin) is sometimes used. Many electric organs have

◁ **Steve Winwood** Vocalist and keyboard player Winwood worked with the Spencer Davis Group and Traffic before making successful solo albums. It was with the Spencer Davis Group that his use of strong organ riffs first came to the fore, particularly on tracks like "I'm a man" and "Gimme some lovin' ".

Electric keyboards

flute voicings that produce almost a pure sine wave, useful for building up a voicing.

Strings usually have a weak fundamental and a fairly full harmonic content. They achieve this with very narrow pipes. They often have "box beards" that surround the mouth of each pipe, and enable it to be driven with a stronger blast of air.

The pipes known as *reeds* contain a vibrating reed at the mouthpiece. The sound this makes is amplified by the air mass in the body of the pipe. The pitch is determined by the length of the reed – the shorter it is, the higher the pitch. Reed stops are rich in harmonics, but their exact timbre varies according to the shape of the pipe and the thickness of the blade.

Registration

Organ stops are labeled in "footages". For example, a certain flute stop might be given the marking 8' (eight feet). This refers to the length of the longest pipe in the rank of that particular stop. Usually this is the pipe that corresponds to the bottom key of the manual. A 16' stop is pitched an octave below an 8' one, while a 4' stop sounds an octave higher. If the 8' pipe is the fundamental pitch (see p. 26), the 4' pipe is the second harmonic, the 2', two octaves above, is the fourth harmonic, and the 1', three octaves above, the eighth harmonic. The 16' pipe, an octave below the fundamental, is known as the sub-harmonic. You will also find mutations, stops that produce uneven harmonics, such as the $2\frac{2}{3}'$.

The way keyboards have changed over the years has depended on a number of advances and inventions in the world of electronics. Perhaps the first of these was the development of the *radio valve* (or *diode*). This enabled keyboard designers to produce circuits such as amplifiers.

The *LC* (or *Hartley*) *oscillator,* developed in 1917, provided a tone generation system that was to be used widely until about twenty years ago.

In the early fifties the *transistor* appeared. This device acted as a replacement for the valve in the control of an electric current. Valves were large, fragile, and awkward to use. Transistors, on the other hand, are small, strong, reliable, and easy to work with. They revolutionized the whole electronics industry. Keyboards got smaller and more attractive for home use.

Compactness was not the only advantage of the transistor. It made it possible for the home organ to become a complete musical system, with features such as percussion sounds.

Technology took another leap forward in the mid-sixties with the appearance of the *integrated circuit.* This incorporates hundreds (or even thousands) of transistors on a small (and cheap) slice of silicon. As a result, home keyboards got even smaller and more gadget-laden.

Pioneering instruments

The first true electric keyboard instrument was called the Telharmonium. It was patented in 1897, weighed about 200 tons, needed six railway cars to move it, and required two people to play it. It was a polyphonic instrument and had a touch-sensitive keyboard. The sound was produced by a series of rapidly spinning alternators driven by banks of electric motors. These rotated at fixed speeds, to govern the frequency of the alternating currents, and therefore the pitch of the sound. These alternators were very noisy, and most of the instrument had to be housed in a separate room from the loudspeakers.

The first popular electric musical instrument was called the Theremin. Invented in 1924, it became the most talked-about instrument of its time. Its sound was produced by two very high-frequency LC oscillators. You controlled the pitch and amplitude of the sound by moving your hands toward and away from a pair of antennae. The Theremin's tone – a haunting, almost-pure sine wave – could not be varied. It was used in 1966 by the Beach Boys to produce the wailing sounds at the end of their "Good Vibrations".

Other instruments used a similar principle to the Theremin. Of these, probably the best known are the French "Ondes Martenots" and "Ondes Musicales". An extra dimension of their sound is controlled by a ring on the player's finger.

The Hammond organ

It was inventor Laurens Hammond and his chief engineer John Hanert who were successful in taking the rotating disk system of the Telharmonium and adapting it to create the tone-wheel organ. The Hammond organ first appeared in 1939 and was very similar to the model used today. It has an electric motor that runs at a precisely defined rate. This rotates a shaft containing 91 metal disks, each profiled with a different pattern of peaks and troughs. These are used to regulate 91 frequencies.

As well as the basic frequencies, the Hammond allows you to control harmonics. Each note operates nine different switches, each corresponding to a particular harmonic and connected to one of nine different harmonic volume controls called *drawbars*. By using these controls you can regulate the timbre by adding together harmonics and produce over 300,000 different sounds.

The makers claimed that the original Hammond organ provided a good alternative to the large and expensive pipe organ. A comparison between a Hammond and the $75,000 Skinner Pipe Organ in Chicago University's Rockefeller Chapel was organized with the Hammond's speakers hidden among the pipes. The Hammond fared well. One third of the experts and half the non-experts present failed to identify the two instruments.

To help fill the broadcasting hours, live electric organ music became one of the most useful assets of the program schedulers. Most studios had their own Hammond organ and organist.

Many variations on the Hammond were made. The B-3 (and its European equivalent the C-3) achieved widest popularity. They became *the* jazz organs of the fifties, before being taken up by the rock musicians.

Portable organs

The fifties saw the birth of the small band. Styles like rhythm and blues, rock and roll, and skiffle had encouraged small groups of players to buy guitars and drums and play music together. The guitar in particular became more and more popular – you could tuck it under your arm and carry it anywhere. But for keyboard players this meant problems. Most amateurs and semi-professional players simply couldn't transport their electric organs around.

The Italian company Farfisa, with their Compact Duo, were one of the first to meet the demand for a really portable electric organ. Vox, with their Continental and Jaguar models, also produced low-cost, portable, transistor organs. These proved popular with both amateur and professional players.

But many musicians still wanted to use their Hammond organs. In the fifties, the Hammond sound couldn't be effectively copied using electronic circuitry. So players had their Hammond organs "split". The lower section would be sawn off horizontally, so that the keyboards, motors, and electrics were housed in the top section. The leg section, containing the pedals, could be transported separately if required.

◁ **Laurens Hammond** The designer of the Hammond organ was a Chicago-based inventor who had spent a lot of time working on devices driven by clockwork and electric motors. His inventions ranged from an electric clock to an automatic card dealer. The organ uses a version of an electric motor originally developed for use in a clock. The original Hammond organ was designed during 1933–4, but made its first public appearance in 1939 at an Industrial Arts Exposition in New York's RCA Building.

◁ **Mike Smith** Keyboard player with the Dave Clark Five, Smith used Vox Continental and Jaguar electric organs. These made an important contribution to the group's sound.

▽ **Madness** The characteristic thin vibrato timbre of the Vox Continental played a part in the evolution of Madness' eccentric sound. They later replaced the Vox with a more versatile Yamaha YC-45D.

Home organs

The market for home organs grew phenomenally in the post-war years. The first commercially produced electronic organ was the Baldwin Model 5. Other companies, still well known in the field of electronic organs, also entered the market at this time. F. C. Lowery produced the Lowery Organo, a device that enabled a piano to be modified to incorporate an organ voicing system. The piano's keys themselves activated the Organo's circuitry, and you could layer organ tones on top of the piano sound. Other manufacturers, such as Gulbrausen, Conn, and Thomas, developed electronic organs, leaving Hammond the only major producer of electric types.

A modern home organ like the one shown on this page is rather like an electronic orchestra. It offers the player an amazing wealth of performance controls and automatic features. But perhaps the most impressive quality of these units is the fidelity of their sounds. Several major manufacturers now use a technology called pulse code modulation. This enables recordings of real sounds to be put into digital code. So the sounds the organ makes are derived from acoustic instruments. If the organ is played in the right way, the overall feel of the sound can be stunningly close to the real thing.

The biggest limitation with most keyboard instruments designed to play bass, chords, rhythm, and melody, is that you only have a single pair of hands. Most of the more sophisticated home organs have not only two separate keyboards but also a pedalboard, at least one swell (or expression) pedal, and a sustain footswitch. Automatic features such as auto chords, arpeggios, and auto bass facilities are common, helping to make it easy to get the full sound. The pedals are usually monophonic and used with your left foot to play the bass line.

A home organ with a comprehensive array of features can look rather like the flight deck of an airplane. The many banks of switches and control knobs give the instrument as much timbral scope as possible. This type of organ is designed as an instrument for live performance, so you have to be able to "play" the controls, changing sounds quickly and effortlessly at the precise moment dictated by the music. The instrument is designed to make such changes as straightforward as possible. But you will still need a lot of practice to master the arts of voicing, arrangement, and being able to make efficient control changes.

Upper manual voicings The basic signal source for most electronic organs is the upper flute section. This model has eight flute footages each providing sine waves, as well as four harmonic percussion sources, a simulated "click" tap, and two string footages.

String ensemble Preset cello and violin string sounds can be assigned to either keyboard.

Vocal ensemble Vocal sounds — with voices either humming or singing "ah" — can be selected for either keyboard.

Bass section Ten preset sounds are employed for the bass. They can be assigned to the pedalboard or to either keyboard.

Rhythm programmer The rhythm section features 22 preset patterns, and you can also create your own patterns using 12 different percussion voicings linking them to form complete rhythm tracks.

Automatics The instrument will automatically generate any bass or chord accompaniment. In addition you can make complete arrangements that can be recalled at the touch of a button.

Percussive presets These consist of a set of voicings that have no sustain facility. In other words, these instruments all have piano-like envelopes. Examples include harpsichord, clavinet, electric and acoustic piano, banjo, and guitar. You can assign these voicings to either keyboard.

Musical display The liquid crystal display gives detailed information about the organ's operating modes, which computer-control functions are running, the rhythm tempo, and other data.

Orchestral conductor You use this to select which individual voice-generation circuits are to be used to produce the desired overall sound. It makes fast changes of texture and voicing much simpler and it enables you to see at a glance which functions are being used.

Voice-setting computer This provides a set of memory locations into which program data can be entered and recalled.

Orchestral presets These preset voices have a sustain facility, are assignable to either keyboard, and are mostly simulations of instruments from the brass family.

Spatial effects Effects such as tremolo, vibrato, chorus, celeste, and phasing are selected by using these controls.

Lower manual voicings Four flute and two string voicings are used for the lower manual.

Solo synthesizer presets These monophonic synthesizer sounds can be used for melody or bass accompaniments. They are mostly imitative sounds.

Digital memory A plug-in memory pack enables you to store program and sequence data permanently in separate modules. You can build up a library of your favorite arrangements on these modules.

Tone generation

Most organs require so many different pitches that it is impractical to have an oscillator for every pitch. There are three main alternative systems of tone generation: top-octave division, master-tone generation, and voice assignment.

With top-octave division, twelve tone generators are used for the pitches of the chromatic scale (see p. 101). These tones are set at the highest pitches for each tone that the organ will require. The problem with this sytem is that the tuning can drift.

The master-tone generation system uses a single, very high frequency oscillator as the main reference pitch. Its oscillation, divided by twelve different figures, gives pitches corresponding to the notes of the chromatic scale. The main advantage of this is that the tuning cannot drift – the instrument is always in tune with itself. But the sound can be rather flat, because all the tones derive from a single pitch.

The third type of tone generation, voice assignment, uses a fixed number of voices that are assigned to particular notes in turn. This method is frequently used in polyphonic synthesizers (see p. 50).

Electric and electronic pianos

As electric organs became more and more successful, it seemed logical to take electric organ technology and adapt it to produce an electric alternative to the acoustic piano.

The electric pianos of the thirties and forties were basically acoustic instruments with the soundboard replaced by electric pickups. There were problems with this system. You couldn't get the lower notes to die away quickly enough with the soundboard removed, so the sound of these pianos was rather muddy and jumbled. Using a conventional piano as a starting point wasn't very satisfactory anyway – the instrument was still far too bulky for many musicians' requirements.

There were two solutions to these problems. The first, developed by serviceman Harold Rhodes during the Second World War, had hammers that struck metal rods. The second used an adapted version of the Everett electric organ mechanism. This blows air over small metal reeds. The first became the Fender Rhodes, the second the Wurlitzer, two of the most popular keyboards of their time – and instruments that still have their devotees.

The Wurlitzer piano

It was engineer B. F. Meissner, working for Wurlitzer, who adapted the Everett electric organ system to make an electric piano. In 1955 he unveiled the Wurlitzer electric piano, the design of which was to remain unchanged for over 20 years.

The reeds he used were made from steel and were about a quarter of an inch wide. Every reed had a different length and therefore a different natural frequency. A small amount of lead solder was applied to the reed tips. By increasing or reducing the amounts of solder, fine-tuning was possible.

A vibrating reed generates a very pure tone. This is fine in an electric organ, but causes problems in a piano. The reason is the acoustic piano's rich timbre – the lack of higher harmonics tends to make the reed's sound rather dull. Meissner solved the problem by setting up the action so that the hammers struck the reeds one third of the way down their length. This introduced odd harmonics. He also positioned the reeds so that they didn't vibrate symmetrically in relation to the pick-up. The result was a very rich waveform.

The Wurlitzer is AC powered and was one of the first commercial instruments to offer a headphone facility, allowing you to practice almost silently.

One of the Wurlitzer's shortcomings is the span of the keyboard. With just 64 notes it was not extensive enough for many traditional pianists. Another problem is that the reeds often break. This can happen a lot if you play heavy-handedly.

Many types of Wurlitzer have been built over the years. The action of the most recent models is very good. It is fast and sturdy, although people used to acoustic instruments find that it is rather light and lacks the acoustic piano's dynamic control.

▷ **Wurlitzer Model 200**
This model has a keyboard of 64 notes. It accepts headphones and has its own internal amplifier and speakers, although there is also an output jack for an external amplifier. The front panel has controls for volume and variable-intensity vibrato. The function of the pedal is to lift the dampers so that the notes are sustained.

▽ **Suitcase Rhodes piano**
With its integral stereo amplifier and speakers snd its stereo vibrato unit, the Suitcase Rhodes is an electric piano that has proved very popular with touring musicians over the years. This model has a keyboard of 88 notes.

The Rhodes piano

It was Harold Rhodes, a serviceman in the US Army Air Corps, who invented this piano during the second world war. He was employed in an army service hospital and decided to try to teach patients to play in order to boost morale. Acoustic pianos were difficult to obtain and were obviously useless to bedridden patients. So Rhodes set about designing a small portable piano, so that patients lying in bed could play.

The original model had bare wooden keys that activated hammers which struck metal rods (called *tines*). Each tine had a different length and so vibrated at a different frequency. At the end of the war Rhodes saw commercial potential for his piano. He lengthened the keyboard and added pick-ups, to make the instrument virtually the same as the one we know today.

The action of the Rhodes produces sounds that are unique to the instrument. When the tine is struck by the hammer it is deflected, causing some distortion in the pick-up and giving a rich harmonic tone during the note's attack phase. This portion of the sound can be controlled by the way you strike the keys – the harder you play, the more deflection occurs, and the brighter the sound.

When the tine's vibration is damped, the waveform is more like the tine's movement. It is this effect that is responsible for the Rhodes' characteristic rather bell-like tone.

In the sixties Leo Fender's company took over the manufacture of this instrument, which then became known as the Fender Rhodes. There were four basic models. The Stage 73 and Stage 88 are 73- and 88-note versions of the basic instrument. The Suitcase 73 and 88 models incorporate a stereo amplifier and speaker on which the keyboards sit. The Suitcase 88 also has a stereo vibrato facility that has become the hallmark of the Suitcase Rhodes. It is still a marvellous instrument, and if you want to try an electro-mechanical keyboard, this is the best one.

Adapting the Rhodes

Although the Rhodes has few controls there are other ways of varying the sound it makes. Rhodes enthusiasts often adapt their instruments in various ways to get a slightly different sound. Coarse tuning is possible by cutting a tine to a specific length. To fine-tune the instrument, you move a small spring along the tine.

You can also adjust the position of each tine in relation to its pick-up. This allows you to set the tone and loudness contour of every note exactly as you wish. By sliding the pick-up closer to the tine, you can adjust the note's amplitude, so that you can balance the piano's volume to suit your particular musical requirements.

Hammer tips come in five grades of hardness and you can fit harder tips for a more percussive sound. This is fairly simple. You have to remove the old tips carefully and glue the new ones in place.

The piano's action can be changed by moving the action rail. One company makes a foot pedal which will actually move the harp (the assembly housing all the tines) so that you can alter the position at which the hammers hit the tines. Naturally, this alters the way the tines vibrate and therefore changes the sound they make.

The Pianet

This machine has metal reeds positioned next to pick-ups. When you press a key, a sticky rubber pad pulls the reed, making it bend, until the force required to bend it is too great. At this point the reed is released, and it starts to vibrate.

The Clavinet

About 1960 Ernst Zacharias, inventor of the Pianet, developed the Clavinet. This works in a similar way to a clavichord (see p. 35), but the striking mechanism consists of a hammer and anvil and there are tuning screws along the front of the instrument, under the keys. You adjust the tuning by altering the tension of the strings.

The Clavinet caught on as a jazz-rock and funk instrument, helped by artists such as Stevie Wonder, who really capitalized on its percussive qualities. The most recent models, the D6 and E7, have a set of rocker switches for selecting different tones. This is achieved by a dual pick-up arrangement, which allows

This system made the Pianet very cheap to produce and until recently it was the cheapest of all polyphonic keyboards. Its sound is a little woolly, there is no sustain facility, and little dynamic control. But it does have a sound similar to a piano and has stood the test of time well.

the machine to mix bass and treble tones.

Touch-sensitive control is a feature of the Clavinet. The harder you strike the keys, the brighter the note. In addition, by applying pressure to a key after playing it, you can raise its pitch. Another effect you can get, by repeatedly increasing and decreasing the key pressure, is vibrato. But the Clavinet is a very percussive instrument, and the notes will not sustain for long after you have played them.

Most preset polyphonic synthesizers feature a voice (labelled ''Clav'' or ''Clavi'') designed to simulate the instrument's biting percussive sound. For this reason, many musicians no longer use a separate Clavinet.

The electric grand piano

For a long time there has been a demand from touring musicians for a portable grand piano that could easily be amplified. In response to this, Yamaha started producing electric grand pianos in the late seventies.

They made these instruments portable by splitting them into two sections, one housing the harp, the other containing the action and strings. The two units are latched together so that the hammers are directly in line with the corresponding strings.

Because it uses short strings to keep dimensions down, the electric grand doesn't sound exactly like its acoustic counterpart. The bass notes are rather punchy and the Yamaha instruments only have two strings per key in the treble notes and one in the bass register.

The absence of a soundboard means that there is less damping of the strings, so that the sustain time of the electric grand is longer. If you play it together with highly amplified instruments, you also get positive feedback (see p. 28).

But many players like the electric grand, finding it pleasing to play.

◁ **Stevie Wonder and the Clavinet** Singer, songwriter and keyboard player Stevie Wonder has made the percussive sound of the Clavinet one of his hallmarks. The role of this instrument is often rather like that of a rhythm guitar.

▷ **A portable piano** This electric grand piano has a full 88 note keyboard, but it is compact enough to pack into two portable units. It has bass, middle, and treble tone controls, and a brilliance level switch, which enables you to balance the piano's sound with your amplifier.

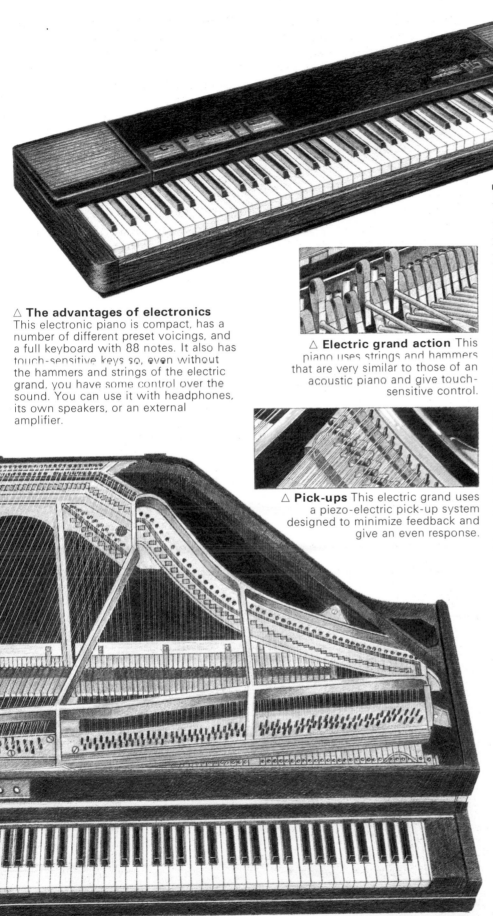

△ **The advantages of electronics**
This electronic piano is compact, has a number of different preset voicings, and a full keyboard with 88 notes. It also has touch-sensitive keys so, even without the hammers and strings of the electric grand, you have some control over the sound. You can use it with headphones, its own speakers, or an external amplifier.

△ **Electric grand action** This piano uses strings and hammers that are very similar to those of an acoustic piano and give touch-sensitive control.

△ **Pick-ups** This electric grand uses a piezo-electric pick-up system designed to minimize feedback and give an even response.

The electronic piano

With the invention of the transistor (see p. 39) there was a boom in the development of electronic pianos. The complex piano sound meant that electronic pianos were a little late in catching on. Unlike an organ, which has a waveform that is quite easy to imitate, the piano is a touch-sensitive instrument that produces a highly complex timbre rich in harmonics.

As with electronic organs, there are several possible systems of tone generation. Tones can be derived from top octave generators or master tone generators (see p. 90) and divided. But these methods do not produce a very lively sound. So one of the first electronic pianos to be made, the RMI Electra-piano, had a separate tone generator for every note.

Italian manufacturers were the first to produce low-cost electronic pianos. These usually had five-octave keyboards with a selection of piano, harpsichord, and honky-tonk piano voicings.

Imitating the acoustic piano

Acoustic pianos have two or three strings per note. This feature gives the piano its rich, full sound. To simulate this, some manufacturers now produce electronic pianos that have two complete sets of master tone generators and dividers. The result is that every time you play a note you can hear two tones that are not phase-related, greatly enhancing the sound's

47

Synthesizers

authenticity. In addition, the system allows you to detune one set of generators against the other, giving a honky-tonk sound.

The traditional piano is fully polyphonic – you can play as many notes at once as you like. Many current electronic models go some way to imitating this feature by having a set number of voices, which can be assigned to different keys (see p. 50). The advantage of this voice-assignment system is that the instrument needs less circuitry to produce the actual tones. Sixteen voices or more are required for serious use.

When you play an acoustic piano, you will notice that the timbre and loudness of the notes vary according to how hard you hit the keys. Some electronic pianos try to simulate this touch-sensitivity by measuring the amount of time it takes for the key to travel a certain distance. The instrument then sends this information to the circuits that govern the timbre and loudness.

To imitate the feel of an acoustic instrument, some of the more professional models have a weighted wooden keyboard.

Advantages of electronic pianos

If you can accept that an electronic piano isn't going to sound exactly like an acoustic one, you will find that the instrument has several positive benefits over its ancestor. It will probably never require tuning. It takes up much less space than an acoustic instrument and, if you are on the move, it is considerably more portable. You can use headphones with most models, which means you don't disturb others when practicing. You can modify the sound quite easily. And if you want to play live with a band an electronic piano will not need miking up.

What exactly is a synthesizer? It is basically an electronic instrument that allows you to shape accurately the pitch, tone, and amplitude of the sound it produces. Instruments such as electronic pianos and organs, although they may use similar technology to produce their sounds, are not normally called synthesizers because they only produce a limited range of timbres.

A synthesizer doesn't have to be a keyboard instrument. There are guitar, wind, and percussion synthesizers, and even synthesizers with no apparent control at all. But the keyboard has become the most widely accepted way of playing the synthesizer. It gives you a convenient way of controlling the electronic circuits that make up a synthesizer simply because the keys are efficient at opening and closing switches.

Most current synthesizers use voltage control to produce the sound (see p. 50). This is an effective and inexpensive control method. But it is not the only one. Some of the most exciting recent synthesizers use digital technology (see p. 64). This type will soon become more common, particularly in conjunction with microcomputers.

The beginnings

The synthesizer as we know it would not have developed without the pioneering work of figures like Theremin, the inventor of the instrument that bears his name (see p. 39), and Hammond (see p. 40). The Telharmonium was a sort of synthesizer, so the instrument is hardly a modern invention. But the true ancestors of the synthesizers we use now were the RCA models that were built in the fifties.

There were two original RCA synthesizers. The Mark I was built in 1954. It was rebuilt the following year as the Mark II and installed in New York's Columbia-Princeton studio. Both machines relied on valves, and were therefore large and expensive. But their output was heard on many recordings of the time.

The RCA synthesizers used a combination of analog and digital systems to produce their sound (see p. 32) and were monophonic. To make polyphonic recordings, you used a multi-track disk recorder. You could record six tracks on this before mixing them down on to a master disk. This master could then take five more sets of six tracks, eventually giving you a 36-track recording.

Robert Moog

Harry F. Olson and Herbert Belar, the designers of the RCA, were important figures in the history of the synthesizer. But in the sixties and seventies there was one name above all that became synonymous with the electronic synthesizer – Moog. It was Robert Moog who made the synthesizer a viable and commercial instrument.

Since childhood, Moog had been fascinated by electronic gadgetry and he had earned money to help pay for his college studies by selling Theremins in kit form. In 1963 he and Herb Deutsch, an electronic composer and lecturer at Hofstra University, decided to produce a small music synthesizer making use of a voltage-controlled circuit that Moog had developed. Their aim was to control the pitch, timbre, and loudness of musical notes using changes in voltage. By 1965 they had set up a small factory to produce the various circuit modules which, when combined, enabled musicians to create their own sounds by defining these three basic parameters. What was more, they managed to produce these models are relatively low cost. Moog's biggest break came in 1967 when Walter Carlos recorded the album "Switched on Bach". This was a record of several of Bach's most popular works using no acoustic instruments at all – just Moog's electronic music modules. The album was a big success and demand for the modules was unbelievable.

▷ **The Minimoog**
Moog had been working on this synthesizer since 1968 and he unveiled it at the AES Convention in 1971. It was the first synthesizer that was designed specifically to be played live and met a massive demand from musicians.

▽ **Moog with his modular synthesizer** Dr Robert Moog, the pioneer of synthesizer design, produced modular units as well as his popular Minimoog and Polymoog models.

The next generation

In 1971 Moog and his fellow designer Jim Scott launched the Minimoog. This was the first synthesizer that could effectively be played live. It is a brilliant piece of design, not only in the circuitry it employs and the sound it makes, but also in terms of "human engineering" – people like using it and it is a real musical instrument. Moog and Scott got it so right that, in spite of radical advances in technology, the Minimoog has remained virtually unchanged over ten years of production, and people still use it today.

At this time several other inventors were perfecting their own instruments. Don Buchla evolved an impressive modular system, while Alan R. Pearlman launched his ARP 2600 which was to be highly popular with musicians over the years.

Synthesizer controls

A synthesizer gets the following information when you press a key on its keyboard: the pitch of the note you require, exactly when the key is depressed, and when it is released – the last two bits of information tell it how long the note is to sound. Only keyboards that are touch-sensitive will transmit other information.

The synthesizer's voice module is responsible for producing a single sound at the pitch determined by the keyboard at the time governed by when you play the note. All the other controls that shape the voice module's final output are regulated by setting switches on the machine's top panel.

Assigning notes to the voice module

If your synthesizer is monophonic, it will have just one voice module. This enables you to play only one note at a time. If you press two or more keys at once, the instrument has to decide which to assign to the voice module. There are three common methods of doing this: low-note priority (the lowest of the notes that you play sounds), high-note priority (the highest note sounds), and last-note priority (the last note is assigned to the voice module).

If your synthesizer is polyphonic, it will probably still have a limited number of voice modules, which it will assign according to last-note priority.

Voltage control

Moog's original circuits, and most synthesizer circuits today, are controlled by changes in voltage. Voltage is a measurement of electrical potential. For example, the two terminals of a battery have a potential difference, so that when a circuit is completed a charge flows.

There are three main elements to an analog synthesizer and they are all controlled by voltage changes. They are: the *voltage-controlled oscillator* (VCO), the *voltage-controlled filter* (VCF), and the *voltage-controlled amplifier* (VCA). The oscillator determines the pitch of the sound, the filter controls the timbre, and the amplifier governs the loudness. The greater the voltage applied to the input stage of the VCO, the higher the frequency of the resulting tone. The greater the voltage applied to the VCF, the higher the cut-off frequency of the filter (see p. 53) and so the more signal the filter lets through. The greater the voltage applied to the VCA, the louder the note sounds.

Low-frequency oscillator This is an oscillator that functions at a very slow rate. You can send its output to either the VCO or VCA, and according to the type of waveform you select and the destination to which you send it, the effect on the sound will be different (see p. 55).

Voltage controlled oscillator The VCO allows you to select a basic waveform that provides the starting point for creating a sound. Many synthesizers have only one VCO (see pp. 52-3).

Performance controls To give you easy control over the sound during performance, the pitchbend and modulation wheels are usually placed next to the keyboard, to the left (see p. 57).

A guide to the controls

The synthesizer shown here is used as a guide to the main controls. Their names vary from machine to machine, and some synthesizers have fewer controls than this one, but the basic format is usually very similar.

Voltage-controlled filter This part of the synthesizer works like a tone control, determining the timbre of the final sound. It works by removing certain frequencies from the VCO's signal while letting others pass through. The controls enable you to determine which frequencies will go through the filter and which are excluded (see pp. 53-4).

Amplifier envelope Envelope generators offer another way of controlling the synthesizer's output. Their control voltage can be sent to both the amplifier and the filter. In each case a group of controls is provided for the four basic elements of the envelope waveform — attack, decay, sustain, and release (see p. 54). Linking the envelope generator to the amplifier allows you to control the amplitude of the sound (see p. 56).

Second VCO The output from a single VCO is pure and continuous and sounds uninteresting. So some models have a second VCO, which gives the sound a much more interesting, lifelike quality (see pp. 55-6).

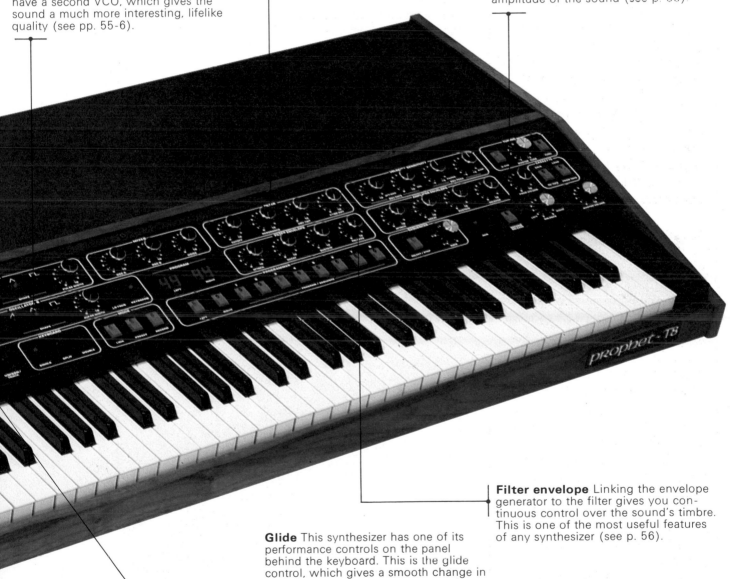

Filter envelope Linking the envelope generator to the filter gives you continuous control over the sound's timbre. This is one of the most useful features of any synthesizer (see p. 56).

Glide This synthesizer has one of its performance controls on the panel behind the keyboard. This is the glide control, which gives a smooth change in pitch between the two notes you play on the keyboard. The glide takes place at the rate you set with this control.

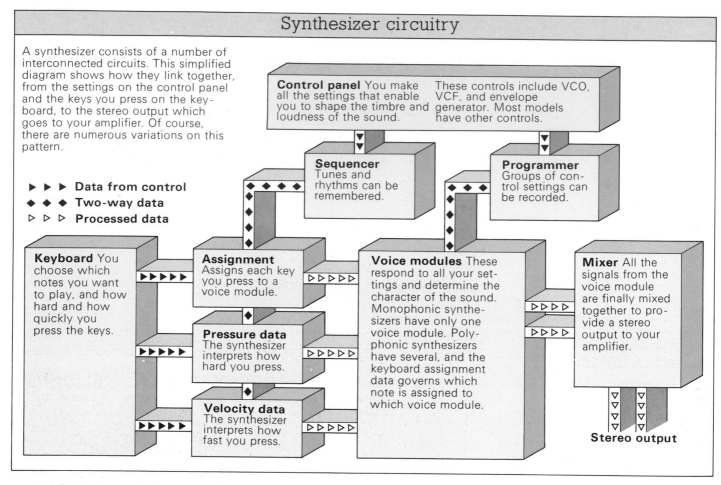

Synthesizer circuitry

A synthesizer consists of a number of interconnected circuits. This simplified diagram shows how they link together, from the settings on the control panel and the keys you press on the keyboard, to the stereo output which goes to your amplifier. Of course, there are numerous variations on this pattern.

▶ ▶ ▶ **Data from control**
◆ ◆ ◆ **Two-way data**
▷ ▷ ▷ **Processed data**

Control panel You make all the settings that enable you to shape the timbre and loudness of the sound. These controls include VCO, VCF, and envelope generator. Most models have other controls.

Sequencer Tunes and rhythms can be remembered.

Programmer Groups of control settings can be recorded.

Keyboard You choose which notes you want to play, and how hard and how quickly you press the keys.

Assignment Assigns each key you press to a voice module.

Pressure data The synthesizer interprets how hard you press.

Velocity data The synthesizer interprets how fast you press.

Voice modules These respond to all your settings and determine the character of the sound. Monophonic synthesizers have only one voice module. Polyphonic synthesizers have several, and the keyboard assignment data governs which note is assigned to which voice module.

Mixer All the signals from the voice module are finally mixed together to provide a stereo output to your amplifier.

Stereo output

The voltage-controlled filter

The VCO produces a pitch that is proportional to the voltage applied to it. It has to control a wide range of frequencies, so a small change in voltage has to result in a large swing in frequency. This means that to change the pitch slightly, the voltage need only be varied by a very small amount. Most manufacturers have adopted a principle of "one volt per octave". This means that if you raise the voltage applied to the VCO by one volt, the frequency of the oscillators doubles, so that the tone rises an octave.

VCO controls

The VCO section of a synthesizer usually has a number of controls, including range and fine-tuning knobs, and a waveform selector.

The range control is normally marked in footages. If you set it at 8' and apply a voltage of 2v, it might produce a pitch corresponding to middle C. Switch the range control to 4' and this will raise the frequency by one octave (in other words the frequency will double).

In order to set the exact pitch of the oscillators, a fine-tuning control enables you to vary the output frequency continuously over the range of one octave. An additional advantage of this is that if your synthesizer has two VCO's, you can set their frequencies apart at any interval.

A VCO produces a signal that you can amplify and feed to a loudspeaker before it is sent to the VCF. But the actual sound it produces isn't very exciting. Although the VCF is mainly responsible for controlling the overall timbre of the instrument's output, the VCO also plays some part in this. Therefore it often features a waveform selector.

A VCO can oscillate between two fixed points producing a square wave, or it can oscillate smoothly tracing out a continuous curve, or it can repeat itself in several other ways. The waveform selector allows you to choose one of these waveforms. Each of them has a different harmonic content and therefore a different tone quality. So when you want to shape the timbre of the sound by using the VCF and you want a sound rich in harmonics, you should use a waveform from the oscillator that provides these from the start – you cannot add harmonics when you are filtering.

In order to give a richer, fuller sound, some synthesizer manufacturers provide a sub-octave source. This is generally a square wave that is pitched an octave below that of the main VCO output. It is particularly useful for generating heavy bass sounds.

Oscillator controls

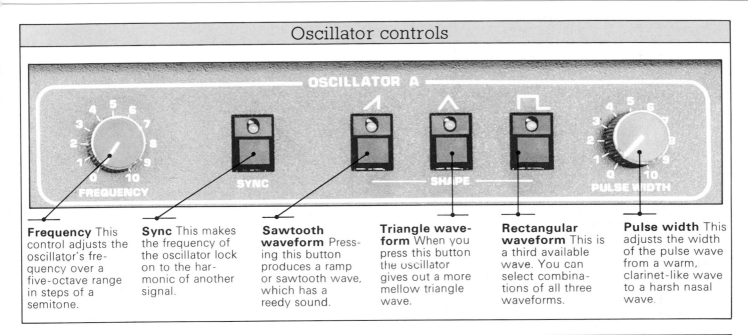

Frequency This control adjusts the oscillator's frequency over a five-octave range in steps of a semitone.

Sync This makes the frequency of the oscillator lock on to the harmonic of another signal.

Sawtooth waveform Pressing this button produces a ramp or sawtooth wave, which has a reedy sound.

Triangle waveform When you press this button the oscillator gives out a more mellow triangle wave.

Rectangular waveform This is a third available wave. You can select combinations of all three waveforms.

Pulse width This adjusts the width of the pulse wave from a warm, clarinet-like wave to a harsh nasal wave.

The voltage-controlled filter

The VCF is in many ways like the soundboard of a piano or the body of a guitar. It determines the character of the synthesizer itself. For example, Moog's original VCF circuit produced a much warmer, more mellow tone than the filters used by ARP, and so it is possible to distinguish between some of the sounds produced by the two different instruments.

This difference in character is very important. An interesting example is the Sequential Circuits Prophet 5, a polyphonic synthesizer. This started life in 1977 with a set of filter circuits made up of SSM chips. Later it was given a new filter and although the instrument looked the same from the outside, this resulted in a change in the Prophet's characteristic sound. For this reason, some people prefer the original Prophets to the newer ones.

How filters work

There are many kinds of filters, but all of them work by letting some things through while restraining others. In a synthesizer, the most common type is the low-pass filter. This allows all the

Filter controls

parts of the signal below a certain frequency (called the *cut-off frequency*) to pass through, while restricting the higher frequencies. You determine what the cut-off frequency is to be by changing the voltage applied to the VCF. A filter's band of operation isn't clearly defined. If the cut-off point is 1,000 Hz, the filter will not simply allow a frequency of 999 Hz to pass and then totally block one of 1,001 Hz – the response is much more gradual.

You will often see the performance of a filter referred to in "decibels per octave" (dB/octave). If a filter has a rating of 6 dB/octave (or −6 dB/octave), a frequency of one octave above

Cut off You set the initial pitch of the low-pass filter by using this control.

Resonance Increasing this gives a ringing sound, until the filter oscillates.

Envelope This control sets the amount of movement of the envelope.

Keyboard This allows the cut-off frequency to be proportional to the note played.

the cut-off point will be reduced by 6 dB (and halved in amplitude), a frequency two octaves above will be reduced by 12 dB (and quartered in amplitude), and so on. A typical specification for an electronic synthesizer VCF is 24 dB/octave.

VCF controls

A synthesizer's VCF normally offers a number of controls that help you to vary the timbre of the sound. In addition to the frequency control, which sets the bias of the cut-off frequency, there are usually resonance and keyboard tracking controls.

It is useful to be able to change the resonance of your VCF.

Resonance operates like audio feedback (see p. 28), with some of the output sent back to the input. It increases the amplitude of the signal near the cut-off point, so that the sound becomes thinner and more "ringing". The greater the resonance, the more frequencies are amplified, until there comes a point, as with audio feedback, when the filter starts to oscillate. The VCF then effectively becomes a VCO. You can use this feature to produce flute-like or whistling sounds.

Keyboard tracking

It is also useful for the filter to be able to track the keyboard. The synthesizer does this by routing the keyboard control voltage to the filter. The most obvious use of this feature is when the filter starts to oscillate as a result of increased resonance. The tracking facility allows you to play the resulting pure tone using the keyboard.

Keyboard tracking is also necessary for most filtering operations, because the ideal amount of filtering varies according to which note you play. For example, if you are producing a brass tone, you will want a fairly mellow, heavily filtered voicing. But if you set the filter's cut-off frequency at around 100 Hz to get a good sound at the bottom end of the keyboard, you will find that when you play a note from the upper end of the keyboard's range, the filter will let virtually no sound through. So the filter must track the keyboard to maintain the correct amount of filtering across the whole range.

The voltage-controlled amplifier

This is a very simple circuit. It takes the audio signal fed to it and amplifies or attenuates this by an amount proportional to the voltage you apply to it.

Often the VCA has no external controls, though sometimes you will find that a gain control is

Envelope generators

An electronic tone generator will produce a constant, rather boring sound. A synthesizer can make this more interesting to the ear by introducing slight variations in timbre and loudness throughout the note's duration.

All acoustic instruments make sounds with continuously changing amplitude and tone, and synthesizers have a way of simulating this effect. The envelope generator produces a control voltage which, when routed to the VCA and VCF, allows the amplitude and timbre to be varied automatically.

When you play a note, the envelope generator receives a signal to say "a new note has just been played". This immediately activates the envelope generator, and also tells the envelope generator when the note has been released. From this information, the circuit can set about producing a control envelope. This can be sent to the VCA and VCF.

The most common form of envelope generator is known as

provided. This allows you to determine the amount of voltage that is presented to the circuit. For example, if 5 volts were applied to the VCA and you set the gain control at the halfway position, only 2.5 volts would get through to the circuit, thus reducing the amount of amplification of the signal.

the *ADSR* (Attack, Decay, Sustain, Release). Its four elements usually have slider or rotary controls on the synthesizer's top panel. You use the "Attack" control to set the time it takes for the voltage to rise from zero to its maximum level. When it has risen to this point, the voltage then drops down at a rate corresponding to the setting of the "Decay" control. With the "Sustain" control, you set the voltage level at which the envelope stays until you release the key. At this point the voltage level falls at a rate determined by how you set the "Release" control.

Some manufacturers use other combinations to govern their envelope generators. One of the most simple is the "AR" type. With this, the voltage rises at the Attack rate to a maximum level. It stays there until you release the key, when it falls away at the decay rate. With the "AD" type the voltage rises at the Attack rate and then falls away at the Decay rate as soon as it has reached its maximum. The "ASR" envelope is also available.

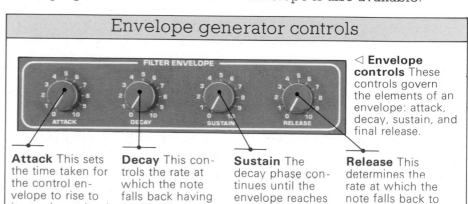

Envelope generator controls

◁ **Envelope controls** These controls govern the elements of an envelope: attack, decay, sustain, and final release.

Attack This sets the time taken for the control envelope to rise to its maximum level.

Decay This controls the rate at which the note falls back having reached its peak.

Sustain The decay phase continues until the envelope reaches this sustain level.

Release This determines the rate at which the note falls back to its initial position.

Low-frequency-oscillator controls

◁ **LFO modifications** The LFO gives you another way to modify the sound, and a choice of the different elements you can modify.

Frequency This governs the LFO's oscillation rate.

Waveshapes These are used as control signals.

Initial amount This sets how much of the LFO's output goes to the voltage-controlled devices.

Destination This group of controls sets the elements to be modulated.

The low-frequency oscillator

Another mechanism that you can use to modify the three basic elements of a sound is the low-frequency oscillator (LFO). This is simply an oscillator that runs at a very slow rate.

The purpose of the LFO is to introduce a continually repeating form of modulation to the tone. The output of the oscillator is usually either a square wave or a sine wave (although sometimes a triangle wave is used instead) and this is normally sent to the VCO or VCA. According to the way it is routed, and the type of waveform produced, it gives different results. Sine wave modulation of the VCO provides vibrato; square wave modulation of the VCO creates a trill; sine wave modulation of the VCA produces tremolo; and square wave modulation of the VCA provides an echo-like effect.

There is another way you can use the LFO – to vary automatically the pulse width of the VCO's square wave output. This can create interesting variations in the harmonic content of the waveform. The audible effect of this is to make the sound a lot thicker and fuller.

The noise generator

In addition to the VCO, most synthesizers have a noise source. Noise is unpitched. Its sound is a powerful, steady hissing and it is made up of a random, continuously changing combination of all the audio frequencies.

The noise generator is most useful for creating sound effects such as wind and waves, but you can also give noise a degree of pitch by filtering it.

Usually the only control on a noise generator sets the level of the circuit's output, but some instruments also offer you a choice between white noise (containing equal amounts of all audio frequencies), and pink (with more lower frequencies).

Dual-oscillator controls

▷ **Dual oscillators – the advantages** An instrument with two oscillators offers far more scope for creating different sounds.

Low frequency This adjusts the oscillator's operating frequency, to make it work at sub-audio levels, like the LFO.

Fine tuning The second oscillator's fine tuning control enables you to de-tune this oscillator against the other one. This gives a much "fatter" sound.

Keyboard You can use the keyboard switch to disconnect the VCO from the keyboard, so its frequency is independent of any note you play.

Dual-oscillator voices

Some synthesizers have two oscillators. This feature is very useful. An acoustic piano has two or three strings for each note. These strings are tuned in unison, but they are not phase related. The result of this is that the sound they produce is harmonically complex – the vibrations from the two strings are continuously interacting with each other to produce a rich sound. Having two oscillators per voice on a synthesizer allows you to enhance the sound in a similar way. By tuning the oscillators as closely in unison as possible you can almost get them to cancel each other out. You will notice how a slight tuning discrepancy makes the sound change. This is a very pleasing effect, especially with a warm, mellow filter like the one on the Minimoog. By detuning the oscillators slightly you can get a very rich sound.

Another advantage of having dual oscillators is that you can set them at intervals apart. For example, you can set one VCO to C, and the other to an A two octaves and a sixth above. This will form the basis of a piano voicing. A good synthesizer will allow you to set different levels, waveforms, and pitches for both oscillators, so that you can make use of the circuitry provided.

Synchronization

If your synthesizer voice module has two oscillators, a facility known as synchronization is often available. This means locking one oscillator on to the harmonic of another. The result can be a very sharp, harsh sound that is rich in higher harmonics. It is a useful effect, but you should use it sparingly since, like distortion, it is easily overworked.

By changing the frequency of just one of the oscillators you can alter the synchronization frequency and affect the timbre of the whole sound. Some instruments allow you to route an envelope waveform directly to one of the oscillators. If you do this when the oscillators are synchronized, you get a very powerful sound – it can be rather like the sound made by a heavily distorted electric guitar.

Contouring

The envelope generators provide a control voltage which you can route to any of the three basic parts of the synthesizer – VCO, VCF, or VCA. Controlling the effect that the envelope generator will have over these elements is known as contouring. The VCA and VCF routes are the most important.

The envelope generators and the VCA

Linking the envelope generators with the VCA is essential with any synthesizer. If no form of envelope is applied to the VCA, the instrument will produce a continuous droning tone. Applying an envelope allows you to vary the amplitude of the sound from zero to maximum for as long as you hold down a key. When you release the key the output returns to zero. This is an envelope known as a gate.

But you may have the type of synthesizer on which, for reasons of economy, only one envelope generator is provided for con-trolling both the VCA and the VCF. On this type of machine the gate pulse is sometimes available as a preset sound envelope.

The envelope generators and the VCF

If you listen to most acoustic instruments you will notice that the start of a note is usually much brighter than the decay and release phases. It is one of the synthesizer's most useful qualities to be able to imitate this change by allowing you to vary continuously the timbre of any note. By applying the control voltage from the envelope generator to the VCF you can immediately brighten a sound as it is played, then remove the higher frequencies as the note decays away.

Some synthesizers offer an optional inverted envelope control. With this, the envelope begins high, then drops to remove the higher frequencies before returning to its high level. This facility is more useful for creating abstract sounds rather

Envelope controls

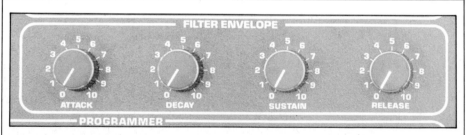

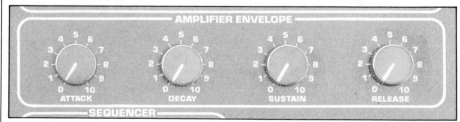

△ **Dual envelope generators** Some electronic synthesizers are provided with dual envelope generator controls on the front panel. The advantage of this is that it enables you to establish different contouring for the filter and amplifier. This is important especially if you are trying to build up realistic imitations of acoustic sounds. This synthesizer provides a full range of controls for attack, decay, sustain, and release. Some models have few adjustable controls, giving less versatility.

than imitating existing acoustic instruments.

The envelope generators and the VCO

Connecting the VCO to an envelope generator is probably something you will want to do less frequently, but there are several options. First, you can use the envelope generator to modulate the pitch of the oscillator, in which case the VCO's frequency will follow the shape of the envelope. This can provide you with a range of gliding and whooping sounds. Second, you can use the envelope generator to control the pulse width of a square or rectangular wave, altering the harmonic content, and therefore the tone of the filter's output. Third, if your instrument has two oscillators, it is often possible to use an envelope control voltage on one of the VCO's. When the two are synchronized (see pp. 55-6), you can hear the modulated tone sweeping across the harmonics of the other oscillator.

Performance controls

The majority of synthesizer keyboards, unless they are touch responsive, are simply rows of switches. When you press a key you are simply turning a switch on or off – there is no expression involved. However most synthesizers also have a group of performance controls near the keyboard, usually to the left. They are commonly quite large, widely spaced, and placed so that you can manipulate them without having to look at them.

These performance controls allow you to inject expression into your playing by giving you real-time control over your sound. In other words, they make your synthesizer a truly musical instrument. The main controls – usually edge-wheels – are for *pitchbend* and *modulation*. Some models also provide facilities for *portamento* and *glissando*.

Pitchbend

This allows you to raise or lower the pitch of any note while you are playing it. You can change the pitch by any amount up to an octave. The effect you get is rather like the sound produced by bending strings on a guitar.

Pitchbend wheels are designed so that you can move them one way to lower the pitch and the other way to raise it. On some models the wheel is spring-loaded and automatically returns to its center position when you release it. On others you reset the control manually. It clicks back into its original position so that you are sure that your instrument is exactly in tune.

Modulation

The modulation wheel is normally set at zero. You turn it to introduce low-frequency modulation to the oscillators. If you use triangle-wave or sine-wave modulation, you get a vibrato effect, while a square wave gives a trill. Vibrato is usually applied to the end of a sustained note.

Portamento and glissando

These effects are usually controlled with an ordinary slider or a rotary knob. Portamento is a continuous sliding effect between notes. Glissando is moving from one note to another in semitone steps. So if you introduce portamento while playing two notes, the machine will start at the first note, then slide up or down to the second. It will reach the pitch of the second note some time after you play it, and the amount of time this takes is determined by how you set the portamento control.

Performance controls

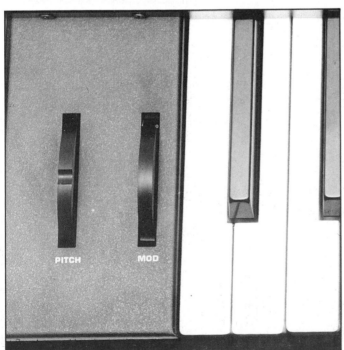

Pitchbend This control is usually designed so that you can move it either up or down to raise or lower the pitch. On this model a small notch is cut in the wheel so that it can be centrally positioned. On other types a spring returns the wheel to the center.

Modulation This controls the amount of modulation sent from the LFO to various destinations. It only requires positive movement, so its rest position is fully back.

Glide control

Glide On this model the glide control determines the rate at which which the oscillators take to move from one pitch to another.

Synthesizer types

There are many different types of synthesizer, each designed for specific tasks. On the following pages, you will find details of the main types of synthesizer and the applications for which they are designed. Remember that these are only guidelines – most of these instruments have been used in many ways.

The original synthesizers were monophonic and so are many current models. A monophonic instrument, with its single voice, can only produce one note at a time. Polyphonic keyboards, on the other hand, allow you to play chords as well as a melody line (see pp. 61-3). But few of these synthesizers are *fully* polyphonic – most allow you to play 6, 8, or 16 notes at a time. However, polyphonic models normally offer a bigger keyboard.

The advantage of a monophonic synthesizer is that it offers you more control over the pitch, timbre, and loudness of the sound. To get exactly what you want from a synthesizer, you have to have complete control over every part of the sound. You can really only do this with one note.

So if you want to be able to control the sound precisely, a monophonic machine is probably the best choice. But if you want to play chords, or if you can afford one of the more sophisticated polyphonic models that does give a variety of sounds, then a polyphonic synthesizer is best for your needs.

Monophonic synthesizer

This fully-variable, monophonic synthesizer has slider controls for most of the sound parameters on the top panel. It has a good range of performance controls, based on a bender that you can use either for pitch bending or for introducing modulation. The optional handgrip, with its own performance control, together with a shoulder strap, make this battery-powered unit mobile. Its other features include a built-in sequencer. This allows you to store and play back a series of notes. On this model, you can store up to 100 musical steps. There is a useful range of control inputs and outputs. By using these you can connect other equipment. Doing this will extend the range of your synthesizer considerably.

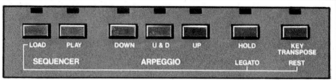

Sequencer and arpeggio controls

LOAD	PLAY	DOWN	U & D	UP	HOLD	KEY TRANSPOSE
SEQUENCER		ARPEGGIO			LEGATO	REST

△ A separate group of buttons controls the built-in sequencer and the automatic arpeggio facility. For the sequencer, you press "Load" to store musical notes and "Play" to play them back. The "Legato" button allows you to store slurs and ties, and there is also a "Rest" button. You can change the tempo by using the modulator section. Three central buttons give you three different arpeggio patterns.

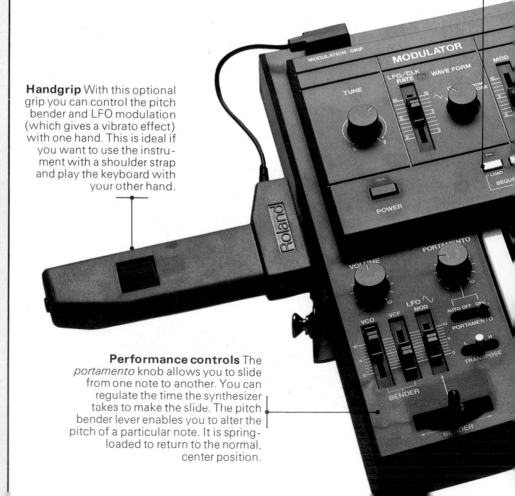

Handgrip With this optional grip you can control the pitch bender and LFO modulation (which gives a vibrato effect) with one hand. This is ideal if you want to use the instrument with a shoulder strap and play the keyboard with your other hand.

Performance controls The *portamento* knob allows you to slide from one note to another. You can regulate the time the synthesizer takes to make the slide. The pitch bender lever enables you to alter the pitch of a particular note. It is spring-loaded to return to the normal, center position.

Source mixer This mixes the waveforms from the VCO, the sub-oscillator, and noise, in the proportions that you require. The resulting mix is then sent to the VCF.

VCF (voltage-controlled filter) You can adjust the timbre of the output from the source mixer by means of the VCF (see p. 53). The VCF is a low-pass filter. In other words it lets through low frequencies and blocks out higher ones. The cut-off point of the filter is adjustable by changing the voltage, which you do with the left-hand slider control.

VCO (voltage controlled oscillator) This controls the pitch (see p. 52). On this model, the VCO governs three types of waveform that make up the synthesizer's sound source. The circular dial controls the VCO's pitch in steps of one octave.

Connections

△ This synthesizer has connections on the top panel, for ease of access. As well as the usual sockets for output and headphones, there are several extra sockets. The "CV/Gate out" sockets allow you to control an external synthesizer or send a signal to a separate sequencer to give you more sequencer capacity. The "CV/Gate in" sockets enable you to drive your synthesizer from an external keyboard.

VCA (voltage-controlled amplifier) This regulates the loudness of the sound (see p. 54). It is usually controlled by the output voltage from the envelope generator. The selector switch gives you the option of controlling the VCA from the gate signal.

Envelope generator Four sliding controls give you a method of regulating the attack time, delay time, sustain level, and release time (see p. 54).

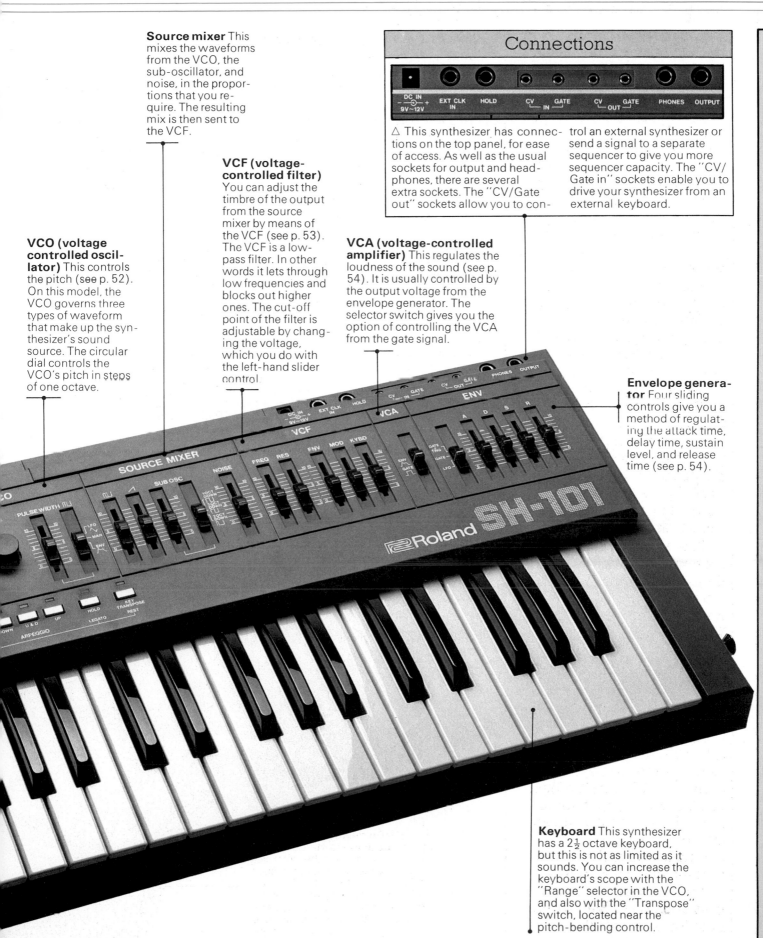

Keyboard This synthesizer has a 2½ octave keyboard, but this is not as limited as it sounds. You can increase the keyboard's scope with the "Range" selector in the VCO, and also with the "Transpose" switch, located near the pitch-bending control.

The synthesizer range

The most basic monophonic synthesizers are preset types. For more control over the sound, you should choose a fully variable monophonic (see also pp. 58-9), or a programmable type with its own memory. Polyphonic synthesizers come in a similar range.

The preset monophonic synthesizer

This type of synthesizer gives you a quick and easy way to change sounds. The front control panel of the instrument contains a set of switches that allow you to produce particular predetermined sounds. The presets usually imitate acoustic instruments, offering sounds like violin, oboe, clarinet, and piano.

The preset synthesizer is good for live performances because it enables you to change sounds very quickly. But it does limit you to a range of factory-programmed voicings. In the seventies many organists used a preset on top of their organ, for lead-line solos.

Probably the best known preset was the Roland SH-2000, which has long since been discontinued. One of the best is the Kawai 100P.

The fully variable monophonic synthesizer

This type gives you controls for the various sound-shaping parameters on the front panel itself. This type of instrument provides a good balance between range of sounds available, ease of use, and cost. However, changing sounds quickly in live performance can be difficult unless you are very familiar with the instrument.

Until recently, the Minimoog was the most popular fully variable machine, and the ARP Odyssey ran it a close second. Later, instruments such as the Korg MS-20, the Moog Prodigy,

▷ **Programmable monophonic** One of the most versatile and impressive monophonic synthesizers is the Oscar. It has many features not found on most monophonic models, including both a programmer and a sequencer that allows you to link various sequences together to give longer tracks. It has two oscillators which will create a number of preset waveforms. You can also produce your own waveforms by adding together harmonics.

▷ **Six-voice polyphonic** The Roland Juno 6 uses oscillators that are digitally controlled. These are cheaper than VCO's and they are also not sensitive to temperature changes and stay rigidly in tune. Other features include automatic arpeggios and a built-in chorus unit, useful to fill out the sound.

◁ **Modular synthesizer** The Roland 100M system is made up of a number of different modules that you link together. These include a basic synthesizer module (containing VCO, VCF, and VCA), separate VCF's and VCA's, an envelope and LFO module, an analog sequencer, and a mixer. This range of units provides a very flexible studio synthesizer.

◁ **Eight-voice polyphonic** The Korg Trident II is divided into three sections — synthesizer, strings, and brass. The synthesizer has eight voices, dual oscillators, and 32 memory locations. The string section is very good for creating a "bowed-string" sound. And the brass section is very powerful, with its own filter and envelope controls.

and the Sequential Circuits Pro-One became popular, but, as with the preset, this type of synthesizer is losing some appeal to the programmable type.

The programmable monophonic synthesizer

Programmable machines combine the flexibility and range of sounds offered by the fully variable synthesizer with the preset's ease of use. They look very much like fully variable units, with the addition of a bank of switches that you use to control a memory. The idea is that you adjust all the controls until you get exactly the sound that you require. Then you "record" this sound into the instrument's memory bank. This is very simple — you just press the "record" button and indicate the memory location where you want the sound to be stored. You have then recorded the control settings for that sound — not the sound itself.

When you have filled up all the memory locations with the sounds you require, you can recall any of these by selecting its specific memory. So, in effect, you've made your own set of preset sounds. These will stay in the instrument's memory even when the power is switched off, though of course you can also change them, or replace them with completely new sounds, whenever you want to. Most programmable synthesizers offer at least eight memory locations — some have 100.

Programmable synthesizers are getting more and more popular. Probably the most enduring machine of this type is the Moog Source.

The modular monophonic synthesizer

Modular synthesizers are used mainly in the studio. They consist of several circuit modules that you link together using patch cords. Their main advantage is that they are highly versatile. Moog's modular synthesizers were the first — and probably the best — of their type, but recently Roland's relatively low-cost 100-M has become popular.

The modular polyphonic synthesizer

These machines are neither very common nor widely useful. Modular synthesizers are essentially studio tools and, since studios offer facilities for multitracking, a polyphonic modular instrument is seldom required.

You can use separate oscillator and envelope modules, together with a polyphonic keyboard. Roland make such a keyboard as an option for their 100-M system. Another type of polyphonic modular system routes signals from the oscillators directly through individual VCA's, but then treats the whole signal together as if it were a monophonic source. This is known as a *pseudo-modular* polyphonic arrangement.

The preset polyphonic synthesizer

Like the preset monophonic instrument, this type has its voices set internally, at the factory. Polyphonic presets are usually voice-assignable types (see p. 50), though one of the first, the Polymoog keyboard, was in fact fully polyphonic.

The fully variable polyphonic synthesizer

Most fully variable polyphonics have voice-assignable keyboards, and their controls are virtually the same as their monophonic counterparts. Probably the most popular synthesizer of this type was Roland's Juno 6, which offered a wide range of sounds at a very reasonable price. But this has now been superseded by the Juno 106, a programmable polyphonic.

The programmable polyphonic synthesizer

This is the boom area of the synthesizer market. At the end of the seventies a keyboard player with a band often had to invest in an electronic piano, a Clavinet, an organ, and a monophonic synthesizer. With a programmable polyphonic you can have all these instruments at the touch of a button.

Nearly all keyboards of this type use voice-assignment (see p. 50). The control panel is very similar to that on a monophonic unit, but with the addition of a set of programming buttons.

A programmable keyboard has obvious advantages in the number of sounds it allows you to create. The polyphonic type gives another bonus: it is far easier to get convincing simulations of some sounds when you can play chords.

The Prophet 5 was the dominant polyphonic programmable synthesizer on the market until recently. Its ease of use, good looks, and clear, bright sound made it the natural choice for many players. But it has been superseded by other machines such as the Roland Juno 106, the Sequential Circuits Six-Trak, and Yamaha's DX synthesizers.

The Roland Juno 106 synthesizer, shown on this page, is a programmable polyphonic synthesizer with 128 memory locations and a facility for cassette dumping which extends the machine's effective memory even further. Such a large memory, together with MIDI sockets for computer control and a very flexible sound-generation system, makes this a very versatile instrument.

Performance controls Moving the center-sprung slider left or right generates a negative or positive control voltage that can be used to regulate the pitch of the DCO, the cut-off frequency of the filter, and/or the modulation.

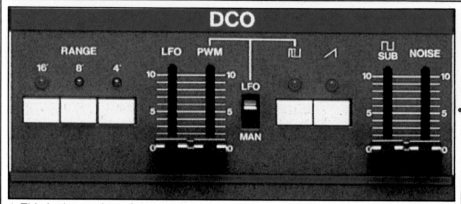

Digitally controlled oscillator (DCO)

△ This is the section of the synthesizer from which the sound originates. On many synthesizers, this section is labelled VCO. The oscillator provides rectangular and sawtooth waveforms.

You can select these at three different pitch ranges (16', 8', and 4'). It is also possible to introduce a noise signal at this stage.

Output panel
This features stereo and mono jack outputs, a headphone socket, footpedal sockets, tape cassette connections, and a trimmer for finely adjusting the tuning.

Keyboard control switches
You use these switches to determine the way in which the synthesizer's voice modules are assigned to the notes being played.

Low-frequency oscillator (LFO)
This gives a continuous modulation source for the oscillators (controlling pitch) and the filter (controlling timbre).

The programmer

△ The programmer features 128 memory locations used to store the panel settings of the LFO, DCO, HPF, VCF, VCA, envelope generator, and chorus circuit. The memories are arranged in two groups, A and B, with eight banks in each group and eight patches in each bank. The display shows which program is selected and any setting can be edited by moving the relevant control. When the programmer is in manual mode the instrument's output corresponds to the positions in which the controls are set.

All the program data can be dumped on to an audio cassette in digital format, freeing the memory for 128 new sounds. The cassette can be replayed into the unit and the former sounds stored on the tape can be recalled as required.

High-pass filter (HPF) To remove unwanted low frequencies from the combined signal of the oscillator and the noise source you use this filter, which acts like a tone control.

Voltage-controlled filter (VCF) This low-pass filter is the main element for shaping the timbre of the sound. It is a voltage-controlled device and its cut-off frequency can be varied either manually or automatically, by the LFO or the envelope generator.

Voltage-controlled amplifier (VCA) Responding to the control voltage applied to it, the VCA amplifies or attenuates the audio signal. On this machine it can be driven either from a gate pulse directly from the keyboard circuitry or by the envelope generator.

Chorus circuit This processes the output from all the instrument's voices. It gives the output a stereo image and also adds an extra degree of depth and movement to the sound. As this model has only one oscillator per voice, this is a very useful device.

MIDI output sockets These are used to connect the instrument to additional devices such as a rhythm unit, a polyphonic sequencer, or a computer.

Cassette interface controls To free the machine's memory for the storage of more sounds, you can download its contents on to cassette using these controls. The data you have stored on cassette can be played back into the synthesizer to recall sounds.

Other types of keyboard

So far we have looked at subtractive synthesis – so-called because you start with a sound, produced by oscillators and a noise source, and then remove, by filtering out or subtracting, the parts of the sound that you don't require. But with the increasing power of the microprocessor, new systems of voice generation are now available. By adding together sine waves of different amplitude and frequency, you can create almost any waveform.

This method is known as additive synthesis. The original problem with it was that the waveform of nearly every acoustic sound is changing continuously. So to create an effective imitation, you have to specify continually the amplitude and frequency of every harmonic. Thanks to high-speed microprocessors, this is now possible.

On the following pages you'll also find information about replay and sampling keyboards. Replay keyboards are elaborate tape-players which allow you to change the sound produced by inserting a new set of tapes. Sampling keyboards can be fed with any sound, which you can then play back at a whole range of different pitches.

FM digital synthesis

Developed in the US and commercially exploited by the Japanese company Yamaha, this type of additive synthesis is one of the most important breakthroughs in the industry.

"FM" stands for frequency modulation. When you take a pure tone (a sine wave – known as the *carrier*) and continually alter its tone with another sine wave (the *modulator*), a complex tone is produced. By accurately controlling the ratio between the carrier and the modulator and by determining how much of one you apply to the other, you can accurately specify the tone the system produces.

Originally the FM system was very difficult to use – the programming of sounds was a hit-and-miss affair. So at first only preset instruments were produced. But the system has now been made much easier to use.

The major breakthrough was the introduction of the concept of the *operator*. This consists of the equivalent of a voltage-controlled sine wave generator

Performance controls The pitchbending and modulation controls are similar to those found on most conventional synthesizers.

Assignment selection This is the heart of the control panel. You use it to determine the functions of the 32 switches to the right.

Algorithm map This shows you how the operators are arranged for each of the 32 algorithms.

Data entry You can link these controls to any element you need to alter. The setting can then be changed according to the position of the slider or moved up and down with the buttons.

Display The LED display indicates which program number you have selected. The LCD panel shows the title of the program and the settings used to create that sound.

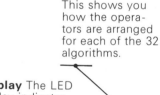

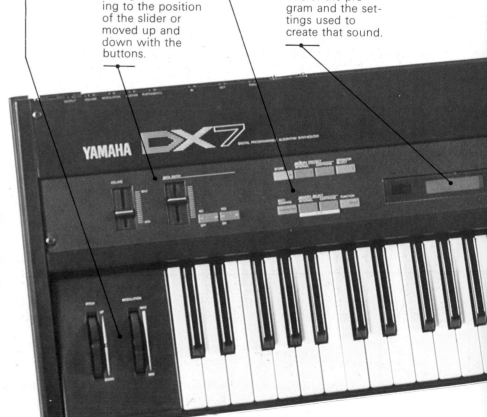

and an envelope generator. You can either use all the operators as carriers or use some of them as carriers and the others as modulators, to determine changes in the timbre produced by the carriers.

Every voice has a certain number of operators (for example, Yamaha's DX-7 has six). You can arrange these in many different ways and the signal paths used are known as algorithms.

FM synthesis is not the easiest system to understand or to program, but the results you can obtain are remarkable. The instruments usually have a much brighter sound than ordinary subtractive synthesizers and some players think the sound is too clinical and unemotional. But the emotional content depends much more on how you play your instrument than on the instrument itself.

Setting pitch, timbre, and amplitude

FM synthesis deals with the same three basic elements of sound as conventional subtractive synthesis, but you have to treat them in a different way.

It is helpful to start by taking only two operators and making one a carrier and one a modulator. You can then set the various elements quite easily. The basic pitch of the tone is governed by the frequency of the carrier. The waveshape produced by the carrier is determined by the frequency ratio between the carrier and the modifier. For example, if the modifier is set at 200 Hz and the carrier at 100 Hz, there is a ratio of 2:1, and if the relative amplitudes are in the same proportion the result is a square wave.

The brightness of the sound depends on the amount of modifier fed to the carrier. So, using the same example, if you reduce the amount of the modifier, the corners of the square wave will start to round off, and the sound will become increasingly mellow. The effect will be the same as lowering the cut-off frequency of the VCF in a subtractive synthesizer (see p. 53).

The modifier's envelope generator corresponds to the filter envelope of a conventional synthesizer (see p. 56). You use it to

Switch panel
You use these 32 switches to select: the programmed sound you want to use; which voice function is to be assigned to the data entry controls so it can be altered; which program function is to be assigned to the data entry controls; and the letters for naming the voicings.

Envelope diagram This is a programming aid that shows you how the eight envelope settings relate to each other.

Cartridge port This allows you to insert a data cartridge. ROM cartridges contain extra preset sounds, while RAM cartridges enable you to store your own sounds.

Keyboard level scaling map This shows how different operators can be amplified or attenuated according to which note on the keyboard is played. The output of a certain operator can be negligible toward the top of the keyboard, and at its maximum at the bottom.

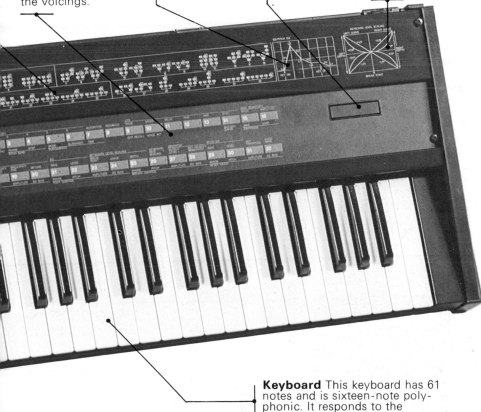

Keyboard This keyboard has 61 notes and is sixteen-note polyphonic. It responds to the pressure and velocity with which you strike the keys.

Conventional	FM synthesis
Pitch	Carrier's frequency
Waveshape	Modifier's frequency in relation to the carrier
VCF cut-off	Output level of modifier
VCF envelope	Modifier envelope
VCA output level	Carrier output level
VCA envelope	Carrier envelope

△ **FM synthesis** This table shows the way the controls on an FM synthesizer roughly correspond to those of a conventional type. An FM synthesizer usually has more than two operators.

vary the timbre over a period of time. In a similar way the carrier's envelope generator shapes the amplitude of the sound in relation to time.

FM feedback

Yamaha's FM system allows you to take the output of one operator and feed it back into itself. You can do this in varying degrees, but if you do it to the maximum point, you get a sound similar to white noise.

By using a modifier in this "full feedback" mode, you can also produce a sawtooth wave. The two operators should be set at the same frequency and the modifier's output level set to a maximum 75 percent. You will then get the characteristic reedy sawtooth sound.

Stacking more operators

You can achieve very complex timbres by stacking up operators. You can think of the sound as flowing downward through the stack of operators, though the actual output of each operator only affects the one immediately beneath it and you will only actually hear the sound of the operators on the bottom row.

Replay and sampling keyboards

Electronic synthesizers can imitate sounds very effectively. But there is another method of getting similar, keyboard-based control over a variety of sounds. This is to use a replay keyboard – one which plays back a recording of a real sound when you press one of the keys.

The Mellotron

The pioneers of this idea were a company called Streetly Electronics, who produced the Mellotron, later renamed the Novatron. The most popular Mellotron, the model 400, has a keyboard of 37 notes, and for each key there is a length of three-track recording tape. A sound was recorded on to each track at a pitch proportional to the key under which the tape was placed. This sound can be made by an acoustic instrument, by a group of instruments, or it can be a sound effect.

When you depress one of the keys, the tape passes between a roller and a rotating drive shaft and is pulled over a replay head. When you release the key a spring mechanism makes the tape move back to its initial position, ready for the next time the key is played.

Another model, the Mark II, works in the same way but has two keyboards, each with 35 notes. The left-hand keyboard is split in two. One half provides the rhythm section and the other half the accompaniment. This leaves you free to play the melody on the right-hand keyboard.

Of course, the length of the note you can produce is limited by the length of the tape – usually about seven seconds in the case of the Mellotron. You could get a continuous sound with a continuously cycling loop of tape. But the Mellotron's system gives a more faithful repro-

duction of the original sound. The attack phase of the sound is crucial for good reproduction. With the Mellotron, you hear a recording of the attack phase as soon as you press the key.

Changing sounds

The Mellotron's tapes are contained in removable racks, so that you can change to a completely new set of sounds by simply changing racks. A wide range of sounds has been recorded for use with the Mellotron, including all the usual instruments and sound effects. Tapes were even produced that contained jazz phrases played by full "big bands", so by pressing a C key you would get a phrase in the key of C. It was even possible to get your own sounds put on Mellotron tapes. Patrick Moraz did this so that he could play live many of the sounds on his "Story of i" album.

Many rock bands used the Mellotron for backing in the days before string machines and brass synthesizers were available. The Moody Blues were among the first to use the instrument. Others to use it included the Beatles (the flutes on "Strawberry Fields Forever" were played with a Mellotron), Genesis, and King Crimson.

Electronic sampling keyboards

The Mellotron, with its bank of tape-playing mechanisms, has many moving parts, and has always suffered from the rigors of touring. So manufacturers tried for many years to produce an electronic version of the instrument that would store sounds in digital form. The problem was the huge amount of memory required. For each second of recorded sound you need a digital memory with a capacity of at least 30,000 bytes (a byte is a digital word).

The solution was found by the

E-mu Corporation, who produce the Emulator. This instrument stores recordings of sounds in digital format and uses computer processing to transpose these sounds to any pitch in the keyboard's range. So the Emulator doesn't have a separate recording for every note of the keyboard.

As you might expect, the transposing mechanism works less well with certain sounds. One example is the human voice. The prime resonances of the human voice stay the same no matter which note you sing. The Emulator cannot make allowances for this when transposing the note into different keys. Nevertheless for most purposes its transposing mechanism is perfectly adequate.

A useful feature of the Emulator is looping, which allows you to extend the maximum length of any note. You have to tell the machine which part of the sound to repeat, and this means that you can retain the attack phase of the note, for a more faithful sound.

Sound sampling

An additional feature of the Emulator is that it can be used to sample sounds. You can feed any sound into the instrument either by using a microphone or by feeding it in directly from an electronic instrument or a tape recorder. The instrument will then make this sound available over the whole range of the keyboard.

The Emulator contains a built-in floppy disk drive which allows you to store your own sounds for later use. It is quick and easy to recall sounds from disk and the Emulator allows you to load a new sound into one half of the keyboard while playing a different sound on the other half. This makes the machine very useful in live performance as well as for creating sounds in the studio.

The main role of the Fairlight CMI (see p. 68-70) is also as a sampling keyboard. Both instruments allow you to use these sounds polyphonically, both systems produce sounds that are far clearer than those of earlier tape machines, and in addition the digital instruments are far more reliable and less bulky than the Mellotron.

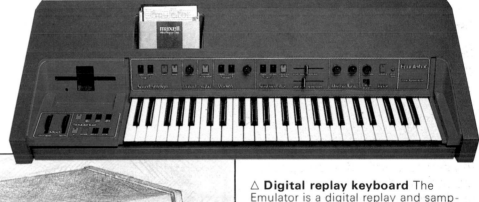

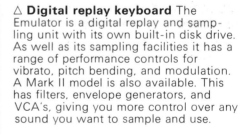

△ **Digital replay keyboard** The Emulator is a digital replay and sampling unit with its own built-in disk drive. As well as its sampling facilities it has a range of performance controls for vibrato, pitch bending, and modulation. A Mark II model is also available. This has filters, envelope generators, and VCA's, giving you more control over any sound you want to sample and use.

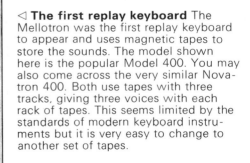

◁ **The first replay keyboard** The Mellotron was the first replay keyboard to appear and uses magnetic tapes to store the sounds. The model shown here is the popular Model 400. You may also come across the very similar Novatron 400. Both use tapes with three tracks, giving three voices with each rack of tapes. This seems limited by the standards of modern keyboard instruments but it is very easy to change to another set of tapes.

Computers in music

The majority of synthesizers and electronic organs have a central "brain" called a microprocessor. This is a tiny computer, but the synthesizer's controls are designed so that you do not have to know anything about computers in order to operate the keyboard. This is because the microprocessor has been told, by means of a control program, exactly what to do in response to how you set the instrument's controls and play the keys. It scans the keyboard and the controls, and sends signals to the relevant parts of the instrument, telling it what to do.

Many people now have access to a personal computer, and these devices can be used for music-making. Unlike the microprocessor in a synthesizer, a personal computer is not a dedicated device. It can perform many tasks, from doing accounts to making sounds, but it can only do these things if you give it the right instructions. These instructions are known as programs, and they need to be fed to the computer before it can make any sense of any further information you want to give it.

Using a computer

A program would be necessary if you wanted to get the computer to produce tones corresponding to the keys on its typewriter-style keyboard. The sequence of instructions would have to ask the computer to look in turn at each of the keys to see if it is being depressed, until it finds a note to play. These instructions would have to be written clearly and unambiguously, using one of the programming languages that the computer understands.

You do not have to write these instructions yourself. Various music programs are available for many microcomputers, including ones that score the notes being played on the computer's screen. Often the system will enable you to construct tunes by specifying the pitch and duration of each note, and with some machines this is possible in three separate channels, so that you can get your computer to play chords, or build up melody, obbligato, and bass lines.

The computer as a control device

To get more sophisticated sounds you will need a device like Roland's Compu-Music. You link this directly to a personal computer. It then accepts information from the computer and uses this information to control chord generators, melody, bass lines, and rhythm patterns. All the control information is derived from the computer, which leads you step by step through the process of constructing a song.

A more comprehensive facility is offered by the alpha-Syntauri and Soundchaser systems. Both are compatible with Apple computers and make use of two circuit cards that plug directly into expansion sockets on the Apple's main circuit board. These cards provide waveforms when you specify the fundamental frequency and harmonic content.

This is a two-channel system, so you can specify two waveforms at any instant, and each will have its own envelope generator. There are eight voices, so you can produce polyphonic chords with up to eight notes. Programs are available that allow you to construct waveforms and see them on the screen, while there are other programs for recording songs in up to eight tracks. A musical keyboard is also supplied, so that you can play the system conventionally in "real time", rather than programming the sounds using the typewriter-style keyboard.

The Fairlight

The computer instrument that has had most impact on professional musicians is the Australian

Fairlight Computer Musical Instrument (CMI). It has two microprocessors, which vastly enhances its processing power. One can control all the input and output of information while the other does the actual manipulation of data.

Instruments like the alpha-Syntauri can produce only two separate waveforms, which you cross-fade to produce tonal movement. The Fairlight, however, can create a waveform that is continually changing. One of the roles in which the Fairlight has proved particularly useful is as a sampling keyboard (see pp. 66-7).

This instrument is so versatile that you can use it as a complete multi-track recording system that provides precise control over all the lines you load into it. You can even see on screen the notes of a tune that you have

◁ **Thomas Dolby**
Innovative solo artist Thomas Dolby started by playing Fender Rhodes and a variety of synthesizers. Now he experiments with sampling keyboards such as the Fairlight CMI.

▽ **Computer musical system**
The Fairlight CMI consists of a musical keyboard, a computer keyboard, a screen with a lightpen, and a main cabinet that contains disk drives, digital sound modules, and the computer system itself. You can sample sounds, type music in using a computer language, or draw waveforms on the screen.

played, and move them around. You can vary the positions within fractions of a second to ensure perfect timing.

The Fairlight is especially suited to studio and movie work because it accepts time codes put down on film and allows the user to synchronize score and sound effects directly to the action – frame by frame.

The manufacturers have promised never to release a Fairlight "Mark II". The instrument is designed so that it will accept software changes simply by feeding in new programs, while any necessary hardware updates can be achieved by simply plugging in new circuit cards. Technology is advancing so quickly, however, that the Fairlight's makers may be forced to reconsider their decision and produce an updated computer instrument in years to come.

It is now possible to construct quite complex pieces of music using a microcomputer alone. A computer's ability to make music depends largely on the programs available for it. The size of the computer's memory is also important. An advantage of some of the older models is that more programs may have been written for them, so it is not always advisable to buy the latest model. A good program will allow you to construct envelopes to give you a variety of different sounds. You should also be able to play chords.

Computers like the Apple II and the Commodore 64 have

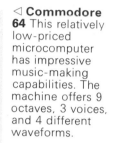

◁ **Commodore 64** This relatively low-priced microcomputer has impressive music-making capabilities. The machine offers 9 octaves, 3 voices, and 4 different waveforms.

▷ **Apple IIe** Apple computers have become well established in the music world as controllers for electronic instruments. They form a central part of the alphaSyntauri and Soundchaser systems and many music programs have been written for Apple machines.

good musical capabilities. You can also use some of them as instrument controllers. The Apple II has become particularly well established for this.

The Yamaha system

The use of computers for controlling musical instruments has continued with the more recent launch of Yamaha's CX-5 system. The package consists of a personal computer, an FM voice module (see pp. 64-5), and a small keyboard.

You can use the computer to program the voice module, giving it all the information it needs to produce the timbre and pitch you require. The system also incorporates a basic rhythm machine to supplement the sound. Equipment that is compatible with the MIDI system (see p. 149) can also be connected to the computer.

You can also use this computer as a programming tool for constructing sounds with Yamaha's FM digital keyboards. With the on-screen editing facility this means that you see instantly the values of all the synthesizer's settings, making programming much simpler.

◁ **The alpha-Syntauri** This system is centered on an Apple computer together with a set of voice cards. There is also a range of musical keyboards and a screen. Preset sounds, additive synthesis, and sequencing are all possible with the system.

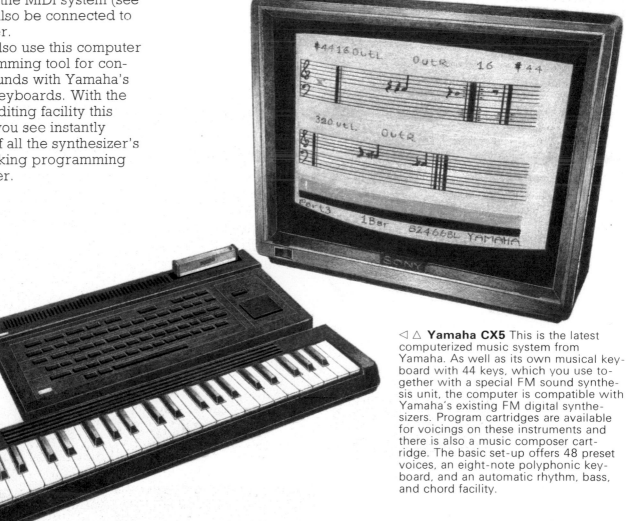

◁ △ **Yamaha CX5** This is the latest computerized music system from Yamaha. As well as its own musical keyboard with 44 keys, which you use together with a special FM sound synthesis unit, the computer is compatible with Yamaha's existing FM digital synthesizers. Program cartridges are available for voicings on these instruments and there is also a music composer cartridge. The basic set-up offers 48 preset voices, an eight-note polyphonic keyboard, and an automatic rhythm, bass, and chord facility.

Controllers

An electronic keyboard instrument is a device that turns electrical impulses into sounds. What sounds it actually produces are determined by the design of the instrument's circuitry, the settings of the controls on the front panel, and the notes that you can play on the keyboard. The first of these factors is predetermined for you, and you usually set the front panel controls before you start playing. So the keyboard is the main interface between you and your instrument while you are playing. Therefore the keyboard is often known as the *controller* mechanism.

A keyboard is a very efficient controller – but it isn't the only one available to you. There are many different types. Guitar, percussion, and even wind-driven synthesizers exist, and none of these uses the chromatic keyboard.

Types of controller

Some guitar synthesizers use an actual guitar, while others employ guitar-like mechanisms for the purposes of control. Wind synthesizers usually consist of a metal tube with a set of switches corresponding to the keys on a wind instrument such as a clarinet. The mouthpiece contains a pressure sensor. As you blow into this, the synthesizer produces a control voltage accordingly. Of course, these instruments have their limitations. Guitar synthesizers are confined to six-note polyphony, while wind synthesizers are monophonic.

So the keyboard is the controller that makes best use of your ten fingers and enables you to produce polyphonic music with relative ease. In other words, it is the best controller for real-time playing.

Sequencers

But this is not the only way to play a synthesizer. In some circumstances it is useful to be able to program your synthesizer to play a particular passage of music – so that you can play a lead solo on another keyboard, for example. To do this, you need a device known as a sequencer. With this form of controller, instead of receiving instructions from the keyboard, the instrument gets them directly from the sequencer, which has been set up previously.

There are three basic types of sequencer: analog, digital, and hybrid-computer sequencers. As with rhythm machines (see pp. 78-9) there are two methods of programming sequencers – real time and step time. A step-time sequencer will divide a passage of music up into equal periods of time. If you require notes of varying durations, you have to divide the sequence up into steps as small as the shortest. Most rhythmic phrases will then be possible if you tie notes together and introduce spaces where neces-

◁ ▽ **Guitar synthesizer** Roland's guitar (left) is designed as a controller for their guitar synthesizer (below). The guitar's unusual shape, with the bar connecting the body and the headstock, is intended to damp any harmonics produced, giving a purer tone from the strings. The signal from each string is translated into a digital code that drives the floor-mounted synthesizer unit. This can be user-programmed with the required voicings and operated using foot switches. You can use an optional programmer to create individual voice programs. The combination can also control other synthesizers via a MIDI output.

◁ **Monophonic sequencer** This monophonic sequencer records voltage and trigger information in the form of analog signals. You can feed these signals back into a synthesizer in order to play it.

△ **DCB sequencer** This polyphonic digital sequencer accepts Digital Control Bus (DCB) data from a keyboard. This data is only available on some Roland instruments.

◁ **Polyphonic sequencer** This digital sequencer can store several polyphonic sequences and record the information in the form of digital codes on small cassettes for future use.

sary. When you are dealing with real-time devices it is possible to specify both the time and pitch of a sequence of notes as you play.

Analog sequencers

This was the first type of sequencer, is generally used with monophonic and modular voltage-controlled synthesizers, and works in step time. You can easily recognize an analog sequencer: it has two or three rows of knobs or slider controls, arranged in columns. Each column corresponds to a step in the sequence, and each row to a certain channel.

So for every step you can set three separate controls, by routing the channel outputs to different parts of the synthesizer's circuitry. For example, you could use channel A for the pitch (by routing it to the VCO), channel B for the timbre (connecting to the VCF), and channel C for the loudness (linking it to the VCA). A clock pulse is used to go through the steps of the

sequence one by one until it reaches the last step, after which the cycle is repeated.

Digital sequencers

You program a digital sequencer by feeding data directly into its memory bank via a keyboard or another controller. You simply set the sequencer into record mode, start playing, and all the control data goes to the sequencer to be stored, as well as to the instrument itself.

The sequencer remembers the exact duration of every note and, on replay it recreates exactly the same output signals as were originally made by the keyboard when you were playing. An additional feature is that you can vary the replay speed, and it is often possible to transpose the sequence into any key.

A variation on the digital sequencer operates in step time,

but is programmed directly from the keyboard. As you play notes or chords, the sequencer assigns them to a particular step. You have to put in spaces in order to program the correct timings and rhythm.

Hybrid sequencers

The hybrid sequencer is a more elaborate device. It enables you to create multi-track recordings using electronic memory rather than tape. With the advent of the MIDI interface (see p. 149), the combining of instruments with this type of controller has been made very simple – you can build up a score in the studio by programming it bit by bit into the central controller.

Portable keyboards

Technology has evolved at such a rate over the past ten years that a whole new generation of versatile, low-priced keyboard instruments has come into being. These machines are designed mainly for home use, but some of the instruments are just as suitable for the more serious musician.

There are several reasons for the enormous popularity of these keyboards: first, many of the smaller machines, being powered by batteries, are easily portable; second, most have built-in loudspeakers, doing away with the need for a separate amplifier and speaker cabinet; third, they are capable of a remarkable range of different sounds; and last, but by no means least, they enable a virtual beginner to produce multilevel versions of simple tunes within a few hours.

The key to the new portable keyboards is miniaturization. Highly advanced micro-circuitry and large-scale integration have meant that the workings of instruments such as a huge console organ can be compacted into a handful of "chips". These keyboards therefore have many of the features that first popularized the home organ – in particular, the automatic, or "easy-play" controls. These allow you to produce not only a melody line, but also simultaneous rhythm tracks, chord accompaniments, and automatic bass and arpeggio lines.

A home keyboard

Numerous portable keyboards are available, all with different features to enhance their ease of playing, versatility, and realism of timbre (see also pp. 76-7). The machine shown here is a mid-priced home keyboard that is also suitable for live performance. It illustrates the kind of things these instruments are capable of. It has a polyphonic melody section with 20 preset sounds, an automatic rhythm unit with 16 different rhythm patterns, automatic generation of chord, bass, and arpeggio lines, and a pseudo-multi-track data recorder for constructing complete arrangements.

Amplification This is a stereo model with a built-in 8 watts plus 8 watts amplifier. It incorporates a pair of monitor speakers for personal use, although a headphone socket is available for private playing and a line output can be used to feed the instrument to a larger amplification rig for public performance.

Display A built-in liquid crystal display indicates such information as tempo rate, auto chord, file number, and stereo selection.

Stereo controls The stereo sound is controlled by ten push-button switches. These position the sound of the melody section across the stereo spectrum. Seven of the options are static. The other three give you a sound that moves around the stereo spectrum.

Chord automatics Various options are available when you select the automatic chord facility. You can create a "figured" accompaniment, so that notes played in the left-hand section of the keyboard can be set to sound continuously or rhythmically in synchronization with the rhythm unit. Another option is to set the machine to generate a chord based on the root that you select.

Rhythm unit Twelve rhythm patterns are provided. You can introduce these manually, by means of the "start/stop" button, or, when in "synchro" mode, by playing a key on the left-hand accompaniment section of the keyboard.

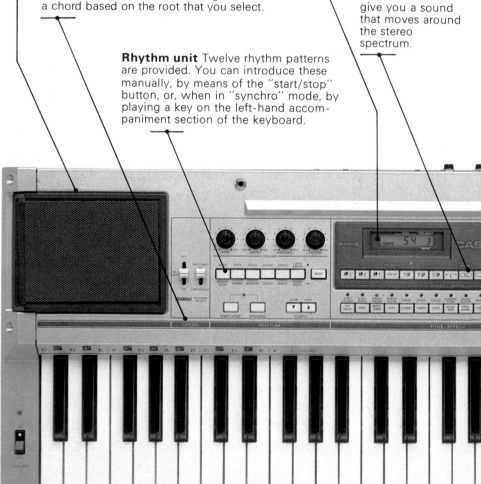

Preset keyboard

When this type of small keyboard first came out in about 1980, the range of sounds and facilities offered was comparable to instruments costing many times the price. This recent addition to the market continues the trend, with twenty preset voices and an accompaniment section offering hundreds of combinations of bass, chord, and arpeggio patterns.

Chord section This allows you to select chords by pressing single keys. Alternatively, you can finger chords using the accompaniment section of the keyboard.

Chords, arpeggios and bass Up to 768 different accompaniment options are available to you by using this group of controls.

Synchro-start This enables you to trigger your rhythm pattern on selection of a particular key.

Preset sounds This keyboard gives you twenty different preset sounds, some of them imitating acoustic instruments, others purely abstract.

Envelope controls By using these switches you can modify the character of the preset sounds.

Effects section Pseudo-reverberation effects, as well as sustain and vibrato, are available with these two controls.

Melody voicings There are twenty pre-set instrument voicings. When activated, the relevant data corresponding to the identity of the selected voicing is fed to the tone-forming circuitry. This keyboard uses what is known as a consonant/vowel system. The machine recreates a sound by considering it as two signals — the attack and the body of the sound.

Cassette interface

Mixer In order to achieve a suitable balance between the various sections, separate level controls are provided as well as static pan controls for the automatics.

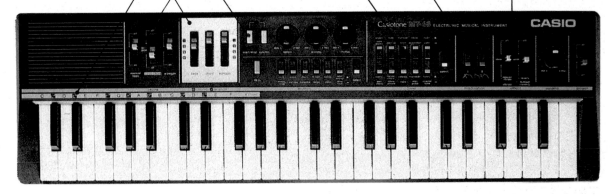

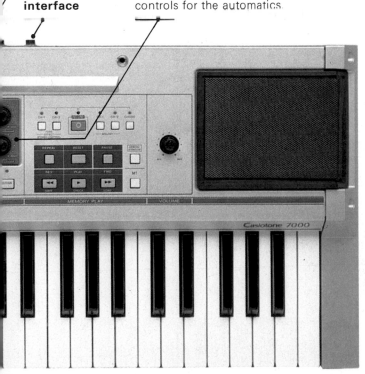

The multi-track data memory

The illustrations below show you how you can build up a single bar of a multi-track arrangement using the built-in digital memory system. You record a melody and an obbligato yourself on channels 1 and 2.

Melody You can play this on the keyboard and store it on channel 1 of the memory.

Obbligato This is a complementary melody, which you also play on the keyboard, but store on channel 2.

Arpeggio The unit generates the arpeggio line automatically, but it is dependent on the programmed chord.

Chord You can either finger chords on the keyboard or produce them automatically.

Bass This is generated automatically, but is also dependent on the chord and rhythm.

Rhythm You can preset a choice of patterns. The rhythm line is usually divided into three separate tracks.

Printing keyboard

With this unit you can actually get a printed version of the notes, chords, and rhythms that you play. This is obviously useful if you want to improvise and keep a written record of what you've played, so you can try out the same tunes again later. The print-out can also be valuable for beginners, since it shows you the relationship between the notes you play and the correct musical notation.

This keyboard also has most of the automatic features that are now common on portable keyboards, from memory to automatic arpeggios.

Music printer Using a replaceable ball-point pen, this gives you a print-out of the melody and chords as you play. You can also use the printer to get a record of the melody and chords you have stored in the instrument's memory.

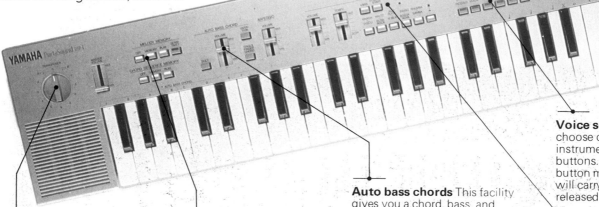

Transposer Altering the pitch by as much as half an octave up or down is easy with the transposer. This allows you to adjust the instrument to the pitch of a singer or another instrument in a different key.

Memory section This allows you to store tunes and chord sequences, which you can play back later. The memory is cancelled out when you switch off the power supply.

Auto bass chords This facility gives you a chord, bass, and rhythm accompaniment, simply by pressing one key. You select a rhythm and press the single-finger chord button. Then, if you press one of the 14 keys on the left-hand side of the keyboard, a chord will play along with the rhythm you have chosen.

Voice selectors You can choose one of ten different instrument voices using these buttons. Pressing the sustain button means that each note will carry on after you have released the key.

Rhythm section Ten different rhythm patterns are available. The tempo control allows you to adjust the speed of the rhythm before you start to play.

Playcard system

You program this ingenious keyboard with a *playcard*. This contains all the information needed to reproduce a particular tune on a magnetic strip. Above the strip, the tune is printed in ordinary musical notation. The machine will "read" the strip and play back all the music on the card. Or it can play back part of the music (for example, the rhythm and chords) so that you can fill in the rest. So although the playcard seems ideal for beginners, it also has some attractions for more experienced players.

Playcard Each of these cards contains a magnetic strip on which are recorded a melody, obbligato, chords, rhythm accompaniment, and bass line. When you have inserted the card the machine can play back the music. You can then try playing along with it yourself. The machine adjusts the tempo of the accompaniment according to the speed at which you play, so you can start off by taking it slowly.

Melody lamps When you play the melody along with a playcard accompaniment, the machine tells you which note to play next by the lights that glow above the keys. Experienced players can turn off the lights completely if desired.

Multi-menu keyboard

This compact stereo keyboard has a feature called "multi-menu" which acts like the programmer found on more sophisticated synthesizers. It enables you to create your own sounds and rhythm patterns, and to store them for use later. Other features include a range of preset sounds and rhythms, a keyboard transposer, and an auto-bass chord facility.

Menu options The menu offers nine different modes. The options are: creating your own sounds by combining envelopes and waveforms; playing two melody voices at once; setting a different chord voice; selecting a bass line instrument; programming a rhythm unit by hitting buttons when you want beats to sound; creating your own bass lines; storing chords and melodies; and putting any information you have programmed into the menu system on to magnetic tape for later use.

Rhythm patterns The 12 preset rhythms can each be varied in three ways, giving 36 patterns.

Preset sounds This keyboard offers 12 different preset polyphonic voices, together with two types of sustain to enhance the voices further.

Stereo sound A pair of built-in speakers provides stereo sound. You can use the stereo symphonic control to enhance the sound. The chorus setting gives a broader stereo chorus effect, while the tremolo creates a wavering sound.

Menu selector The nine different menu options are selected easily and quickly using a quick turn of the thumbwheel control. As you rotate the wheel the display changes to show which option you have selected.

Combined unit

This machine includes a cassette deck, radio, and detachable stereo speakers as well as a small computerized keyboard.

The cassette deck is useful for storing tunes, rhythms, chords, and other information, acting as the unit's memory. Both the tape deck and the keyboard section have a number of sophisticated features. But many players will find the keys too small.

Selection controls The function of the keyboard changes according to which of these buttons you press. If you press "Tone", you can choose one of nine different voices by depressing one of the black keys. If you press the "Rhythm" button you can select one of twelve rhythm patterns with the labelled white keys.

Auto-chord accompaniment A group of controls is provided that allows you to select a variety of different chords. As well as twelve keys labelled with musical notes, there are ten keys that determine the chord type. So if you want an F♯ major seventh, you simply press the F♯ key and the maj7 key. You can also link the chord and rhythm sections of the machine, for automatic accompaniments.

Program search buttons With this facility, you can find tracks on a tape very quickly. The tape winds on rapidly until the mechanism finds silence between tracks. You can also key in a number on the search buttons to find a particular track. The tape unit has a number of other computer-play features. For example, you can set the machine to single play, so that only one section of the tape is played back.

Programming controls You use these controls when programming music into the computer's memory. They include two keys that allow you to program repeats and two that enable you to delete and insert information.

Rhythm units

Devices that imitate the sound of drums, cymbals, tomtoms and similar percussion instruments have existed for some time. Early units had unrealistic voicings and produced very limited preset rhythm patterns.

The first professional-quality rhythm unit was the Bentley Rhythm Ace, developed by the American Bentley corporation for use in one of their organs. It was later marketed as a free-standing unit and used by Elton John on his recording "A song for Guy" and also by Arthur Brown, who replaced the drummer in his band Kingdom Come with this unit.

The Rhythm Ace was so successful that other companies soon started producing rhythm units incorporating the latest technology. Whereas the Rhythm Ace was a preset instrument, many of these new machines allowed you to program in your own rhythm patterns. The new generation included popular machines from manufacturers such as Roland, Korg, and Electro-Harmonic, and professional units like the LM-1 Drum Computer from Linn Electronics. The latest drum machines continue to make use of recent technology, and units are now available with which you can sequence your rhythm patterns to create entire rhythm tracks, and even program the tuning and amplitude of individual beats.

Types of rhythm unit voices

The voices of a rhythm machine can either be electronic simulations of percussion sounds or digital recordings of real acoustic instruments. Simulated voices, created by oscillator, noise, filter, and envelope circuits, can be very faithful to the sounds that they are copying. Manufacturers often provide fine-adjustment controls for these units, enabling you to change the tuning, amplitude, and color of the sound.

Digital voices are more expensive to produce than electronic simulations, but, because they are recordings of actual instruments, they sound much more realistic. The digital system does have its disadvantages. A very large computer memory is required. A two-second sample of a sound takes about 50 k of memory, so you rarely find samples lasting longer than

△ **The Linn Drum** This programmable unit uses digital recordings of real drum and cymbal sounds. Each drum sound is contained in a separate memory chip, and you can buy new sets of chips to change the whole character of the instrument. You can even get tapes of your own drum sounds put on chips for insertion into the machine.

◁ **Electronic percussion** The playing pads have pick-ups that sense how hard you hit the pad and send trigger pulses to a central control unit. This fires analog or digitally recorded sounds.

this. In addition, if you want to change the tuning of a digitally recorded sound you adjust the speed replay rate – and this naturally varies the duration of the sound as well.

Controlling rhythm units

Rhythm machine control systems are always digital. There are usually two programming modes – real time and step time.

In the real-time mode, you usually set the length of the pattern (for example, two bars), and the time signature. Then you run the unit. It gives you a metronome pulse and you treat the unit like a miniature drum kit, hitting buttons corresponding to the percussion voices when you want them to sound. In this mode you can split the bar up into very small parts. This means that the patterns you can create have a very realistic feel.

To program in step time you use a very simple digital code. If your rhythm pattern's shortest beats are sixteenth notes, and

you are working in 4/4 time, you have to divide your pattern up into sixteen equal steps. Then you simply key in which instruments you want to sound during each step. You can do this either by looking at each step in turn, or by going through a specific instrument voicing and telling the machine on which beats it is required to sound.

Preset machines have the codes for these patterns stored in a memory that you cannot alter. So simply selecting a "Rhumba" voice will give you a rhumba rhythm.

On more advanced models you can store sequences as well as patterns. So you can number your patterns and then call up pattern 1 for four bars, pattern 2 for one bar and pattern 1 for another three bars. Doing this is only a matter of keying in the appropriate pattern numbers as often as you want them to occur (in this example you would key in "1, 1, 1, 1, 2, 1, 1, 1"). Recent machines allow you to use large numbers of patterns in this way, so that you can create and store the rhythm tracks for a number of entire songs.

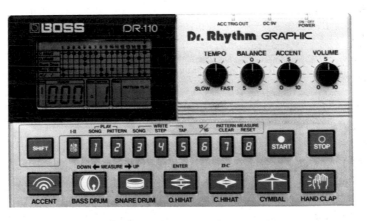

◁ **Low-cost unit** This is a programmable drum machine that enables you to construct 16 of your own patterns and assemble them, together with 16 preset patterns, into songs up to 128 measures long. Each measure can have 12 or 16 steps; you can use the unit in step or real time.

Vocoders

A device that gives a sound vocal characteristics is called a vocoder. These machines were developed in wartime as scrambling devices for coded messages. But they have since found a home in some types of electronic music.

To understand how a vocoder works, imagine that you could remove your vocal cords and replace them with a small loudspeaker. Any sound coming out of the loudspeaker

would be changed by the shape of your throat, and you could alter it further by changing the shape of your mouth and by moving your tongue and lips.

In reality a vocoder consists of a bank of analyzers connected to a row of filters. Each analyzer responds to a certain frequency and has its own filter. A "carrier" signal is fed to the filters. Any signal detected by the analyzers is fed to the filters and takes on the char-

acter of the carrier, while retaining its original shape. Ideally the carrier should be rich in harmonics. To make the sound more sibilant, white noise is often used when dealing with more percussive sounds. Many vocoders use sounds derived from a keyboard as the carrier source. A prime example of this is Roland's successful vocoder, the VP-330. Other models are designed for rack-mounting.

▷ **Rack-mounted vocoder** This unit analyzes a vocal input using tuned filters. The program signal is fed into corresponding filters to give it a vocal quality.

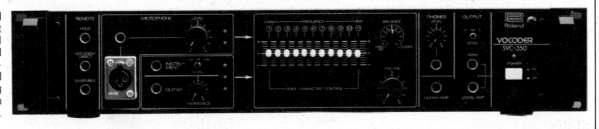

Choosing a keyboard

Keyboards for home performance

If you want an instrument for use at home, one with a polyphonic keyboard is probably the best investment. You might find the variety of sounds possible with a monophonic machine initially attractive, but if you only have one keyboard instrument, you will find the inability to play chords is a real limitation.

Many people would ideally choose an acoustic piano (see pp. 35-7). But these are large, make a lot of noise, and need regular tuning. Electronic instruments, which allow you to use headphones and do not require tuning, provide an attractive alternative.

Electronic pianos (see p. 47) have touch-sensitive keyboards, but this is an expensive feature. In addition, remember that an electronic piano will never sound really like an acoustic one. But does it have to? All that really matters is whether you find the sound pleasing.

An electronic organ, with all its automatic features and its variety of orchestral sounds is more versatile than a simple electronic piano (see pp. 42-3). Good dual-keyboard organs are costly, but single-keyboard portables offer good value.

The many small portable keyboards now available are inexpensive (see pp. 74-7). Their small keys can be a limitation. If you go on to a larger instrument you may find it hard to adjust, so choose full-size keys if possible.

Keyboards for home recording

For home recording there are two essential features – versatility and the ability to make connections with as wide a variety of devices as possible. When recording you can take as long as you like constructing a sound, so choose a keyboard with as many sound-shaping controls as possible. Many home recording enthusiasts use a monophonic synthesizer because it offers more control over the sound for its price (see pp. 58-9). But it is often useful to have a polyphonic instrument available as well (see pp. 62-3). Depending on the type of music you play you may also require a rhythm unit (see pp. 78-9) and possibly a sequencer (see pp. 72-3). The ability to link all these is especially useful, so instruments compatible with the MIDI system are best (see pp. 149-50).

Keyboards for playing in a group

Here your choice will depend on the type of group with which you're playing. A polyphonic programmable synthesizer is the best all-round instrument (see pp. 61-1). You probably won't need rhythms, automatics, or built-in amplification. If you use a synthesizer with a touch-sensitive keyboard you will not need an electronic piano. But if you are required to solo or take the melody line, a monophonic performance synthesizer is a very useful second instrument (see pp. 58-9).

Keyboards for professional recording

For this type of work you need to be able to call on as wide a variety of different sounds as possible. Several different electronic instruments are usually required (you can rent extra keyboards if you don't own them). The newest model is not necessarily the best – producers like to work with equipment they are familiar with. But it is also true that recording companies are always looking for new sounds.

In the store

When you have decided what type of instrument you want, visit a few dealers to try out some machines. As you do so, ask yourself these questions.

☐ Are you listening to the instrument "straight", with no reverberation or signal processing applied? If you do not do this you will not get a true idea of the sound.

☐ Does the keyboard feel right? How far do the keys move when you press them? This varies a lot from one instrument to the next and can make a big difference to how comfortable a keyboard feels when you're playing.

☐ Is the level of hiss and hum acceptable? Instruments with a built-in stereo chorus can be particularly noisy.

☐ If it has internal amplifier and speakers, how good are they? Turn the volume up and see if there is a rattle.

☐ How many notes can you play at once? Even eight notes can be a limitation if you play sustained runs.

☐ If there is a pitch bending wheel, does it return the pitch exactly to the "in-tune" position?

☐ Are there adequate servicing and guarantee arrangements? You should find out if the store is a main dealer, and if imported instruments have come in via an official importer. If not, you may have problems with servicing.

☐ Does the instrument do exactly what you want it to do? If not, there will almost certainly be another one that does.

Playing technique

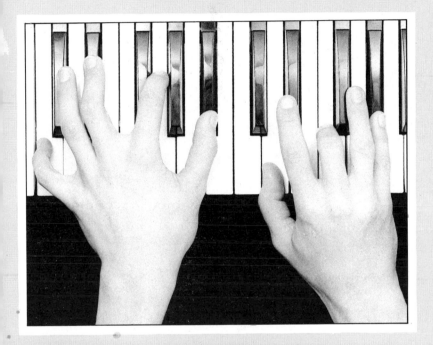

Whether you have a piano or a synthesizer, a large electronic organ or a small portable machine, mastery of the keyboard is essential for success. In this section of the book you will find the main elements of keyboard technique and musical theory explained. The section starts by looking at some of the things you should know first of all – the best instruments to use when practicing, the recommended posture to adopt when sitting at the keyboard, and some hints and tips on the best methods to use for practicing.

Next the section covers the language of music itself, showing you how to translate the signs and symbols of printed music into notes on your keyboard. After some hints on simple fingering techniques and tuning, the basic elements of music theory are covered one by one. This takes you from the simplest scales, through key signatures and the various chords, to rhythm. At the end of each topic there is a summary to remind you of the most important points. The summaries are also useful if you want to look at the book later.

The music theory in this section will be useful to you in a number of ways. For example, the scales are invaluable in practicing and also help provide structures for songs and other compositions; chords form an essential part of all but the simplest pieces of music; and knowing about rhythm, as well as being vital for both keyboard playing and writing music, will enable you to write out parts for electronic rhythm machines.

Getting started

If you do not have a keyboard instrument, think carefully about which type to buy. On this page, you will find some information about the best instruments on which to learn to play. If you can play, you may need advice about which keyboard to use for which purpose (see p. 80).

Keyboard practice is vital if you want to develop your technique. On the following pages you will find some information about the best way to practice, and also about playing posture and warming up.

Which keyboard?

What sort of keyboard should you use? There are many "new-technology" keyboards on the market, mostly with "easy-play" facilities. These are tempting, but if you start with an easy-play keyboard, you will find it difficult to play more sophisticated instruments. So it's advisable to learn on a conventional keyboard instrument, such as an acoustic piano, that gives you touch control and allows you to play chords.

Advantages of the acoustic piano

This instrument has several advantages for the beginner. First, it has a touch-responsive keyboard – the harder you strike a key, the brighter and louder the note sounds. You therefore have to develop the correct playing technique right from the beginning. If you learn on a keyboard that is not touch-responsive, you'll find that you will have to change your technique. Second, acoustic piano keyboards usually have at least six octaves, allowing you to play most existing keyboard pieces. Third, acoustic piano keyboards are fully polyphonic – you can play as many notes at once as you like. Fourth, it's relatively easy to change from a piano to an electronic keyboard instrument, whereas people often find it difficult making the opposite transition. So although playing a piano may not at first seem an

attractive prospect, it may be the best long-term choice.

Drawbacks of the acoustic piano

The piano does have some disadvantages. Good instruments are costly and if you economize with a secondhand piano, you must make sure everything works. Acoustic pianos are not portable, take up a lot of room, and need tuning from time to time. In addition, although you can play a piano at low volume levels, you cannot play silently, as you can with an electronic keyboard using a pair of stereo headphones.

Some alternatives

A good compromise is to use an electric or electronic piano. These instruments are polyphonic. They are usually compact, and often provide a degree of touch sensitivity. Electric pianos suffer from similar tuning problems to acoustic pianos, but most current electronic pianos are designed so that it is impossible for tuning to drift. An additional advantage of electronic types is that you can use a pair of headphones.

If you want to start with a synthesizer, it is best to begin by using a polyphonic instrument, so that you can finger chords as you would on an acoustic piano. Ideally, you should use a synthesizer with a touch-sensitive keyboard, but unfortunately this is a costly feature.

◁ **New beginnings** Musicians don't always start with the kind of music for which they are best known. For example, the original Human League, formed in 1977, had an electronic sound rather like the German band Kraftwerk. It was only when they reformed, working with their new line up and producer Martin Rushent, that their familiar synth-pop sound emerged.

How to practice

Practicing should always be a pleasure. But it involves spending a lot of time working with the instrument and many people find it a frustrating chore. This often leads to inefficient practice, and sometimes to the player abandoning the instrument completely.

To get the most benefit and pleasure from practice, you should always feel you are achieving something. You should be able to monitor your progress, and for this reason practice sessions should consist of modest tasks that are realistically attainable, not attempts at things that are a long way outside your capacity.

So when you are starting a practice session, keep the words "practice slowly" in your mind. Begin each piece of music at a very slow tempo, and build up speed only when you can play the notes accurately. You will gain nothing at all by racing

ahead at the beginning.

If you're still having problems even at snail's pace, break up the piece into smaller sections, and work on each in turn. Then, when you're happy, reassemble them, and you will have made a noticeable, if small, step in your progress. It is often a good idea to stop and restart if you make a mistake in a passage – any small upset will disturb the flow of a piece. But beware of spending all your time on just the first notes, while neglecting the end of the piece. If you are constantly returning to the start, break the passage up into smaller sections and work separately through each one.

The right attitude

One of the most useful skills you can have is the ability to listen to yourself play and criticize your performance. Initially, you may find it helpful to use a tape recorder to assess your performance. Watch out for bad habits at this early stage – they are much easier to correct now than later.

Relaxation is the key to successful practicing. If you get angry or frustrated, your muscles get tense, and it becomes harder to get the results you want. You should aim to practice regularly and for as long as you're enjoying it and feeling that something is being achieved. When this stops, so should you. The correct playing posture (see p. 84) will help keep you relaxed.

◁ **Practicing** Whether you are an established multi-keyboard player like Geoff Downes, or a beginner with only a single keyboard instrument, practicing is a vitally important activity. In fact the amount you practice and the way you do so will probably be the two most important factors in the quality of your keyboard playing.

Playing posture

The first thing to sort out is the actual seating arrangement. Most piano manufacturers produce backless stools for use with their products. These are fine, but if you are sitting at the keyboard for a long time, some form of back support will be welcome. So if you prefer a backed chair, choose one with a firm, rigid back, perpendicular to the seat, that provides as much support as possible.

With both your feet on the ground and with a straight back, adjust the height of the seat so that your forearm is parallel to the floor when you place your fingers on the keyboard. This is an ideal position because it requires virtually no muscular action. You will be comfortable and able to concentrate on the keyboard itself.

Hand positioning

To find the most relaxed position for your fingers, let your arms hang down to your sides. Your hand will now have a cupped shape, and this is the shape you should adopt when positioning your hands over the keys. You will notice that if you straighten your fingers a physical effort is required – muscles are being used. Beginners tend to play the keys by pushing with straight fingers and a rigid wrist. This soon leads to uncomfortable, aching arms.

The thumb has a special role. It acts as the focal point of the

whole technique (see p. 87). It can do this because of its ability to move freely in all planes. This allows it to act as a pivot for the rest of the fingers.

As well as moving up and down, the fingers must be able to spread out to form spans. You also have to be able to detect the position of your fingers in relation to the keyboard. The more practice you get, the more these skills will come naturally.

The final major action that you need to practice is rotating your wrist. It is particularly useful to be able to do this when you are playing octaves, and especially for "stride" and other popular left-hand accompaniments.

Warming up

You cannot start from "cold" and expect your muscles to perform at maximum efficiency. For one of the simplest and best ways to warm up you don't even need a keyboard. Simply clench your fist as tightly as possible. Then, using your other hand, bend each finger in turn gently but firmly backward. This will stretch your muscles, which will soon start to operate more efficiently. Don't crack the joints when you are doing this – it will cause damage over a long period of time. If you have double-jointed fingers, take a little more care when doing this exercise – double-jointing indicates a probable weakness that it is unwise to aggravate by exercising too strenuously.

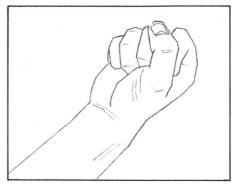

△ **Starting to warm up** A good way to start warming up is to clench your fist as tightly as you can.

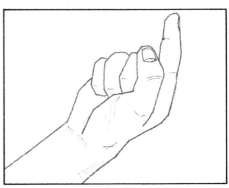

△ **Opening out** Open out each of your fingers in turn.

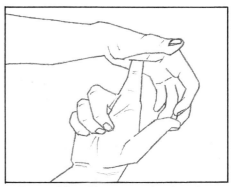

△ **Stretching** Use your other hand to bend back each of your fingers. Do this gently, otherwise you may strain the muscles. Exercise both hands in the same way.

PREPARING AND PRACTICING—SUMMARY

☐ Resist the temptation to start with an "easy-play" keyboard – you will learn more on a manual instrument.

☐ The acoustic piano, with its touch-sensitive, polyphonic keyboard, is probably the best instrument on which to start.

☐ An electric or electronic piano is a good alternative.

☐ If you choose a synthesizer, remember that only a polyphonic model will allow you to play chords.

☐ If you are a more experienced keyboard player, you may still want to know which type of keyboard is best for which task. See p. 80 for more information on choosing keyboard instruments.

☐ Practice slowly.

☐ Break up the music into small

manageable sections and play each one in turn.

☐ Stay relaxed – if you're enjoying it you will achieve more.

☐ Adjust your seat or stool to the best position.

☐ Adopt a cupped hand shape before starting to play – if your fingers are straight they will tire.

☐ Use warming-up exercises, but don't strain your fingers.

The language of music

To communicate in any language you don't have to be able to read and write. The medium we use to talk to each other is speech, and many people, even in the "civilized" world, manage quite happily without reading or writing at all. But if you can't read, you are completely cut off from a wealth of information and entertainment, and your horizons are set by your immediate surroundings and by film, television, and radio.

Music is a language – probably the most widely understood language in the world. As with the spoken word, you don't have to be able to read or write to understand it. Even some top players can't read music, although they are the exceptions.

But most of us are not prodigies. We need to develop our musical skills by practicing the skills and understanding the basics of music. The only way to achieve this is to be able to converse in the language – to be able to read music.

The more music you read, the better you will be at reading music. In addition, you will get all kinds of information about performance and composition, and, perhaps most important of all, you will be able to reproduce a melody or an accompaniment on demand. The ability to read music isn't vital for a musician, but without it music loses a whole dimension.

Musical notation

To be completely literate in the language of music you must be able to write down the music you play and hear. The system of symbols used to write music down is called musical notation; it can be used to communicate or record three musical qualities of every note you play. These are: its pitch, its duration, and when it is played. How the notation system works in general terms is explained below. You will find more information about pitch throughout the following pages, and more information about note duration and when to play notes in the section covering rhythm (see pp. 124-8).

The staff

Over the years a simple system of naming notes with letters of the alphabet has evolved. This system developed when the keyboard was made up of only seven notes (named from A to G). The black notes on the keyboard, the sharps and flats, were a later development, and so they were named with reference to the original seven notes, instead of being given their own letters.

Each of the notes is allotted a position on a five-line grid known as the *staff* (or *stave*). The vertical position of the note on the staff indicates its pitch – higher-pitched notes are placed higher on the staff. The note's horizontal position shows you when it should be played – you read the staff from left to right, just as you do when you are reading the text of a book.

To represent all the notes you can play on a keyboard, you need more than one staff. So symbols called *clefs* are used to "bias" the lines. For example, the bass clef sets the following notes to a lower register than those following an alto, soprano, or treble clef. In addition, extra lines (called *leger lines*) can be added to the staff if the range of the piece requires it.

The *key signature*, placed immediately after the clef, tells you what key the piece is in (see pp. 98-9). After this comes the *time signature*. In conjunction with the bar lines that divide up the music, this indicates the rhythm (see p. 124).

▽ **Notes on the staff** This example (which isn't intended to be played) shows many of the different musical symbols you will encouter in this section of the book.

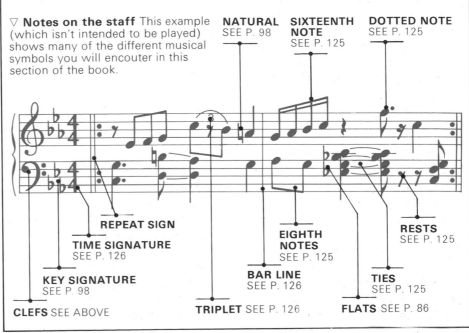

NATURAL SEE P. 98

SIXTEENTH NOTE SEE P. 125

DOTTED NOTE SEE P. 125

REPEAT SIGN

TIME SIGNATURE SEE P. 126

KEY SIGNATURE SEE P. 98

CLEFS SEE ABOVE

EIGHTH NOTES SEE P. 125

BAR LINE SEE P. 126

TRIPLET SEE P. 126

RESTS SEE P. 125

TIES SEE P. 125

FLATS SEE P. 86

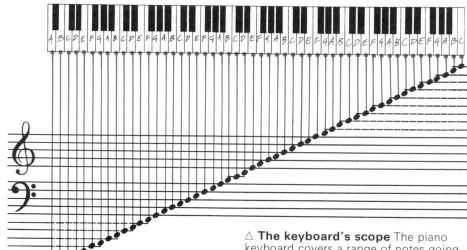

Finding notes on the keyboard

When looking for a note on the keyboard the first thing to do is to find *Middle C*. The staff is centered on this note. Finding Middle C is simple on a piano, since it is the most central C on the keyboard. But many electronic instruments that have keyboards of five octaves or less employ octave-shift switches that raise or lower the keyboard's range in octaves. This effectively extends the span of the instrument, but at the same time moves Middle C. This makes location a little difficult, but your instrument manual should help you find Middle C.

All the C's on the keyboard sit to the left of a pair of black notes (the black notes are in groups of twos and threes). You should be able to locate these notes without looking at the keyboard. Once you have found them, it is a simple matter to discover where all the others lie in relation to C.

Relating the staff to the keyboard

Finding your way around the keyboard is easiest if you use the black notes and the position of Middle C. It is worth sitting down at the keyboard, putting your hands on the keys at random, and trying to identify the notes as quickly as you can. Don't just try to give the notes their letter names – try to visualize their positions on the staff too. Remember that the letters are only an intermediate labeling system – to perfect your reading ability it is important to

△ **The keyboard's scope** The piano keyboard covers a range of notes going far beyond the treble and bass clefs. If you have a synthesizer, the keyboard may be smaller, but there may be a transposing switch (see p. 76).

concentrate on the staff itself. You will soon notice that the C above Middle C falls in a different position on the treble staff to the C an octave below Middle C on the bass staff. The spaces and lines represent different notes for each staff. Beginners often find this confusing. One solution is to work from Middle C and not to learn the names of each space and line, but to translate directly from the staff to the keyboard itself.

The black notes

When you have mastered the white notes look at the black notes, or *accidentals*. Again, you can identify them by finding their position in relation to other notes. But the scoring of the accidentals on the staff is less straightforward. For example, the note between C and D is higher in pitch (or *sharper*) than C and lower in pitch (or *flatter*) than D. This note can therefore be called either C sharp

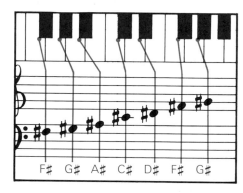

△ **Accidentals** The black notes are named according to the adjacent white notes. You will also find F♯, G♯, A♯, C♯, and D♯ called G♭, A♭, B♭, D♭, and E♭ respectively.

(written C♯) or D flat (written D♭). The same principle is used to name the notes played by the other four black keys. Which of the two alternative names you should use for each accidental depends on the context of the note. You usually use the sharp if ascending to the note and the flat if descending.

THE LANGUAGE OF MUSIC – SUMMARY

☐ Musical notes are written out on a five-line grid called the staff.

☐ The higher the pitch of a note, the higher its position on the staff.

☐ For instruments (such as key-boards) that span more notes than a single staff, an additional staff and leger lines are used.

☐ Clefs are used to show the pitch value of the lines on each staff.

☐ The key signature tells you what key the music is written in.

☐ Find Middle C and locate the

other notes in relation to it.

☐ Use the raised black notes to find your way around the keyboard.

☐ The black notes are also known as accidentals.

☐ These notes are named in relation to the white notes on the keyboard.

Fingering technique

In common with most skills the physical process of acquiring a good fingering technique can't be rushed. The aim of all the practice you will have to put in is quite simple. You are trying to relegate to your subconscious all the effort required to play a piece accurately and you are striving to reach a point where your fingers hit the right notes automatically. So you should study fundamental fingering conventions and "etiquette".

However, although rules do exist on which you can base your approach, many keyboard players develop their own individual fingering techniques. This may be because they find their own method more comfortable, or more suited to the size and strength of their hands and fingers. The "rules" are therefore more like guidelines. To start with, you will need a reference system to indicate which finger to use for which note. A finger numbering system is helpful.

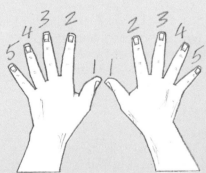

△ **The fingering numbering system**
The general convention is to refer to the thumbs of both hands as 1, the forefingers as 2, and so on. Some music scores print finger numbers above each note. Initially, this can be useful, but beware of not paying enough attention to the notes themselves with this type of score.

Hand positions and the "home key"

Playing a keyboard instrument is in some ways similar to using a typewriter. Perhaps the most obvious link lies in the use of the "home key" concept, which gives a focal point for your technique. In keyboard playing,

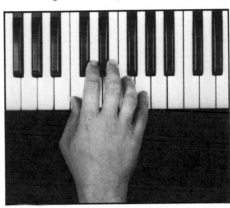

Closed position The fingers fall next to one another on adjacent keys. With your right hand, for example, your thumb plays C and your fingers D, E, F and G. As soon as you know where your thumb falls – on the home key – you should know instinctively the notes your other fingers are covering.

"Jumps"

Though useful for smooth transitions when moving up and down scales, the thumb-under and finger-over pivot techniques (see p. 88) are not always very appropriate. In the context of a particular piece of music, it may be more sensible and more economical to reposition your hand completely and to make a "jump" along the keyboard.

the thumb is the focal point of fingering technique; when you move your hand up and down it forms a floating home key.

There are two patterns in which the fingers of your hand can lie – the "closed" position and the "open" position. The home key theory applies to both.

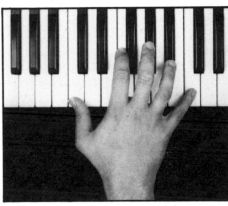

Open position The fingers open out to cover a wide span. For example, while your thumb plays C, your fingers might play D, E, A and B – though the spaces between notes will, of course, vary with the music. Open-position fingering again uses the thumb as a reference point.

The two examples here show how this might work in practice. One shows a jump from G to the A one key up, the other shows how jumps can work with a repeating pattern.

Generally speaking, it is better to keep your fingers in the closed position from jump to jump, rather than trying to accommodate continually varying spans.

△ **Making jumps** In the first example, you use all five fingers, and jump from finger 5 on G to thumb on the A one key up. In the second, a simple pattern is repeated throughout the phrase. You select the best three fingers and use them repeatedly by making three quick jumps, up one semitone each time.

Pivoting

To play notes that fall outside a span of about one octave, you must move up and down the keyboard, changing the position of your thumb and, thus, your point of reference. The obvious method is simply to "jump" (see p. 87), but you can also employ an alternative technique known as *pivoting*.

As an example, let's say you want to play in smooth succession all the white notes from middle C to the C an octave above. Although it is possible to play the first five notes (C, D, E, F, and G) in the closed position and then move your thumb up to the A, it means you have to make an awkward jump in the middle of the phrase. The transition from finger 5 on the G to thumb on the A is very clumsy and would be difficult to disguise. So, instead, try making the switch to your thumb earlier in the run – after the E. This way, you can make a pivot by moving your thumb from the C on which you started to a new position on the F. The top C will then be played by finger 5. The pivot itself is made by tucking your thumb under fingers 2 and 3 while holding down the pivot note with finger 3.

Though this may sound fairly simple, competent keyboard players are always looking ahead to see where they need to go next. This must be taken into account when considering a pivot. For example, if the run of notes had to go past the top C to the D, then you might decide to pivot on the F instead of the E, thus making the G the new home key for your thumb and playing the top D with finger 5. When confronted with a piece of music for the first time, it is best to break it down into small phrases and work out the best fingering.

When traveling down the keyboard – say, from a high C down eight white notes to the C one octave lower – the technique is slightly different. You can still pivot at the same place, but this time finger 3 should reach over your thumb to play the E.

Pivoting is bound to upset the feel of the playing slightly, but, as the new note is introduced, you should try to transmit the right expression even though your hand is momentarily in an awkward position. This will come only with practice, and you should be super-critical when listening to your own playing.

FINGERING TECHNIQUE – SUMMARY

☐ Keep your fingers in the closed position when you are jumping from one key to another along the keyboard.

☐ Use the thumb as the focal point of your fingering technique.

☐ Use pivoting for smooth transitions up and down the keyboard.

☐ Try to develop your own fingering methods.

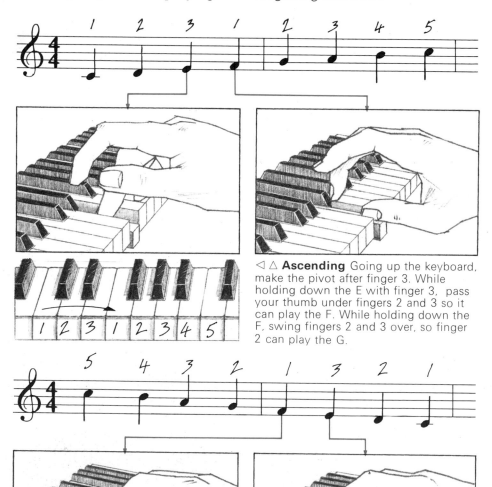

◁ △ **Ascending** Going up the keyboard, make the pivot after finger 3. While holding down the E with finger 3, pass your thumb under fingers 2 and 3 so it can play the F. While holding down the F, swing fingers 2 and 3 over, so finger 2 can play the G.

◁ △ **Descending** Going down, make the pivot after your thumb. While holding down F with your thumb, pass fingers 2 and 3 over, so finger 3 can play the E. While playing E, swing your thumb under fingers 2 and 3 so it can play the final C.

Tuning

A keyboard instrument should be in tune in two ways. It should be in tune with itself, so that all the notes are pitched at specific intervals apart. And it should be in tune with the other instruments with which you are playing.

Tuning can be a problem with acoustic and electric instruments. They are sensitive to movement and to abrupt changes in temperature. An acoustic piano, for example, should be tuned regularly and whenever it is moved. As a matter of course, concert pianos are retuned for every major performance. This is a difficult and time-consuming operation, best left to an expert. In a similar way, the early synthesizers needed elaborate techniques to keep them in tune. But today's electronic instruments pose fewer tuning problems. You may simply have to turn a control to adjust the tuning of your instrument to make it compatible with other instruments.

Most Western countries use a standard reference frequency to tune their instruments, so that a standard A has a frequency of 440 Hz (see p. 26).

Tuning and tempering

Different instruments have different tuning methods. An oboe, for example, is tuned by adjusting the overall length of the instrument's body. This naturally affects the tuning of all the notes. But with a keyboard instrument it is possible to adjust the pitch of each note independently. This opens up a number of different tuning options.

Just intonation

The scale is divided into twelve equal parts, with the thirteenth note twice the frequency of the first (see p. 26). Each division is known as a *semitone*, and originally each of these steps was set so that it had a close relationship with all the others, without the actual steps being equal.

This system of tuning is known as "just intonation". Harmonically it is a very pleasing way of tuning. But unfortunately the system poses problems for the keyboard player. In particular, a keyboard instrument that is tuned in this way is restricted to playing pieces in closely related keys. If you want to change to an unrelated key, the entire instrument has to be retuned, one note at a time.

Equal temperament

This system divides the scale into twelve equal steps so that the ratio between any two adjacent notes is the same. Consequently any interval will have the same fixed frequency ratio no matter which key you are playing in.

Equal temperament is a much more versatile way of tuning than just intonation. Because of this most current electronic instruments are tuned in this way.

▽ **Tuning flexibility** Vince Clark is playing a Sequential Circuits Prophet 5, one of the few instruments that allows you to tune each note individually, as on an acoustic piano.

Tuning methods

The variety of keyboard instruments available today have a number of different tuning methods. It is best to leave some of these methods to an accredited engineer or piano tuner. But some are simple enough for you to do yourself.

Tuning free-phase fully polyphonics

These instruments have a separate sound-producing device for each note. These instruments include the acoustic piano, harpsichord, pipe organ, electric pianos such as the Fender Rhodes and Wurlitzer, and electronic instruments such as the RMI ElectraPiano. With this type of instrument, each note has to be tuned separately. You can tune some types of electric pianos yourself (see pp. 44-5), but in most cases the tuning of these instruments should be left to a professional.

Tuning octave-divider polyphonics

This type has a set of twelve electronic oscillators set to produce the pitches for the top octave of the keyboard, and all the other pitches are derived from these oscillators. Most electronic organs of the 1960s and 1970s fall into this category. With only twelve notes to tune, the process is simpler than with free-phase fully polyphonic instruments.

Tuning master-tone-generator polyphonics

These primarily use a single oscillating medium as the source of all the pitches. Examples include the Polymoog, the Hammond organ, and recent electronic organs, pianos, and string machines that are not voice-assignable keyboards. These instruments do not go out of tune with themselves. There is a single control to adjust the overall tuning of the instrument, to ensure that you are in tune with other members of a group or with other keyboards you are using.

Tuning voice-assignable keyboards

These instruments have "floating" oscillators that adopt the pitch of any note to which they are assigned. Most current polyphonic synthesizers fall into this category. Computer-controlled tuning is often a feature of these instruments.

Tuning meters

Electronic tuning meters are getting increasingly popular and accurate. There are three main types: stroboscopic tuners, metered tuners, and frequency counters. Tuning meters are most useful when you are using several keyboards together and you want to check that they are all in tune with each other. With electronic instruments, you can even do this during a live performance. However, many professionals scorn the use of tuning meters, and it is certainly true that a trained ear is more sensitive to good tuning than any mechanical device.

The stroboscopic tuner

This consists of a spinning disk with concentric striped bands. You play the note you want to tune and feed its pitch into the tuner using a microphone (or a direct connection if the instrument is electric). The pitch then controls a light that flashes at the same number of times per second as the frequency of the note. The disk rotates at a constant speed and the pulsating light shines on to it. If you look at the correct band on the disk for the pitch you are tuning, it

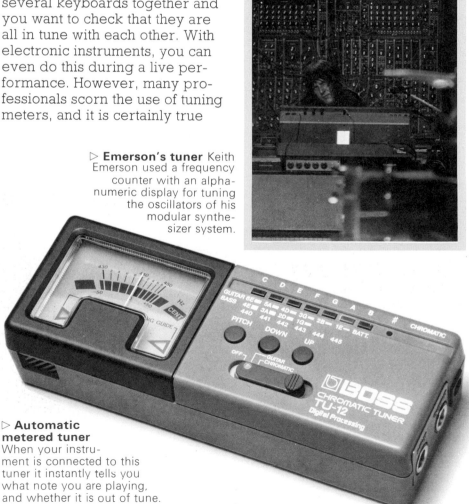

▷ **Emerson's tuner** Keith Emerson used a frequency counter with an alphanumeric display for tuning the oscillators of his modular synthesizer system.

▷ **Automatic metered tuner**
When your instrument is connected to this tuner it instantly tells you what note you are playing, and whether it is out of tune.

Scales

should appear to stand still when the pitch is tuned correctly.

The main problems with these tuners are that they need AC power and are usually expensive. But they are undoubtedly the best type for acoustic and electric pianos.

The metered tuner

This device uses a moving-coil meter to show the pitch of the note. Usually you set the meter to the required note and it shows you how close to the exact tuning position you are. Some tuners work on the same principle but use an LED display rather than a meter.

Metered tuners are usually less expensive than strobo-scopic tuners, but are not as accurate. One advantage is that most metered models produce an audible tone for each note, so that you can check that you are tuning in the right region.

The frequency counter

This is really a piece of laboratory equipment. It gives a digital readout of the frequency of any signal you apply to it. Frequency counters work well for electronic instruments, but they can often be misleading when used with acoustic and electric instruments. This is because the initial attack phase of the note, which can be slightly sharp, tends to mislead the counter.

TUNING – SUMMARY

☐ With just intonation you must retune to play pieces in un-related keys.

☐ With equal temperament you can play in any key.

☐ Leave the tuning of free-phase, fully polyphonic instruments to a specialist.

☐ Octave-divider polyphonics have only twelve notes to tune.

☐ Voice-assignable keyboards often have computer-controlled tuning.

A *scale* is a progression of notes leading from an initial pitch to one an octave above or below. In fact the word "scale" comes from the Latin word *scala*, meaning "ladder", and a musical ladder is exactly what a scale is. Scales are invaluable finger exercises for the musician. But they are more than this.

Why scales are useful

All today's popular music is tonal – it is written with reference to a particular *key*. A tune in a certain key is made up of notes from the scale of that key. For example, a piece that uses the notes of the scale of C major is in the key of C major (see pp. 98-9). The first note of the scale is called the *key note* or *tonic* and all the other notes of the piece are heard in relation to the key note. This makes scales very important whenever you play, write, or even listen to, a piece of music.

Differences between scales

There are two variables that make one scale different from another: the number of steps to be used between the notes and the size of the gaps between each step.

An octave consists of twelve distinct notes, and there is a gap of one semitone between each note and its neighbor. So you might think that the most useful scale would be the one that takes in all the notes (thirteen including the octave) and is made up of twelve semitone steps. This is called the *chromatic* scale. But, like the *whole-tone* scale (made up of 7 notes, each of which is two semitones apart), the chromatic scale is of little practical musical importance (see p. 101).

Because of the traditions on which most popular music is based, our musical structure is founded on scales that employ eight notes and have seven un-equal steps between them.

△ **Versatility** British keyboard player Jools Holland plays in a range of styles from boogie woogie to rock and roll. Whatever your style, a knowledge of scales will help you.

The major scale

This scale is undoubtedly the most pleasing to our ears. Its notes follow a rational order, so that when you listen to it, the scale seems to make musical sense. This is mainly because we are used to hearing it and it is smoothly constructed.

The major scale derives from the Ionian mode (see p. 96). In the Middle Ages, the church disapproved of the Ionian mode since, because of its structure, it had a popular, bright, cheerful air and was used for folk and dance music.

The mood of music written in the major scale is in many ways similar to that of the Ionian mode. For the keyboard player, the simplest major scale is the major scale of C. It uses only the white notes of the keyboard. It is easy to see from the keyboard how the scale is constructed. The keyboard is divided into semitones. So if there is a black note between two white notes, this means that you've stepped an additional semitone.

If you play a major scale on a keyboard instrument it initially sounds smooth, as if all the steps are equal. But if you are listening for them, the semitone gaps are quite distinct.

Each step in the scale has a name that describes it in relation to the key center (see pp. 98-9). Roman numerals can be used for intervals (see below).

Degree names	
I	Tonic (root)
II	Supertonic
III	Mediant
IV	Sub-dominant
V	Dominant
VI	Sub-mediant or relative minor
VII	Seventh or leading note
I	Tonic (octave)

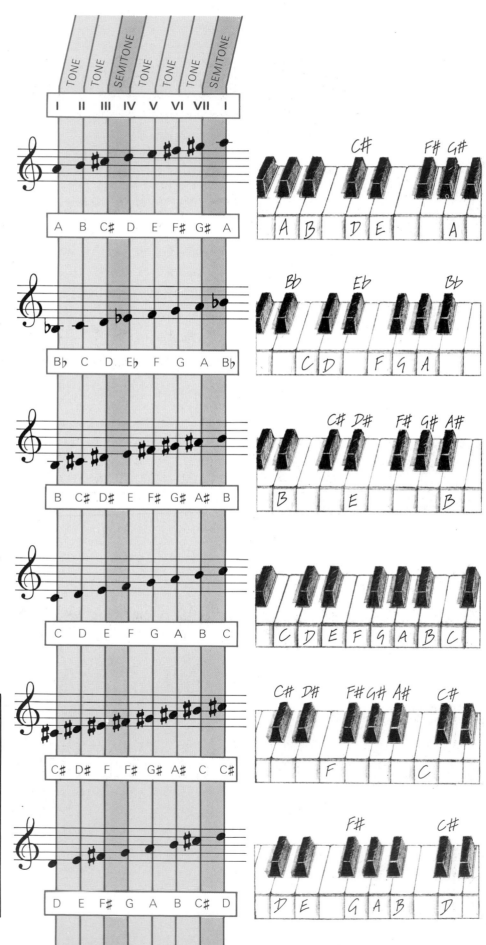

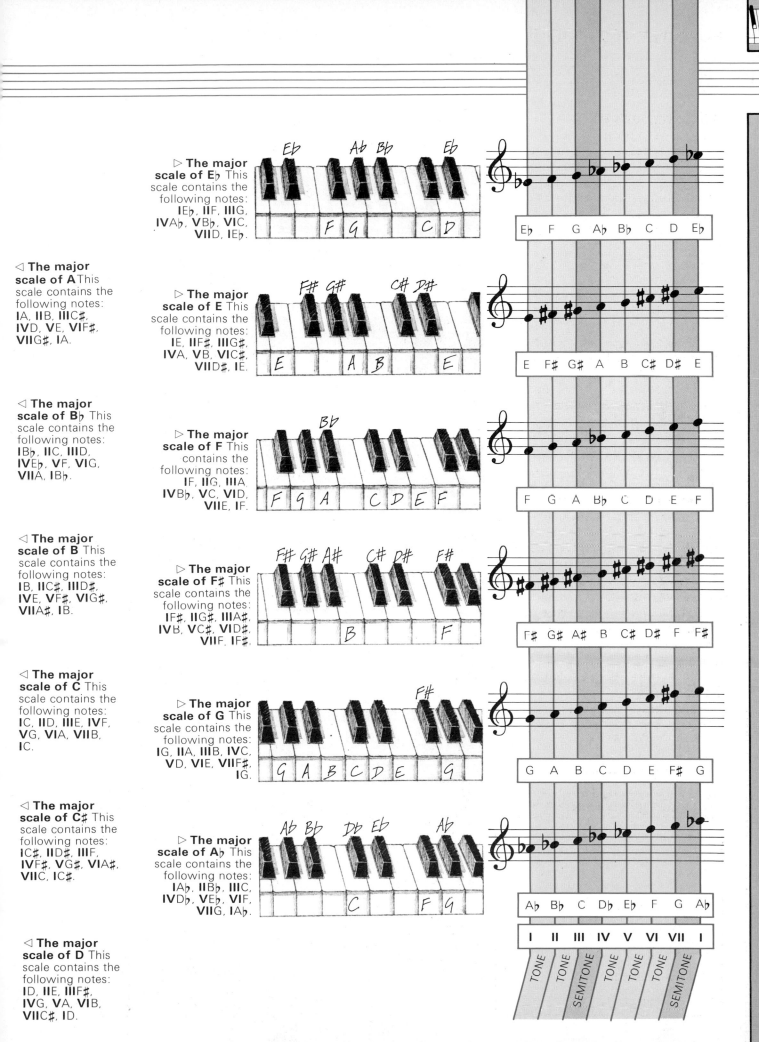

◁ **The major scale of A** This scale contains the following notes: IA, IIB, IIIC♯, IVD, VE, VIF♯, VIIG♯, IA.

◁ **The major scale of B♭** This scale contains the following notes: IB♭, IIC, IIID, IVE♭, VF, VIG, VIIA, IB♭.

◁ **The major scale of B** This scale contains the following notes: IB, IIC♯, IIID♯, IVE, VF♯, VIG♯, VIIA♯, IB.

◁ **The major scale of C** This scale contains the following notes: IC, IID, IIIE, IVF, VG, VIA, VIIB, IC.

◁ **The major scale of C♯** This scale contains the following notes: IC♯, IID♯, IIIF, IVF♯, VG♯, VIA♯, VIIC, IC♯.

◁ **The major scale of D** This scale contains the following notes: ID, IIE, IIIF♯, IVG, VA, VIB, VIIC♯, ID.

▷ **The major scale of E♭** This scale contains the following notes: IE♭, IIF, IIIG, IVA♭, VB♭, VIC, VIID, IE♭.

▷ **The major scale of E** This scale contains the following notes: IE, IIF♯, IIIG♯, IVA, VB, VIC♯, VIID♯, IE.

▷ **The major scale of F** This contains the following notes: IF, IIG, IIIA, IVB♭, VC, VID, VIIE, IF.

▷ **The major scale of F♯** This scale contains the following notes: IF♯, IIG♯, IIIA♯, IVB, VC♯, VID♯, VIIF, IF♯.

▷ **The major scale of G** This scale contains the following notes: IG, IIA, IIIB, IVC, VD, VIE, VIIF♯, IG.

▷ **The major scale of A♭** This scale contains the following notes: IA♭, IIB♭, IIIC, IVD♭, VE♭, VIF, VIIG, IA♭.

93

Minor scales

While there is only one major scale, there are three distinct minor scales. These are known as the natural, harmonic, and melodic minor scales. They have several similarities. The most important is that the first four steps are the same in each scale, so that the first five notes are common to all three. It is therefore the sixth and seventh notes that tell you what type of minor scale you are dealing with.

The natural minor scale

This scale evolved from the Aeolian mode. It has the same step pattern of tones and semitones. The Aeolian mode with C as its key center uses only the white notes and runs from A to A. Thus the natural minor scale of A, like the major scale of C, uses only the white notes.

This relationship is called the relative principle. Every major

▷ **Two examples of the natural minor scale** The natural minor scale is shown in the keys of A and C both on the keyboard (right) and on the staff (far right). You use the same notes ascending as you do descending. The natural minor scale of A is easiest to play because it contains only the white notes of the keyboard. If you compare the major scale of C (see pp. 92-3) with the natural minor scale of A, you will see that the third note of the minor scale (C) is the first note of the major and that the major scale's sixth note (A) is the first note of the minor. A natural minor is the relative minor scale of C major.

▷ **Two examples of the harmonic minor scale** The harmonic minor scale is shown in the keys of A and C, both on the keyboard (right) and on the staff (far right). You use the same notes when ascending the keyboard as you do when descending. The harmonic minor is almost the same as the natural minor scale. The only difference is that the seventh note is raised a semitone, giving a three-semitone jump between the sixth and seventh notes.

▷ **Two examples of the melodic minor scale** The melodic minor scale is shown in the keys of A and C, both on the keyboard (right) and on the staff (far right). This scale is formed by raising the harmonic minor's sixth note. But the main difference between this and the other two minor scales is that its form changes. When you are descending the keyboard the step pattern is exactly the same as that of the natural minor scale (see above).

ASCENDING — DESCENDING

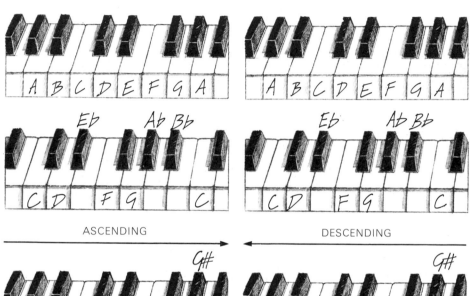

ASCENDING — DESCENDING

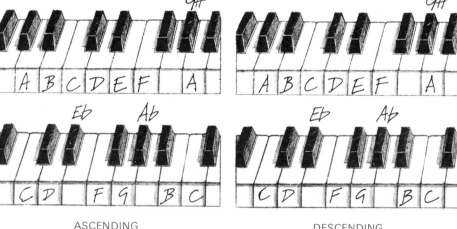

ASCENDING — DESCENDING

key has a relative natural minor. So A is the relative natural minor of C. Although both scales share the same notes, the step patterns are different, which gives the two scales their different "flavors". The major scale and its relative natural minor also share the same key signature

(see pp. 98-9).

The third note of every natural minor scale is also the first note of the relative major. Conversely, the sixth note of the major scale represents the first of the relative natural minor. So it is a simple matter to find the related scales. The relative minor is

always three semitones down from the major.

The harmonic minor scale

The dominant fifth triad chord (see p. 111) is a very useful harmonic tool. But in the natural minor scale of C, this triad (made up of the notes G, B♭, and D) is itself minor. This can cause problems if you want to keep the harmonic structure of a composition flowing, so the harmonic minor scale evolved. This scale is virtually the same as the natural minor, except that the seventh note is raised a semitone to preserve the dominant fifth triad as a major chord. As you can see from the step pattern, this does produce a large, three-semitone jump between the sixth and seventh notes. The gap makes the scale sound rather erratic when you play it as a sequence.

The melodic minor scale

Sometimes you will need a minor scale which, like the harmonic minor, is harmonically acceptable, but which is also melodically much smoother. To get away from the three-semitone gap between the sixth and seventh notes, the sixth note is raised to form the melodic minor scale.

Raising the sixth note in this way is only necessary when the harmony is running up the scale. When descending, the leading note is no longer so important in the harmonic structure. So there is no need to raise the sixth note in the melodic minor scale when you are descending. As a result, the melodic minor scale reverts to the same step pattern as the natural minor when running down the scale. For example, the melodic minor scale of A runs "A, B, C, D, E, F♯, G♯, A" when you are ascending, and "A, G, F, E, D, C, B, A" when you are descending.

The modes

The ancient Greeks developed a system of musical scales that they called *modes*. A mode consists of a series of notes in sequence, including one to which all the others are related. This is always the first (and last) note of the mode. Early keyboards had only white notes, and each mode was made up of seven notes. For example, the original Ionian mode went from C to C, while the original Aeolian mode went from A to A.

The essential difference between the various modes is in the sizes of the steps (either a tone or a semitone) between each of the notes. By using a modern keyboard instrument with black notes, you can play a particular mode by starting with any note – it is the pattern of steps that is important in distinguishing the character of one mode from another. If you look at the steps in each mode, a clear pattern emerges.

The specific modes are related to certain types of music. The Ionian mode clearly corresponds to today's major scale (see pp. 92-3), and the Aeolian mode corresponds to the natural minor scale (see p. 94).

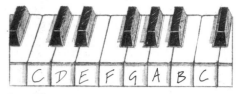

▷ △ **The Ionian mode in C** This mode has the same step pattern, and consequently the same sound, as the diatonic major scale (see pp. 92-3). So in the key of C it uses only the white notes of the keyboard.

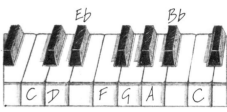

▷ △ **The Dorian mode in C** The Dorian is a minor mode. The difference between it and the natural minor scale (the Aeolian mode – see opposite) is that its sixth note is sharpened. The Dorian mode is suitable for minor chord sequences and is often used to form the basis for blues and rock numbers.

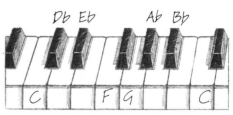

▷ △ **The Phrygian mode in C** Like the Dorian, the Phrygian is a minor mode. It is the same as the natural minor scale (the Aeolian mode – see opposite), but its second note is flattened.

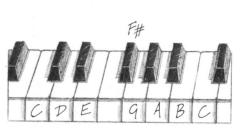

▷ △ **The Lydian mode in C** The Lydian mode is a major scale, but it is different from the diatonic major scale (or Ionian mode – see above) because its fourth note is sharpened.

Using the modes

▽ The seven Greek modes are shown in relation to the major scale of C. These original modes use only the white notes. Each one starts on a different note.

▷ **The Ionian mode** This mode runs from C to the C an octave above.

▷ **The Dorian mode** This mode runs from D to the D an octave above.

▷ **The Phrygian mode** This mode runs from E to the E an octave above.

▷ **The Lydian mode** This mode runs from F to the F an octave above.

▷ **The Mixolydian mode** This mode runs from G to G.

▷ **The Aeolian mode** This mode runs from A to the A an octave above.

▷ **The Locrian mode** This mode runs from B to the B an octave above.

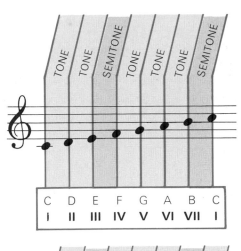

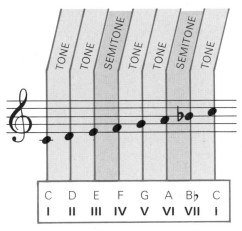

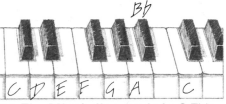

◁ △ **The Mixolydian mode in C** This is a major scale. It differs from the diatonic major scale (the Ionian mode — see opposite) because its seventh note is flattened. The Mixolydian mode also corresponds to the major blues scale and lends itself particularly well to jazz and blues improvisation.

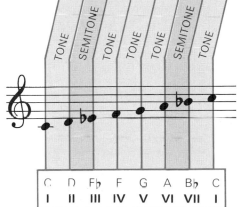

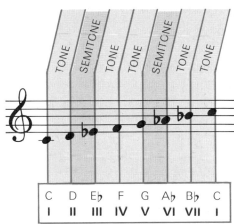

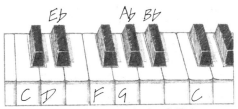

◁ △ **The Aeolian mode in C** This mode has the same step pattern, and consequently the same sound, as the diatonic natural minor scale (see pp. 94-5).

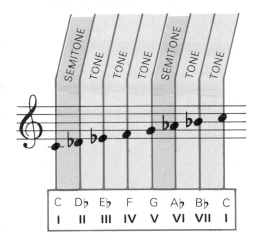

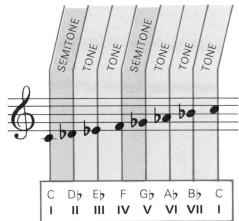

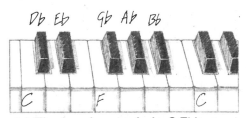

◁ △ **The Locrian mode in C** This mode, with its five flattened notes, is used less in Western music than any other mode. But it is heard in some types of Eastern music, particularly in Japanese and some Indian styles.

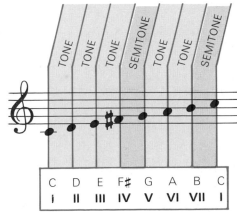

SCALES – SUMMARY

☐ One scale is different from another because of the number of steps and the size of the gaps between them.

☐ The C major scale is easy to play – it uses only the white notes of the keyboard.

☐ There are three different minor scales in each key – the natural minor, the harmonic minor, and the melodic minor.

☐ Each minor scale has the same step pattern for the first four steps.

☐ The melodic minor changes its step pattern according to whether you are ascending or descending the scale.

☐ There are seven modes.

☐ As with scales, modes differ from one another according to the size of the steps.

☐ You can play a mode starting with any note, provided that you keep to the right step pattern.

Key signatures

Most pieces of music follow closely the structure of one of the major or minor scales. The relationship of the music to a particular scale determines what key the piece is written in. The *key signature* tells you what the key is.

Recognizing keys

If a piece uses primarily the white notes of the keyboard and seems to relate strongly to the note C (with phrases beginning or ending with a C), then the piece is probably in the key of C major. If the piece had E♭'s and A♭'s instead of E's and A's, but still tended to use the note C at beginnings and ends of phrases, it would be in the key of C minor.

The scale of C features the notes C, D, E, F, G, A, B, and the C the octave above. These notes are said to be *diatonic* to the key of C major. The remaining notes (C♯, D♯, F♯, G♯, and A♯) do not form part of the C major scale. They are *chromatic* to the key of C major. Similarly, the scale of A minor contains only the white notes. So if the piece contained the same white notes, but was more biased toward the note A, it would be written in the key of A minor. You could also tell that it was in a minor key from the overall feel of the music. Pieces written in the minor keys tend to sound a little less bright and rather more solemn than pieces written in the major keys.

Writing down tunes in a particular key

The major scale of G major contains the notes G, A, B, C, D, E, and F♯, while the notes G♯, A♯, C♯, D♯, and F are chromatic to this key. A piece in G major will probably have no more than a handful of notes that are chromatic to the key.

So when it comes to writing down the music on the staff, it would get untidy to put a sharp symbol in front of every F. This problem would be even greater in a key such as B, which contains five sharpened notes. To overcome this difficulty, you indicate the notes you want to sharpen or flatten at the beginning of each line of the staff, alongside the clef. The resulting combination of clef and the sharps or flats required is called the key signature. All the notes following it must conform to the instructions it dictates. If you wish to play or write a chromatic note outside the key signature, then a sharp, flat, or natural sign (♮) must be drawn alongside the relevant note. In this way you can recognize all adjusted notes as being chromatic to the key signature.

The key signature system provides a vital signpost. You instantly know from the number of sharps or flats in which key a piece is written. With practice, you will automatically adjust yourself to play the sharps or flats. Playing a piece with five or six sharps or flats may be daunting at first, but you will soon get used to it.

◁ **Key signatures on the staff** No matter how many sharps or flats there are in a key signature, you write them down in the order shown here, starting with either F♯ or B♭ and writing in the required number of sharps or flats.

F C G D A E B

B E A D G C F

The order of sharps and flats

There is a fundamental relationship between the notes of the various scales. Every time you move up a fifth (see p. 105) an extra sharp is added to the key signature. So C major has no sharps, G major (a fifth up) has a single sharp, D major has two sharps, and A major has three sharps (see below). This system, called the *order of sharps*, maintains the step pattern of the major scale, and it is always the fourth note of the old scale (or the seventh note of the new one) that has to be sharpened to keep

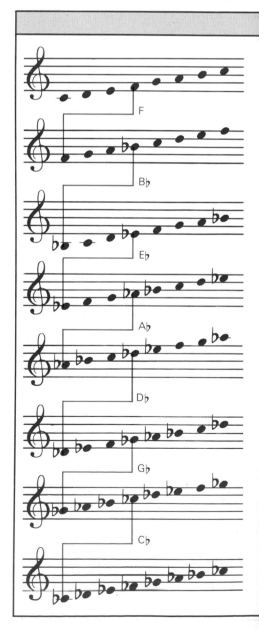

the pattern of sharps consistent.

Similarly, if you move down a fourth (for example, from C to F), the fourth note of the new scale has to be flattened to keep the major scale step pattern the same as in the previous scale.

The order of sharps is a useful device, as it enables you to work out the key signature of a piece of music very easily. You can see that it moves up in perfect fifth intervals (see p. 105) and runs ahead of the progression of key signatures by two steps. It shows that a piece featuring D sharps must contain the three previous sharps (F, C, and G) for it to be written in the key of E major.

On the staff the relative positions of the sharps are always the same (see below). So when there are three sharps, the third (the G) will always be the last. And of course all the sharps refer to those same notes in octaves across the entire staff, not merely in the treble and bass clefs.

The order of flats is similar to the order of sharps, but instead of moving up you move down fifths. Again, you can calculate what key you are in from the number of flats. For example, if you see three flats, the last will be an A♭. You need only move forward a fifth (or back a fourth) to find what key you are in – in this case, E♭. In fact, identifying the key is even simpler than this. If you look at the previous flat, you will see that it is always a fourth below the last flat. So all you have to do to identify the key is to look at the flat immediately before the last one, and this will tell you the name of the key. This holds true with all the keys with flats except for F major, which has only one flat. With this key you have to go back to the other method, counting a fifth forward to work out the key.

Key relationships

◁▷ The keys are shown in relation to the key of C. Each scale with flats starts at the 4th note of the one above. Each scale with sharps starts at the fifth note of the one above.

◁ **The key of F major** This contains one flat. Its relative minor is D minor.

◁ **The key of B♭ major** This contains two flats. Its relative minor is G minor.

◁ **The key of E♭ major** This contains three flats. Its relative minor is C minor.

◁ **The key of A♭ major** This contains four flats. Its relative minor is F minor.

◁ **The key of D♭ major** This contains five flats. Its relative minor is B♭ minor.

◁ **The key of G♭ major** This contains six flats. Its relative minor is E♭ minor.

◁ **The key of C♭ major** This contains seven flats. Its relative minor is A♭ minor.

▷ **The key of G major** This contains one sharp. Its relative minor is E minor.

▷ **The key of D major** This contains two sharps. Its relative minor is B minor.

▷ **The key of A major** This contains three sharps. Its relative minor is F♯ minor.

▷ **The key of E major** This contains four sharps. Its relative minor is C♯ minor.

▷ **The key of B major** This contains five sharps. Its relative minor is A♭ minor.

▷ **The key of F♯ major** This contains six sharps. Its relative minor is E♭ minor.

▷ **The key of C♯ major** This contains seven sharps. Its relative minor is B♭ minor.

Identifying key signatures

Unlike most instruments, the keyboard can be employed as a useful calculating device when you are counting fifths. You can use the keyboard to mark out the various fifth steps. In fact it isn't really necessary to learn any key signatures by heart, since you can work them out from first principles. For example, all you need to know about the key of G major is that it contains one sharp. You know that this is two

Relative minors

Every major key has a corresponding relative minor key. So any key signature will represent two different keys. For example, the key signature used to represent the key of C major, with no

Parallels

It is useful to know the relationship between the key signatures of the major and minor keys of the same note. It is best to think of the sharps as plus points and the flats as negatives. The difference between a major and a minor key is always three. So if you are playing in F♯ major, which has six sharps, you will know that F♯ minor must have

fifths below G. Therefore the note will be an F♯.

There is a quicker trick that helps if you want to identify a key signature. Look at the last sharp, and move up to the next position on the staff. This note will tell you which major key you are playing. For example, if you see seven sharps, the last will be a B♯. Move to the next space above and you are at C♯ (not C, because there is a preceding sharp in the key signature). So the key you are in is C♯ major.

sharps or flats, will be the same as that for A minor. The E major key signature (with four sharps) also represents the key of C♯ minor. The relative minor keys of all the major keys are indicated on p. 99.

three sharps, to balance the equation (6−3=3). Similarly, if you are playing in D major, which has two sharps, you will know that D minor must have one flat. This is because the two sharps represent two plus points. So if you subtract three you get −1, giving you one minus point, or a single flattened note (the resulting equation is therefore: 2−3=−1).

Notes with two names

You may have noticed that the notes E♯ and B♯ have two names – they appear on the keyboard as F and C respectively. Notes referred to by two names are called *enharmonic*. There are two reasons for using this device. First, it helps to give clarity, especially when you are dealing with the relationships between the various key signatures. It helps visually because it allows you to place every note in a particular key on a different line or in a different space. For example, the key of F♯ major has six sharps (F, C, G, D, A, and E). If we were to abandon the idea of E♯, and call it F, we would get two notes on the "F" line (F and F♯), which would lead to great confusion.

KEY SIGNATURES – SUMMARY

☐ A piece written in a certain key will probably have only a few notes that are chromatic to that key.

☐ The notes that are regularly sharpened or flattened in a key are indicated in the key signature.

☐ Every time you move up a fifth an extra sharp is added to the key signature.

☐ Every time you move down a fourth, a new flat is added to the key signature.

☐ You can tell what key you are in from the number of sharps or flats in the key signature.

☐ On the staff, the relative positions of the sharps and flats are always the same – for example, if there are three or more sharps, the third will always be a G.

Transposing chart

When you are playing with other musicians, or arranging music, you will sometimes want to transpose notes or chords in one key to corresponding notes and chords in another. The

chart below is designed to help you to do this, giving equivalent notes in 11 of the most useful keys. The key of C is placed in the center, for ease of reference.

▷ **How to transpose**
To transpose a note or chord from one key to another, you first find the key you are in at the top of the chart and then look across the chart horizontally to find the key you require. You can then look down the two columns to find the corresponding notes.

	SHARPS				C	FLATS				
B	E	A	D	G	**C**	F	B♭	E♭	A♭	D♭
C♯	F♯	B	E	A	**D**	G	C	F	B♭	E♭
D♯	G♯	C♯	F♯	B	**E**	A	D	G	C	F
E	A	D	G	C	**F**	B♭	E♭	A♭	D♭	G♭
F♯	B	E	A	D	**G**	C	F	B♭	E♭	A♭
G♯	C♯	F♯	B	E	**A**	D	G	C	F	B♭
A♯	D♯	G♯	C♯	F♯	**B**	E	A	D	G	C
B	E	A	D	G	**C**	F	B♭	E♭	A♭	D♭

(KEYS)

More scales

As well as the major scale and the three minor scales, it is worth having a working knowledge of some of the other musical scales that you may encounter. You can create many different musical scales, simply by varying the step pattern between the individual notes. But only a few of the possible combinations make real sense when it comes to writing and playing music.

Among the other musical scales that you should learn are symmetrical scales, in which the step pattern has its own internal repetitions, and non-symmetrical scales, where this is not the case.

With these additional scales, it is not simply the step pattern that varies – many of them have a different number of notes to the major and minor scales. It is the combination of step pattern and number of notes that gives these scales their own character.

Remember that the scales shown on these pages only represent a selection of all the possible scales. When you have mastered the ones in this book, you may find it worthwhile to experiment with others.

The chromatic scale

This is the most obvious example of a symmetrical scale, since it contains all twelve notes, and therefore has equal semitone steps between them. Conse-quently, there is only one chromatic scale, and any note within it can be taken as the first note. If writing this scale, sharpen the accidentals going up and flatten them going down.

Whole-tone scales

As their name implies, these scales are made up of notes that are spaced a tone apart. It therefore follows that there are six notes (plus the octave) in the scales. Like the chromatic scale, these scales are completely symmetrical and any note can be taken as the key note.

There can only be two whole-tone scales because the whole-tone scale for any other key is contained within these two. No notes are common to both of these scales.

The whole-tone scales do not feature any perfect fifth intervals (see p. 105). So they are often used for solos over diminished and augmented fifth chords (see p. 114). They naturally sound very even and are therefore very useful compositional devices.

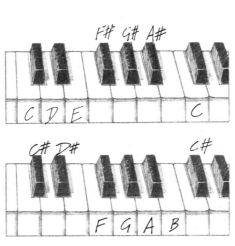

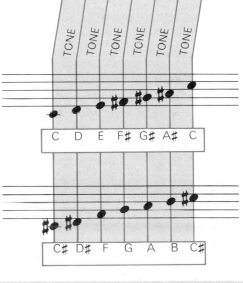

△ **The two whole-tone scales** There are only two whole-tone scales, one starting at C and the other starting at C♯. If you start at any other note and take whole-tone steps the resulting scale will follow one of these two patterns.

▷ **Oscar Peterson** Jazz keyboard player Oscar Peterson emphasizes the importance of scales in keyboard technique whatever your level of ability.

Diminished scales

A symmetrical scale with $1\frac{1}{2}$ tone steps would be impractical because the scale would have to consist of only four notes. Instead, the step pattern adopts alternating tone and semitone steps, and is called the *diminished* scale. If you analyze a diminished scale, you will find that it is made from two diminished seventh chords (see pp. 114-5) – hence the name.

Again, this is a symmetrical scale. This time it has four key centers (the first, third, fifth, and seventh notes), so that there need only be three separate scales to encompass all the key centers.

Diminished scales are rather lively and you can use them to freshen up passages of music that might otherwise be boring or conventional. They are particularly useful for fills and improvisation over diminished chord progressions. Initially they appear quite difficult to master on the keyboard, but their sound will soon become familiar to you, and automatically adopting their shape quickly becomes second nature.

△ **Using diminished scales**
Jazz pianists, such as Dave Brubeck, sometimes use melodies and chords based on diminished scales. The effect of diminished scales seems rather disorienting at first, but if you practice using them you will soon get used to their unusual form.

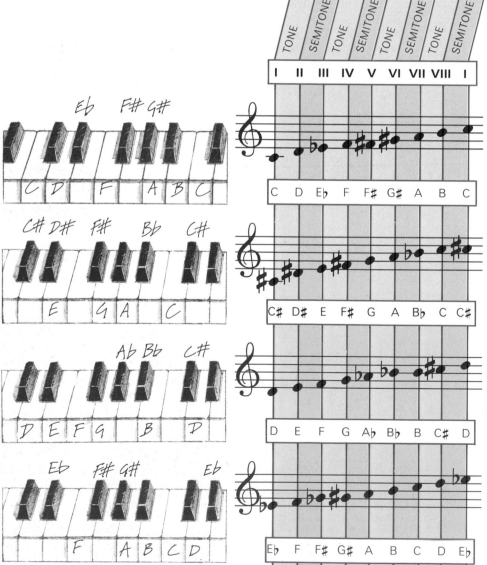

◁ **The diminished scale of C** This scale contains the following notes: **I**C, **II**D, **III**E♭, **IV**F, **V**F♯, **VI**G♯, **VII**A, **VIII**B, **I**C. The diminished scales of E♭ (see below), G♭, and A all share the same notes as this scale.

◁ **The diminished scale of C♯** This scale contains the following notes: **I**C♯, **II**D♯, **III**E, **IV**F♯, **V**G, **VI**A, **VII**B♭, **VIII**C, **I**C♯. The diminished scales of E, G, and B♭ all share the same notes as this scale.

◁ **The diminished scale of D** This scale contains the following notes: **I**D, **II**E, **III**F, **IV**G, **V**A♭, **VI**B♭, **VII**B, **VIII**C♯, **I**D. The diminished scales of F, A♭, and B all share the same notes as this scale.

◁ **The diminished scale of E♭** This scale contains the same notes as the diminished scale of C (see above).

Pentatonic scales

As you might expect from their name, *pentatonic* scales consist of five notes and the octave. They are not symmetrical, so that each scale has only one key center. In addition there are both major and minor forms of these scales. So there are 24 different pentatonic scales in total.

If you look at the step patterns of the pentatonic scales you can see that they are virtually the same as the respective major and minor scales, except that some notes are missing. The major pentatonic scale omits the fourth and seventh notes of the scale, while the minor pentatonic leaves out the second and sixth notes.

The pentatonic scales make a useful foundation for solos against the respective major and minor diatonic chords. These scales are valued for their melodic feel.

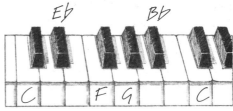

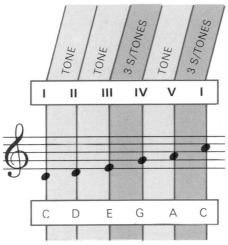

△ **The Pentatonic scale of C major**
This scale contains the following notes: IC, IID, IIIE, IVG, VA, IC. This is equivalent to leaving out the 4th and 7th notes from the major scale of C.

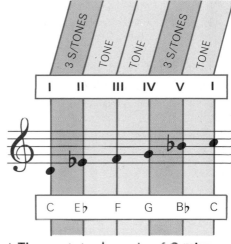

△ **The pentatonic scale of C minor**
This scale contains the following notes: IC, IIE♭, IIIF, IVG, VB♭, IC. This is equivalent to leaving out the 2nd and 6th notes from the natural minor.

The blues scale

This is not a scale in the strict sense, but it provides a useful musical structure if you are sitting in on a session. There is no hard-and-fast step pattern for the blues scale, nor is there even a standard number of notes. There is some resemblance between the blues scale and the pentatonic major scale (see above). But the blues scale is so loose that such comparisons are not very helpful. The structure features prominently in blues and certain jazz pieces, but non-scale notes are very common, particularly as lead-ins to the main notes.

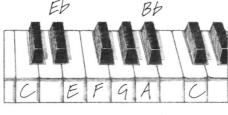

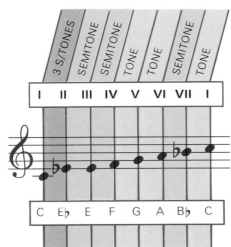

△ **A blues scale in C** This is just one example of a blues scale in this key. You can experiment with other patterns and notes.

▷ **Using blues scales** These scales have provided the basis for a variety of blues and rhythm and blues artists, such as Billy Preston.

Some other scales

By varying the step pattern you can make up any scale you like, but in many cases the results you obtain will not be very useful. But there are one or two additional scales that you can try out.

Their structure makes them sound rather dissonant, and so they are not used widely. But you may find them worth experimenting with.

All these are non-symmetrical scales and are shown here based on the note C. None of them contain other key centers, so you will have to transpose them, using the step pattern, in order to derive the corresponding scales for other key notes that you want to use.

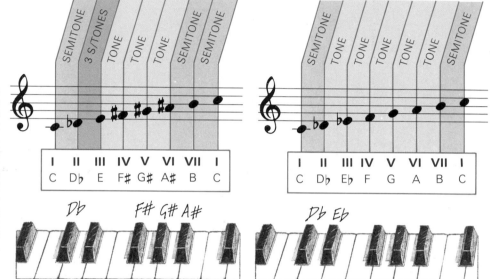

▷ **The enigmatic scale in C** This scale contains the following notes: IC, IID♭, IIIE, IVF♯, VG♯, VIA♯, VIIB, IC. Its difference from the diatonic major scale is its flattened 2nd note and its sharpened 4th, 5th, and 6th notes.

I	II	III	IV	V	VI	VII	I
C	D♭	E	F♯	G♯	A♯	B	C

◁ **The major Neapolitan scale in C** This scale contains the following notes: IC, IID♭, IIIE♭, IVF, VG, VIA, VIIB, IC. Its difference from the diatonic major scale is its flattened 2nd and 3rd notes.

I	II	III	IV	V	VI	VII	I
C	D♭	E♭	F	G	A	B	C

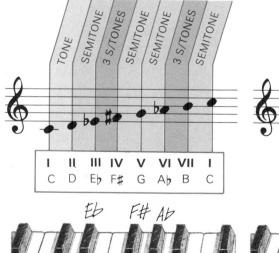

▷ **The Hungarian minor scale in C** This scale contains the following notes: IC, IID, IIIE♭, IVF♯, VG, VIA♭, VIIB, IC. Its difference from the diatonic major scale is its flattened 3rd and 6th notes and its sharpened 4th note.

I	II	III	IV	V	VI	VII	I
C	D	E♭	F♯	G	A♭	B	C

◁ **The minor Neapolitan scale in C** This scale contains the following notes: IC, IID♭, IIIE♭, IVF, VG, VIA♭, VIIB, IC. Its difference from the diatonic major scale is its flattened 2nd, 3rd, and 6th notes.

I	II	III	IV	V	VI	VII	I
C	D♭	E♭	F	G	A♭	B	C

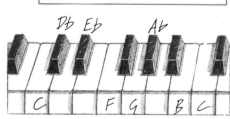

MORE SCALES – SUMMARY

☐ The chromatic scale includes all twelve notes of the keyboard, with equal semitone gaps between them.

☐ The two whole tone scales are each made up of six notes a tone apart. Any note can be taken as the key note of a whole-tone scale.

☐ Diminished scales have alternating tone and semitone steps.

☐ Pentatonic scales are made up of five notes plus the octave. They include two steps of three semitones each.

☐ Though not a true scale, the blues scale provides a useful structure for composition and improvisation and can take many different forms.

☐ Try experimenting with other scales when you have mastered all the scales that are covered in this book.

Intervals

The effect of three or more notes sounding at the same time is vitally important in music. When you play more than two notes simultaneously you are producing a chord. Chords are especially relevant if you are using a polyphonic instrument, but the principles involved are also important even if you are playing a monophonic keyboard (one that can only produce one note at a time).

In order to understand how chords work, you need to know about *intervals.* In musical terms, an interval is the difference in pitch between any two notes. Every interval has its own characteristic sound, although of course the overall effect depends not only on the actual pitch differences, but also on the instrument you are using. This is because, although the fundamental pitch stays the same, the harmonic content of each note, and therefore the timbre (see pp. 27-8), varies from one instrument to another.

Interval names – the major scale

The names used to describe the different musical intervals are simple to grasp. You can work them out by counting the number of notes in the scale that the interval bridges. Take, for example, the fifth, one of the most common intervals. In the scale of C major, G is a fifth above C because five notes (C, D, E, F, and G) bridge the gap between them.

You can count all the intervals in the scale in this way, and this will give you the second, third, fourth, fifth, sixth, and seventh spans. If two notes have the

Interval names – other scales

So far we have looked only at intervals involving the eight notes of the major scale. But the octave is made up of twelve semitones. For our method of calculating intervals, it would appear that the spans from C to G and from C to G♯ would both be fifths. Obviously these intervals are different, so some new names are needed to cover all possible intervals.

The fourth and fifth intervals

Using intervals

Some intervals sound more pleasing than others, and some can be changed by simple modifications. The information below tells you what the various intervals sound like, how to modify them, and how to work them out on the keyboard.

Consonance and dissonance

The fifth and the octave are very pleasing to the ear and are known as *perfect consonances.* These intervals form part of the natural harmonic series (see p. 27), and this gives them their satisfying quality. So their acoustic nature justifies the term "perfect".

same fundamental pitch, they are said to be in unison. The eighth interval is naturally known as the octave.

The layout of the keyboard can at first make it a little difficult to determine the intervals in different keys. But working out intervals on the staff is very much simpler, because of the way the musical notation system works. You merely have to count the number of notes in the scale that lie on different adjacent lines or spaces. So the interval from C to A would encompass six notes, and would therefore be a sixth; that from C to D, spanning two notes, is a second.

are the same in both major and minor scales (as are the unison and the octave). So the fourth and fifth are referred to as the *perfect* intervals.

The second, third, and seventh intervals vary according to whether they are in a major or minor key, and so can be called either *major* or *minor* intervals.

To incorporate the other notes of the chromatic scale, musicians use the terms *augmented* and *diminished* to indicate the variations (see pp. 106-7).

Thirds and sixths are also consonant, but they do not have the same natural qualities as the fifth and the octave, so they are known as *imperfect* (or *soft*) *consonances.*

Seconds, sevenths, and all the augmented and diminished intervals are usually considered to be rather unstable, with a slightly unsatisfying sound. Therefore they are called *dissonances* and can be qualified as being either mild or sharp. The fourth interval can be either consonant or dissonant depending on the musical context.

Compound intervals

There is no reason why an interval should be confined to a

single octave. Spans of an octave plus an interval are known as *compound intervals*. The span from C to the G one and a half octaves above is written C to G' and is a perfect 12th. Similarly, the interval the interval C to D' is a major 9th.

Interval inversions
Raising the pitch of the bottom note of a pair of notes by an octave (or lowering the top note by an octave) creates an inverted interval. This type of interval has an interesting relationship to the original, because the sum of both intervals always totals nine. For example, a fifth always inverts to a fourth (5+4=9), while a second inverts to a seventh (2+7=9).

The following rules also apply to interval inversion. Perfects always invert to perfects; majors invert to minors and vice versa; diminished intervals invert to augmented intervals and vice versa. An augmented fourth inverts to a diminished fifth, which is essentially the same interval. As with notes that have

two alternative names, two intervals that share the same name are called enharmonic intervals (see p. 100).

Intervals on the keyboard
Although it is simplest to work out an interval on the staff, you can calculate it quite easily using the keyboard. If you are a beginner, the most straightforward method is to count semitones. But you should also familiarize yourself with the actual sound of the different intervals and train yourself to recognize the span distances by ear.

To help you to recognize intervals by ear you should practice playing two notes at random, one after the other, without looking at the keyboard. Then try to name the interval. When you have mastered this, try identifying the interval while you are playing two random notes at the same time.

Usually a particular interval will sound basically the same no matter which key you are playing in (for example, a C to G fifth will have a similar quality to a D to A fifth). The intervals do sound slightly different because

differently tempered scalings create minor discrepancies (see p. 89). But for most purposes the equal tempering used on the majority of electric and electronic keyboards keeps these differences to a minimum.

The keyboard's design means that some intervals do not automatically span the same physical distance when you transpose them to different keys. This happens when an interval incorporates a black and a white note. For example, the fifth between C and G (two white notes) spans a shorter distance than the fifth from B♭ to F, but has the same distance as the one from C♯ to G♯ (two black notes).

This can make playing the intervals difficult at first. But with practice it soon becomes easy to gauge the compensation required when spanning black and white notes.

Intervals are the basic elements in chord construction and it will help you to use intervals when building up chords if you can recognize intervals by their actual sound. Their different sound characteristics are shown in the table below.

INTERVAL CHART							ENHARMONIC
NUMERICAL SYMBOL	I (1ST)	ii (♭ 2ND)	II (2ND)	iii (♭ 3RD)	III (3RD)	IV (4TH)	IV+ (♯ 4TH)
DEGREE	TONIC	SUPERTONIC		MEDIANT		SUB-DOMINANT	TRITONE
PITCH IN KEY OF C	C	D♭	D	E♭	E	F	F♯
INTERVALS FROM C	C to C	C to D♭	C to D	C to E♭	C to E	C to F	C to F♯
DISTANCE OF INTERVAL	ZERO	1 SEMITONE	2 SEMITONES	3 SEMITONES	4 SEMITONES	5 SEMITONES	6 SEMITONES
NAME OF INTERVAL	UNISON	MINOR SECOND	MAJOR SECOND	MINOR THIRD	MAJOR THIRD	PERFECT FOURTH	AUGMENTED FOURTH
SOUND CHARACTERISTIC	OPEN CONSONANCE	SHARP DISSONANCE	MILD DISSONANCE	SOFT CONSONANCE	SOFT CONSONANCE	CONSONANCE OR DISSONANCE	NEUTRAL OR RESTLESS

INTERVALS – SUMMARY

☐ To work out an interval's name you count the number of notes in the scale that it bridges.

☐ Two notes of the same fundamental pitch are said to be in unison.

☐ The fourth and fifth (the perfect intervals) are the same in both major and minor scales.

☐ Seconds, thirds, and sevenths vary according to whether they are in a major or minor key.

☐ Intervals that sound pleasing are called consonances.

☐ Intervals that sound less satisfying are known as dissonances.

☐ By raising the pitch of the bottom note of an interval by an octave you create an inverted interval.

◁ **Ray Charles and Howard Jones**
These two players have widely different styles. But all music involves intervals and a knowledge of intervals will enhance your musical vocabulary.

▽ **Interval chart** This chart shows the range of intervals with reference to the key of C. The pairs of enharmonic intervals are effectively the same since they involve notes with two different names (see p. 100).

ENHARMONIC		ENHARMONIC		ENHARMONIC				
V° (♭5TH)	V (5TH)	V+ (♯5TH)	vi (♭6TH)	VI (6TH)	vii° (♭♭7TH)	vii (♭7TH)	VII (7TH)	I (1ST)
TRITONE	DOMINANT	SUBMEDIANT				SUBTONIC	LEADING NOTE	TONIC
G♭	G	G♯	A♭	A	B♭♭	B♭	B	C
C to G♭	C to G	C to G	C to G♯	C to A	C to B♭♭	C to B♭	C to B	C to C
6 SEMITONES	7 SEMITONES	8 SEMITONES		9 SEMITONES		10 SEMITONES	11 SEMITONES	12 SEMITONES
DIMINISHED FIFTH	PERFECT FIFTH	AUGMENTED FIFTH	MINOR SIXTH	MAJOR SIXTH	DIMINISHED SEVENTH	MINOR SEVENTH	MAJOR SEVENTH	OCTAVE (8VA)
NEUTRAL OR RESTLESS	OPEN CONSONANCE	SOFT CONSONANCE		SOFT CONSONANCE		MILD DISSONANCE	SHARP DISSONANCE	OPEN CONSONANCE

Simple chords

A chord is generally considered to be a set of three or more notes played simultaneously. Any three notes will do, but different combinations of notes produce a wide range of concordant and discordant effects.

Chords are important because they allow you to back up your tunes by adding notes below. Listen to any song, and you will notice that it consists of a basic tune and chords. Usually, if you play this on a keyboard, the tune (or *melody*) will be played by the right hand, while the chords (or *harmony*) will be played by the left.

It is best to start with the simplest chords. These are triads, which consist of three notes, and sevenths, which are four-note chords. Triads are important because their sound is acceptable to the ear and because they form the basic building blocks of other, more complex chords.

Chord notation

As well as the symbols used in this book, you will find other methods of showing chords. Any chord letter with no supporting sign represents a major chord – the major chord of C is simply written "C".

The plus symbol used for augmented chords usually refers to raising the fifth, but can be used to raise any note in the chord. "C7 +" or "C7 +5" describes a C seventh with an augmented fifth, while "C +11" is an augmented eleventh – the eleventh interval is raised.

The minus symbol used for altered chords flattens the number it precedes. So "Cmaj7 −5" describes a C major seventh diminished fifth. With suspended chords, it is usually the fourth that is suspended (see p. 120).

It is becoming common to define the bass note to be used in conjunction with a chord. This is done either by putting the appropriate letter below the chord name, under a line or putting it in brackets.

CHORD SYMBOLS		
MAJOR	M, Maj, maj,	C
MINOR	m, min	Cm
DIMINISHED	dim, d, −,	Cdim
HALF-DIMINISHED	Cø	Cø
AUGMENTED	Aug, aug, +,	C+
SIXTH	6	C6
SEVENTH	7	C7
NINTH	9	C9
ELEVENTH	11	C11
THIRTEENTH	13	C13
SUSPENDED	sus	Csus
ALTERED	−	C −5

△ **Indicating chord types** For some types of chord a number of different symbols can be used. The table shows the basic chord symbols that you are likely to come across in musical scores and books.

Triads

The triad consists of three notes, but not every combination of three notes constitutes a triad. There are firm guidelines as to which groups of notes you can use to make up a triad.

Usually the most acceptable chords are those made up of intervals a third apart – superimposed thirds. The two do not make a sixth because they overlap. As there are two kinds of third intervals, major and minor, you can construct four different types of triad. These are the only possible combinations of the superimposed major and minor intervals. You can see their relationship to each other quite clearly if you look at the keyboard.

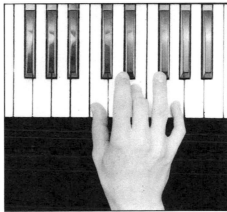

△ **C major triad** This consists of the notes C (the root), E (the major third), and G (the fifth). The interval between C and E is a major third, that between E and G a minor third.

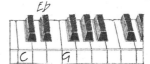
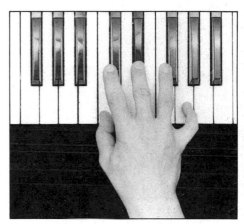

△ **C minor triad** This is based on the minor scale (see pp. 94-5). The notes are C, E♭ (the minor third), and G (the fifth). The lower interval is a minor third, the upper a major third.

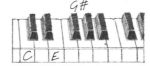
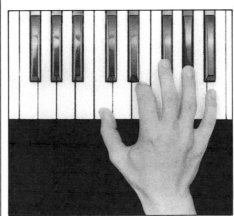

△ **C augmented triad** The fifth is raised a semitone to G♯, making an augmented fifth interval with the C. This triad is found in the whole-tone scale as root, third, and fifth.

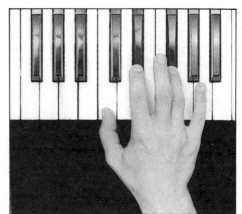

△ **C diminished triad** The fifth is lowered a semitone to G♭, giving two minor third intervals and an interval from C to G♭ of a diminished fifth.

◁ △ **The importance of chords** Whether you are playing a grand piano like Floyd Cramer (above) or an accordion like Tom Bailey of the Thompson Twins (left), chords should be a major part of your musical vocabulary.

109

Working out triads in other keys

On the keyboard a major third interval always spans five keys – counting the root as the first key and the major third as the fifth key, and including both black and white keys. On the other hand, a minor third interval always spans four keys on the keyboard.

As long as you remember which two intervals make up each triad, working out chords becomes easy – whatever key you are in. The chart (far right) tells you the intervals that make up each type of triad and how many keys you need to count for each of them. It's worth memorizing this information – it will help you when using chords.

Let's take an example. Suppose you want to play a G minor

triad. You know that the root must be G, so this gives you your starting point for constructing the chord. You also know that a minor triad is made up of a minor interval with a major interval on top. A minor interval is four keys on the chromatic keyboard and this will

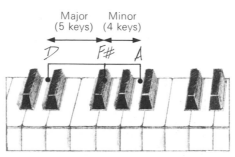

△ **Working out the D major triad**
Starting with D (the root), count five keys, including the root, to take you to F♯ (the third). Then count four keys, including the third, to take you to A (the fifth).

bring you to B♯ – so this is the next note in your chord. A major interval is five keys on the keyboard, so, starting this time from B♯, five keys bring you to D – the last note of the chord. So now you have worked it out: a G minor triad is made up of the note G, B♯, and D.

Counting keys to locate triads		
Triad	First interval	Second interval
Major	Major (5 keys) +	Minor (4 keys)
Minor	Minor (4 keys) +	Major (5 keys)
Augmented	Major (5 keys) +	Major (5 keys)
Diminished	Minor (4 keys) +	Minor (4 keys)

Triad inversion

The examples of the four basic types of triad (see p. 109) are shown with the root or tonic note as the lowest note in the chord. In the same way that you can invert an interval (see p. 106), you can also invert triads, so that the lowest note is no longer the root. But when you have three notes, as in a triad, you can produce two different kinds of inversion. By moving the root up an octave the third becomes the bottom note (the first inversion); by taking the third up an octave the fifth becomes the bottom note (the second inversion). With the C major example, any arrangement of the notes C, E, and G still forms a C major triad.

Triad inversion in practice

By simply playing the three variations of the C major triad you will hear the different characters of the inversions. For the electronic keyboard player, the use of the triad in these different configurations is particularly important. Straight root triads

can sound flat and lifeless on many electronic instruments, and any means you have of varying the chordal accompaniment will enliven your performance.

If you have a polyphonic synthesizer and want to simulate a

complete section of instruments (such as a string section) you should also try using inverted forms of the triad as much as possible, in order to "spread" the parts over a wider range of different pitches.

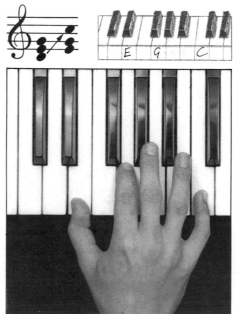

△ **C major triad – first inversion** In the root position the C is the lowest note. For the first inversion this moves to the next C up, making the 3rd (E) the lowest note.

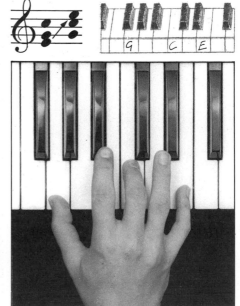

△ **C major triad – second inversion** In this inversion the E also moves up an octave. This leaves the 5th (G) as the lowest note in the chord.

Diatonic and chromatic triads

The notes of a particular scale are said to be diatonic to that scale, while other notes are said to be chromatic to the scale. So a C major chord, made up of the notes C, E, and G, is naturally diatonic to the scale of C major, because the notes it employs form part of the C major scale. But a B major triad (B, D♯, and F♯) would be chromatic to the scale of C major because the scale doesn't include D♯ or F♯, even though it does include B.

The distinction between diatonic and chromatic chords is useful because it helps you work out the structure of what you are playing. It is especially relevant when you are playing chord progressions and in addition is helpful when you are writing music or improvising.

Labeling types of triad

Roman numerals are used to represent the various triads of the scale, with upper-case numerals for major triads and lower-case numerals for minor triads. Upper-case numerals with the addition of a plus sign (+) indicate augmented triads, while diminished triads are shown with lower-case numerals followed by a degree sign (°).

Triads in major keys

The simplest diatonic triads to play are those in the scale of C major, since each triad keeps exactly the same shape. You simply advance one step along the scale each time. But you should notice that although this is a major scale, the diatonic triads it contains are not just major triads of the root notes. The diatonic chordal pattern runs: I, ii, iii, IV, V, vi, vii°, I. This sequence is the same for all keys. In other words, the I, IV, and V chords are major, the ii, iii, and vi chords are minor, and the vii chord is diminished. In sequences of chords you will get a good concluding sound if you move from the V to the I, from the IV to the I, or from the V to the iii, IV, or vi. Try experimenting with other patterns.

Harmonized scales

In any key you can build a series of triads using the notes of the scale as the root notes. The resulting set of chords is called a harmonized scale. You construct a harmonized scale by building two intervals of a third on each note in the scale. You only use the notes of the scale to build the thirds, so the size of the steps between each note of the scale will determine whether the intervals are major or minor thirds (see pp. 106-7), and so will also determine the type of each triad.

Harmonized scales are important because, just as each note of the ordinary diatonic scale has its own particular sound in relation to the tonic, so each triad of the harmonized scale has its own sound in relation to the tonic triad. Moving from one triad in the scale to another can change the mood of the music, so getting to know how harmonized scales work can prove useful whenever you are using chords.

In most music the three major chords of the key are commonest. These give the *three chord trick*, useful in a variety of musical contexts.

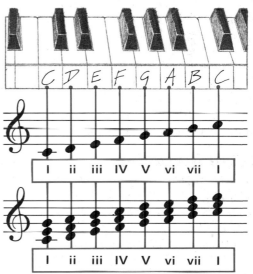

△ **Harmonized scale of C major** This is simply the scale of C major with three-note chords built on each note. These chords use only the notes of the C major scale. The only major chords are I, IV, and V.

The three-chord trick			
Keys	I	IV	V
Keys with sharps	**A**	A	D	E
	D	D	G	A
	G	G	C	D
	C	C	F	G
Keys with flats	**F**	F	B♭	C
	B♭	B♭	E♭	F
	E♭	E♭	A♭	B♭

The three-chord trick in different keys You do not have to restrict your use of the three-chord trick to the key of C. You can use it in any key. All you have to do is select the major chords (I, IV, and V). This chart shows you the major chords in a selection of keys together with those in the key of C, for comparison.

Triads in minor keys

While the diatonic triads of the major scale are fairly easy to follow, those for the minor keys are more difficult to grasp because there are three different types of minor key (see p. 94). So there are four different sets of triads for the minor keys, the tonic triad being the only one common to all three minor scales.

In minor keys the V (dominant) chord is a minor triad, so it cannot have the same role in chord sequences as in major keys (see p. 111). This is why the harmonic minor scale was created by raising the 7th note (see pp. 94-5).

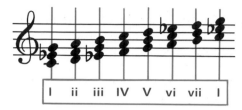

◁ **The harmonized C melodic minor scale** Building triads on the notes of the melodic minor scale of C gives this result.

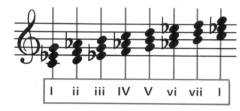

◁ **The harmonized C harmonic minor scale** This is the scale that you get when you build triads on the harmonic minor scale of C.

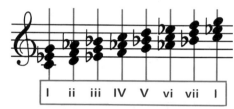

◁ **The harmonized C natural minor scale** This harmonized scale is the result when you construct triads on the natural minor scale of C.

Selecting chords for harmony

All triads contain three different notes, the root, third, and fifth, and any note can play any one of these three roles in a triad. Any note can belong to three different triads. So if you want to use a chord to harmonize a particular melody note or bass note, you immediately have a choice of three chords containing that note. The fact that you can also invert triads (see p. 110) gives you further possibilities.

In the examples on this page, the notes of the major scale of C are used as the root notes and different chords are built on these roots. Try the various chords for each root note to find how you can harmonize the same note but get different effects.

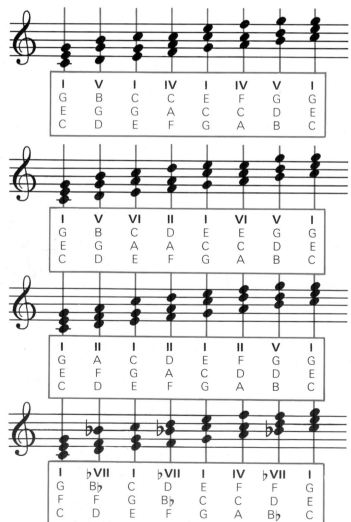

◁ **Using primary triads** This harmonized scale is constructed using the notes of the C major scale as roots and employing inversions. In this way only the primary triads (I, IV, and V) are used.

◁ **Using both primary and secondary triads** These three harmonized scales draw on a wider range of chords and inversions. The first includes inversions of the ii and vi triads. The second uses inversions of I and ii. The third employs inversions of the subtonic B♭ triad, although this falls outside the major scale.

Adding notes to a triad

Any of the four basic triads can exist in three forms – the root, the first inversion, and the second inversion (see p. 110). So this gives 12 different possible triad forms for each key. To add further variations you can introduce an extra note – this is known as *triad doubling*. It is a very useful technique that helps to give variety to chord accompaniments.

Triad doubling involves adding an extra note one or more octaves above or below one of the notes in the fundamental triad. There are three types of doubling – doubling the root, the third note, and the fifth. Each has its own special quality, which you can best understand by playing the doubled chords on the keyboard.

Root doubling provides straight emphasis to the key note of the triad. You should use it at the beginning of a passage, or at the end, to round things off. Third doubling stresses whether the chord is a major or a minor triad – in other words it emphasizes the chord's tonality. Fifth doubling is often used in chord progressions, particularly as a lead-in to a new key.

Doubling enables you to create a wide variety of new chords. But beginners often find it difficult to select the most suitable inversion for the music they want to play. The highest and the lowest notes are the most important, because they determine the overall character or sound of the chord. The note in the bass determines the inversion of the chord, while the top note influences the melodic flow of the chord progression. (The melody is usually in the treble clef, so the ear instinctively tends to use the top note of the chord as a melodic guide.)

◁ △ **Doubling the 3rd note**
To double the C major triad in this way, you play an extra E. You will have to play this with your other hand. Adding this note makes it more obvious whether the chord is major or minor.

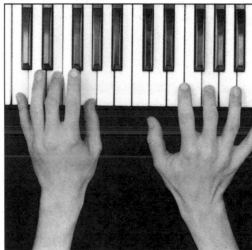

◁ △ **Doubling the 5th note**
To double the C major triad in this way, you play an extra G. Again, you will have to use two hands. Adding this note will make it easier for you to change to another key.

Sevenths

You can play most simple pieces of music with triads alone. But sole use of these chords will probably sound rather dull and uninteresting. Chords that contain more than three different notes will add variety to any piece of music – whatever the style.

Chords are built up by adding or superimposing thirds. So, when building more complex chords, it is logical to work from the triad, with its two thirds, to a chord which has three intervals of a third. This gives us the *seventh*, a four-note chord with a seventh interval between the root and the new note.

The seventh note of the scale is very important. It is called the leading note, because when it is played it needs to be "resolved" in order to satisfy the ear. In other words, it leads us to something – usually the tonic. The seventh note gives con-

siderable color to a chord, and playing a seventh chord can give a passage of music a very strong feeling of tension.

A diatonic seventh chord can be formed only from those notes that make up a particular diatonic scale, and these notes are the root, third, fifth, and seventh. From the four basic triads (major, minor, augmented, and diminished) you can see that adding either a major third or a minor third to the fifth would generate a total of eight seventh chords for each key note. (There are other seventh chords, but they are not diatonic – they cannot be constructed using the notes from any single major or minor scale.)

In fact there are only seven basic options. This is because the final seventh chord would be made up of the notes C, E, G♯ and B♯. This is the equivalent of adding a major third interval to an augmented triad, thus raising the major seventh to an octave above the root.

The names given to each chord are easy to understand, because they are determined by the type of interval the seventh makes with the root, and by the form of the basic triad. If you look at the diatonic seventh chords based on the major and minor scales of C, you will see that all the types of seventh chords listed in the chart (see p. 108) appear. Roman numerals are used to refer to the chords (see p. 111), and the figure ''7'' indicates that the chords are sevenths.

Dominant sevenths

A dominant seventh chord is built from a major triad and a minor seventh. The dominant interval (see p. 107) is the fifth from the root. So the dominant seventh chord of the scale of C major would be G (the dominant), B (the leading note), D (the supertonic), and F (the subdominant).

The word ''dominant'' comes from the Latin word meaning ''to lead'' and this type of chord, when used in a progression, has the quality of leading the music on toward another chord to build up a sequence.

Why does it play this transitional role? The leading note (B) always has a tendency to resolve to the tonic above (C); the dominant (G) also has an affinity toward the tonic, though usually to

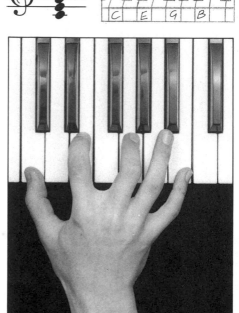

△ **C major seventh (Cmaj7)** This chord is built by adding a major seventh on top of the major triad. It therefore contains the major third, perfect fifth, and major seventh intervals.

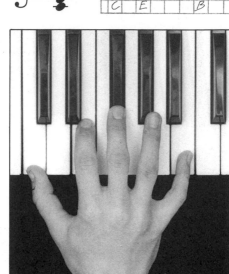

△ **C major seventh diminished fifth (Cmaj7-5)** In this chord the fifth is flattened, giving the major third, diminished fifth, and major seventh intervals with the root.

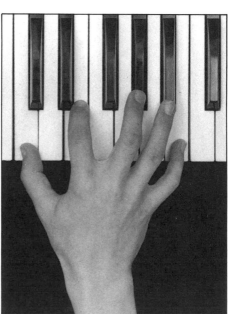

△ **C major seventh augmented fifth (Cmaj7+5)** In this chord the fifth is sharpened, giving the major third, augmented fifth, and major seventh intervals with the root.

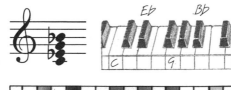
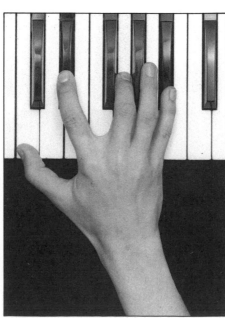

△ **C minor seventh (Cm7)** This chord is built by adding a minor seventh on to a minor triad, giving the minor third, perfect fifth, and minor seventh intervals with the root.

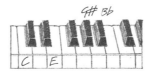

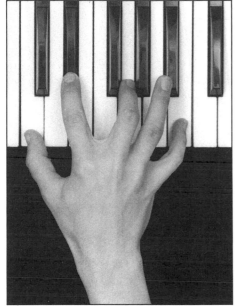
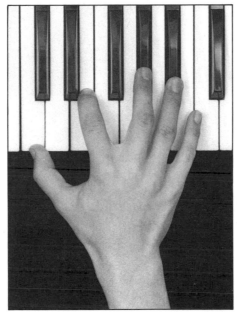
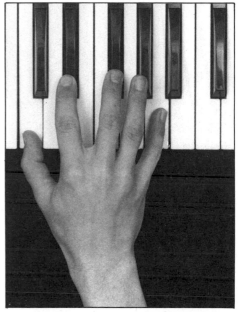

△ **C minor/major seventh (Cmin/maj7)** This chord is built by adding a major seventh interval on to a minor triad, giving the minor third, perfect fifth, and major seventh intervals.

△ **C seventh augmented fifth (C7+5)** In this chord the fifth is sharpened, giving the major third, augmented fifth, and minor seventh intervals with the root.

△ **C diminished seventh (C dim)** This chord is built by adding a diminished seventh to a diminished triad, giving the major third, diminished fifth, and diminished seventh intervals.

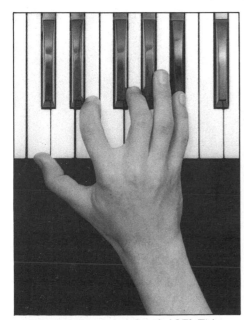
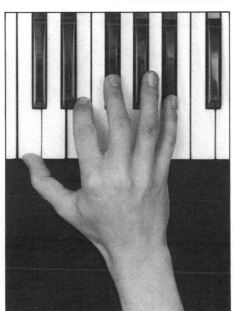
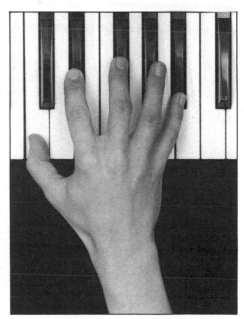

△ **C seventh (dominant) (C7)** This chord is built by adding a minor seventh interval on to a major triad, giving the major third, perfect fifth, and minor seventh intervals.

△ **C seventh diminished fifth (C7−5)** In this chord the fifth is flattened, giving the major third, diminished fifth, and minor seventh intervals with the root.

△ **C half diminished (Cø7)** In this chord only the triad is diminished, not the seventh, giving the minor third, diminished fifth, and minor seventh intervals with the root.

the tonic beneath it. In addition, the chord contains two rather dissonant intervals. These are a diminished fifth (B to F) and a minor seventh (G to F), and in a musical context, the ear usually prefers these to move toward a greater consonance.

So the dominant seventh chord in C major would be resolved well by the major triad. In fact, there is a simple rule that tells you how to resolve the dominant seventh chord in any key: a dominant seventh leads to a chord a fourth up. The result of this "direction of traffic" is called the Perfect Cadence. A cadence (the term comes from the Latin word meaning "to fall") is useful because it gives you a good way of ending of chord sequence.

There are two other seventh chords that are derived from the dominant figure. These are the seventh augmented fifth and the seventh diminished fifth. (You should not confuse these chords with the major seventh augmented fifth and its diminished counterpart.) These chords cannot be constructed solely from the notes of any major or minor scale, so they are not diatonic sevenths. In fact they are based on the whole-tone scale (see p. 101) and they consist of a seventh on top of a triad.

Minor sevenths
Like the dominant seventh family, the minor seventh group contains three chords: the minor seventh itself, the half diminished seventh, and the diminished seventh.

These chords are based on a minor triad. They all have an initial minor third interval. The minor seventh is formed by superimposing a minor seventh interval on a minor triad. The half diminished (or minor seventh diminished fifth) uses a seventh on top of a diminished triad. And the diminished

seventh employs a diminished seventh interval with a diminished triad.

Major sevenths
The major seventh family of chords earns its name from the fact that all its members have a major interval between the lowest and highest notes. The basic triads (major, minor, augmented, and diminished) are used in combination with this interval to provide four major seventh chords.

Diminished sevenths
The diminished seventh, often referred to simply as "the diminished", is a symmetrical chord – it is formed by stacking up three major thirds.

As with symmetrical scales (see p. 101), any note of a diminished seventh chord can

therefore be taken as the root of a new chord. Thus, the chord of C diminished contains exactly the same four notes as the chord of E♭ diminished. The order of the notes is simply rearranged so that either C or E♭ is the lowest or tonic. So you only have to learn three diminished seventh chords in total. By inverting these you can obtain the diminished chord for all the key notes:
(1) Cdim   E♭dim   G♭dim   Adim
(2) C♯dim   Edim   Gdim   B♭dim
(3) Ddim   Fdim   A♭dim   Bdim

▽ **Jan Hammer** For players who are renowned for their technique, like Jan Hammer, a mastery of the various chords and their musical roles is second nature.

Seventh inversions

In the same way that you can create inversions of a triad (see p. 110), you can also create seventh inversions. The technique is similar to triad inversion except that you are now dealing with a chord of four notes, so there are three inversion options as well as the original root position.

The first inversion takes the third note as the bottom note (in other words the root is moved up an octave). The second inversion has the fifth note as the bottom note, and with the third inversion, the seventh note is the lowest. You will notice when you play them that the inversions of most seventh chords will set up rather dissonant intervals (though this is not so with diminished sevenths, since each inversion merely forms a new diminished seventh chord).

For example, the first inversion of a simple Cmaj7 would produce a minor interval at the top of the chord between the B and the C. This sounds rather unresolved. But with the second inversion this minor second moves to the middle of the chord, and is less prominent.

You should experiment with various inversions of the seventh voicings. But remember that the musical context of a chord can change its character.

You can create inversions of chords on the keyboard simply by adding a bass note. For example if you play a simple root Cmaj7 chord and add a bass C, you are still in the root position. But playing an E, G, or B in the bass inverts the chord. This can be very useful when you want to vary the structure of an accompaniment for a piece of music. Similarly by playing a C major chord you can turn it into a Cmaj7 (third inversion) by playing a B bass note, or a C7 (third inversion) by playing a B♭ bass note, or an Amin7 by playing an A bass note.

SIMPLE CHORDS – SUMMARY

☐ Triads are three-note chords which are made up of intervals a third apart.

☐ You can invert triads in two ways – by moving the root or the third up an octave.

☐ A triad that is diatonic to a particular scale is made up of notes from that scale.

☐ In the scale of C major, each triad keeps exactly the same shape.

☐ Adding an extra note that is one or more octaves above or below one of the notes in a triad is known as triad doubling.

☐ Adding another interval of a third to a triad produces a seventh chord.

☐ Dominant sevenths tend to lead you on to a chord a fourth up.

☐ Like triads, sevenths can be inverted, but there are three different inversion options with a seventh, because of the extra note in the chord.

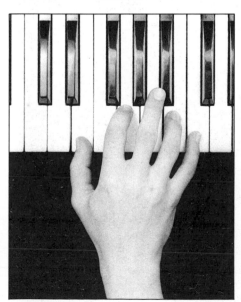

△ **C major seventh – first inversion**
In the root position the C is the lowest note. In the first inversion this moves to the next C up, making the E the lowest note.

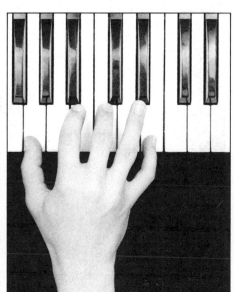

△ **C major seventh – second inversion** In this inversion the E also moves up an octave, leaving the G as the lowest note. The minor second interval between B and C is less prominent.

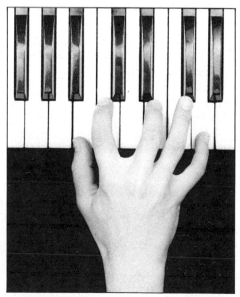

△ **C major seventh – third inversion**
In this inversion of the chord, the G also moves up an octave, leaving only the B in its original position.

Other chords

The triads and sevenths are the most useful chords in the musical vocabulary. But a chord can be made up of any combination of three or more notes, so you can construct other types of chords using the notes of the scale.

You can build additional chords by adding notes to existing chords. So if you start from a chord you already know, it is easy to construct further chords.

As you will have noticed, neither triads nor sevenths use the second, fourth, or sixth notes of the scale. The types of chords produced by using these notes are called added sixths, added ninths, and suspended fourths. When you have mastered these, you may want to go on to more complex chords, stacking notes on top of these chords to produce the so-called extended chords – the ninths, elevenths, and thirteenths.

Added sixths

These chords get their name because an extra note is added to the basic triad, and this note does not replace the fifth. A major sixth combines the sixth note of the scale, the *submediant*, with the major triad. For example, C6 is made up of the notes of the C major triad (C, E, and G) with the addition of A. In a similar way the minor sixth combines the sixth note with the minor triad (giving a chord made up C, E♭, G, and A). So a C chord containing an A must be some kind of a sixth.

The major sixth chord has a satisfying sound. You will often find that it gives you an effective way of concluding a passage. The major sixth is the same as the first inversion of the relative minor seventh. The minor sixth, on the other hand, usually requires resolution; like the dominant seventh, it generally leads to the major chord.

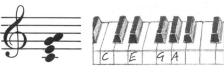

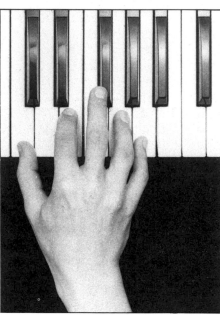

△ **C sixth (C6)** This chord is constructed by adding the sixth note of the scale to the major triad. The sixth is an extra note and not a substitute for the fifth.

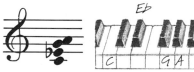

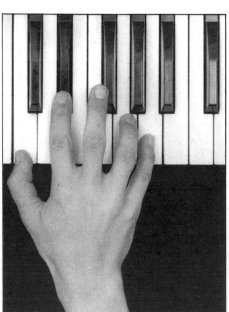

△ **C minor sixth (Cm6)** This chord is constructed by adding the sixth note of the scale to the minor triad. As with the major sixth, this is an additional note.

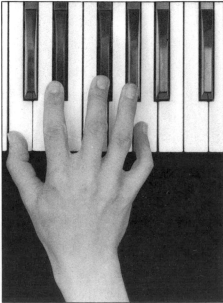

△ **C diminished sixth (Cdim6)** This chord is constructed by adding the sixth note of the scale to the diminished triad, again producing a chord of four notes.

Added ninths

The idea of an added ninth chord may sound rather daunting. But these chords don't necessarily involve ninth spans using a single hand. The added ninth uses the second note of the scale, combined with the major triad; the minor added ninth combines the second note with the minor triad. Again these are added chords – the second does not replace the third. So any C chord that includes a D must be some kind of ninth. In the root position the minor added ninth sets up a minor second interval between the second and third notes of the chord.

The minor second is the most dissonant of all intervals, and so this chord can sound rather harsh in the majority of musical contexts. On some instruments, this gives an interesting sound. In most keyboard pieces the chord is inverted or extended to break up this interval.

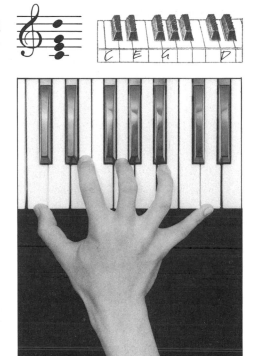

△ **C added ninth (Cadd9)** This chord is constructed by adding the second note to the major triad. It is shown in this example played with the second note (the true ninth) an octave above.

Alternative

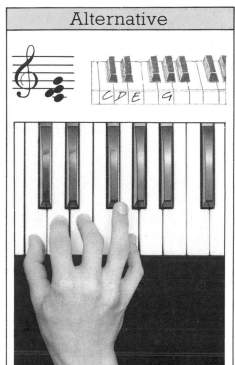

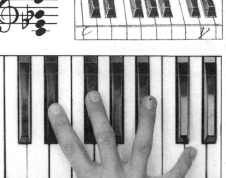

△ **An alternative** In this example, the added ninth is played with the second note itself, to give a smaller fingering span.

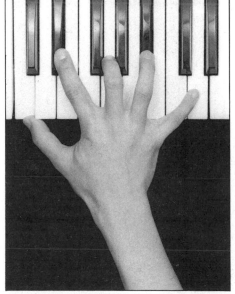

△ **C minor added ninth (Cm9)** This chord is constructed by adding the second (or ninth) note to the minor triad. You can also try playing it with two hands.

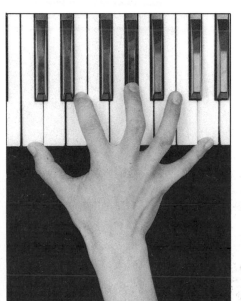

△ **C augmented ninth (Caug9)** This chord is constructed by adding the second (or ninth) note to the augmented triad. Try a two-handed version of the chord if you find the span difficult.

△ **C diminished ninth (Cdim9)** This chord is constructed by adding the second (or ninth) note to the diminished triad. Again, you can try a two-handed version of the chord.

Suspended fourths

The term "suspended" means that one of the notes in the chord has been moved – we are not adding extra notes to make up the new chord. So a suspended fourth can consist of only three notes. It is formed by replacing the third note of any three- or four-note chord with the fourth. The C suspended fourth is made up of the notes C, F, and G (the E in the major triad is replaced with an F). The C seventh suspended fourth comprises the notes C, F, G, and B♭ (the E in the dominant seventh chord is replaced with an F).

The third note of the scale, the mediant, plays an important role in the chord. When you replace it with a fourth the chord automatically sounds unresolved, suggesting that it should return to its original form.

△ **Joe Jackson** Singer and songwriter Joe Jackson writes at the keyboard. A grasp of chord construction is important for this and all other forms of musical composition.

Extended chords

The chords we have looked at so far are formed with three or more notes of the scale, arranged so that they fall within the octave above the root. If you add notes that are more than an octave above the root, you set up larger intervals, and these lead to *extended* chords.

If a second note, inverted an octave above the root, is added to a triad, the result is called a ninth. If the extra note an octave above is a fourth, you produce an eleventh chord. And if you add a sixth an octave above, you get a thirteenth chord.

All these extended chords belong in one of three groups: dominant, major, and minor. They are formed by adding the extra notes to the dominant seventh, major seventh, and minor seventh respectively.

The tonality of the third and seventh intervals determines the tonality of the extended chord. If both these intervals are major, the chord belongs to the major group. If both the intervals are minor, the chord belongs to the minor group. And if the third is major but the seventh is minor, the chord belongs to the dominant group.

You can produce further variations on these chords by raising or lowering the fifth note or the extra note, to produce what are called altered chords. But before you try these, you should get to know the extended chords themselves.

Ninths

There are three types of ninth chord: the ninth (sometimes called the dominant ninth), the major ninth, and the minor ninth.

The ninth itself is formed by finding the second (two semitones) above the root and the note that is an octave above to the seventh chord. So the C ninth is based on the C seventh (C, E, G, and B♭), with the addi-

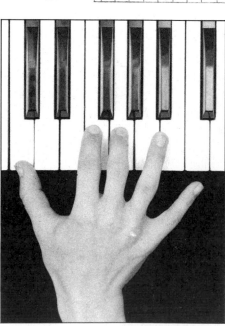

△ **C suspended fourth (Csus4)** This chord is constructed by replacing the third note of the major triad with the fourth, giving the perfect fourth and perfect fifth intervals.

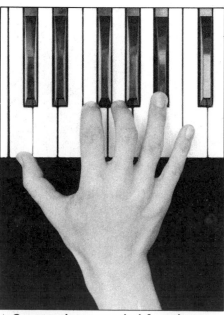

△ **C seventh suspended fourth (C7sus4)** This chord is built by replacing the third note in the dominant seventh chord with the fourth note of the scale.

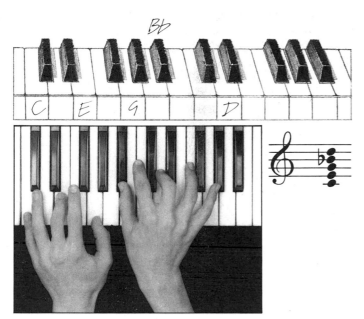

◁ **C ninth (C9)** This chord is constructed by adding to the seventh chord the note that is a third above the seventh. This note is an octave above the second and so is called the ninth.

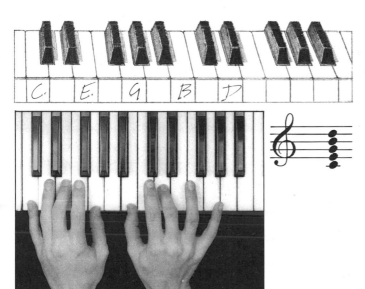

◁ **C major ninth (Cmaj9)** This chord is constructed by starting with the major seventh chord and adding the ninth note.

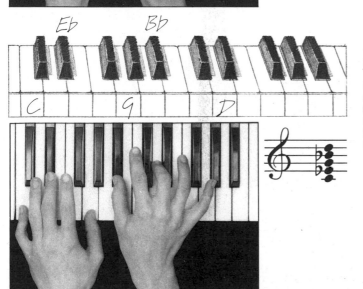

◁ **C minor ninth (Cm9)** This chord is constructed by starting with the minor seventh chord and adding the ninth note.

tion of D. To form the C major ninth, you add D to the C major seventh (C, E, G, B), and to form the C minor ninth you add D to C minor seventh (C, E♭, G, B♭).

So there are five notes in each ninth chord. But it is unusual for a keyboard player to play all five notes. These chords are difficult to finger with one hand, because they require a fairly wide span. In addition the sound can become rather muddled since the chord's notes are so close together. This is especially true on electronic instruments on which the notes are "phase-locked" together.

One solution is to leave out the seventh note. You can then use the chord in an inverted format, with the ninth below the root acting as the bass note for a straight triad. This is a simple but very effective way to use the ninth chord.

Elevenths

If you take a ninth chord and add a fourth note on top, the interval from the root to the fourth will be an octave plus a fourth – an eleventh. The chord you produce is therefore called an eleventh. Like ninths, elevenths fall into three groups – dominant, major, and minor. So to produce a C eleventh chord, you simply add an F to the relevant C ninth chord.

When you play all six notes of an eleventh chord the overall sound picture gets rather confused. A bass note is often required to give the chord some definition. You can think of an eleventh chord as two separate triads. For example, a dominant C eleventh chord (made up of the notes C, E, G, B♭, D, and F) is basically a C major triad (C, E, and G) and a B♭ major triad on top (B♭, D, and F). This type of chord is often called a *polytonal chord* or *polychord* (see p. 123). But the C major eleventh doesn't fall into this simple, two-triad

121

category. For this reason it is rarely used. You can simplify the chord, and make it sound better, by augmenting the eleventh to make the F into an F♯. This gives you a C major triad and a B minor triad. This sounds far more effective than a straight C major eleventh. The resulting chord – the C major augmented eleventh – is often encountered.

You will rarely have to use all six notes of an eleventh chord in an inverted format. Usually the fifth or ninth notes (or both of these) are omitted. Both of these notes set up two separate minor seventh intervals within the chord and this can become a little too dissonant.

Thirteenths

This is another example of an extended chord and incorporates the sixth above the root plus an octave. The thirteenth note is a major third above the eleventh, so the thirteenth chord is simply an eleventh with a note added four semitones above. This makes it a seven-note chord. So the C thirteenth is made up of the notes C, E, G, B♭, D, and F (the C eleventh), plus A (the thirteenth).

With such a large number of notes, the number of possible inversions, doublings, and omissions is endless. Thirteenths often evolve into simpler combinations of other chords.

▷ **C eleventh (C11)** This chord is constructed by adding the eleventh note to the ninth chord, to give a six-note chord. You will probably not use this particular two-handed chord very often. But a modified version in which F♯ replaces the F is more common (see left).

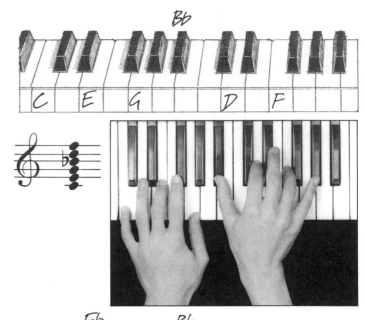

▷ **C minor eleventh (Cm11)** This chord is constructed by adding the eleventh note to the minor ninth chord. Like the other eleventh chords, this is not a very common chord. Sometimes you will find it used with one of the notes left out.

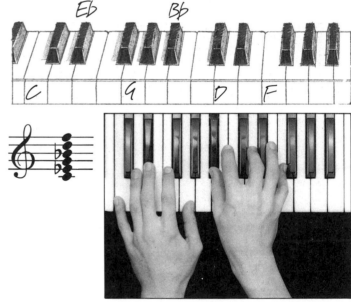

▷ **C major ninth augmented eleventh (Cmaj9+11)** This chord is constructed by adding the twelfth note to the major ninth chord.

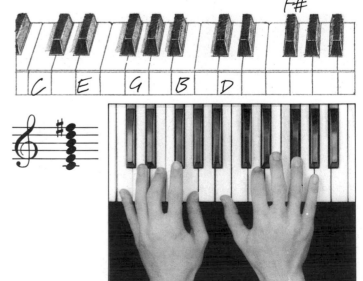

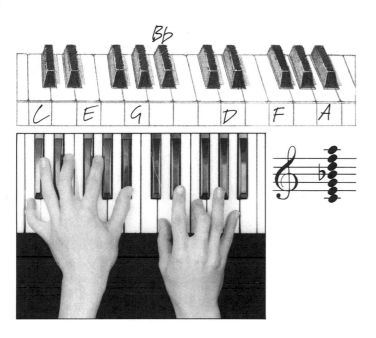

◁ **C thir- teenth (C13)** This chord is constructed by adding the thirteenth note (the sixth plus an octave) on top of the eleventh. This gives a seven- note chord.

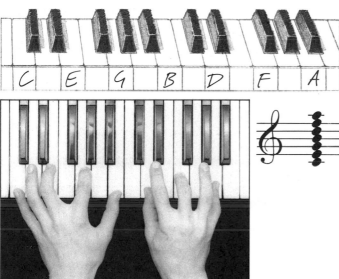

◁ **C major thirteenth (Cmaj13)** This chord is con- structed by adding the thirteenth note to the major eleventh.

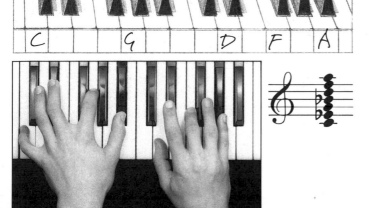

◁ **C minor thirteenth (Cm13)** This chord is con- structed by adding the thirteenth note to the minor eleventh chord.

Bitonal chords

It is often useful to think of a chord as being made up of its constituent parts. This is parti- cularly true with polychords such as ninths, elevenths, and thirteenths, which are made up of two more simple chords such as triads.

A *bitonal* chord is a polychord that is played over a non-related bass note. For example, a C major seventh with the C drop- ped an octave is a bitonal chord. It is easier to think of this as an E minor chord with a C in the bass. This chord is written Emin/C.

Using bitonal chords

The bitonal chord is one of the most useful devices if you want to be able to play professional- sounding accompaniments in a short space of time. Armed with the basic triads for each key note you can easily play accom- paniments for most popular tunes. Bitonal notation is common in popular music. You can use these chords with modern ''easy- play'' keyboards, especially by using the auto-bass facilities. The bass note is played automatically according to the way you pro- gram the machine, while you can finger the accompanying chord using the melody section. If you are using bass pedals, or a dual manual instrument, the bass can be voiced on the pedal- board or lower manual, and you can give the chord a different voicing on the main keyboard. This combination of bitonal chord and bass produces a clean, uncluttered impression that can be very pleasing – the listener can clearly decipher the bass and the chord.

There are no rules dictating which bass notes you should set against which chord. If you ex- periment you will soon discover which combinations work best and how you can use them to ''lead'' in chord progressions.

Rhythm

OTHER CHORDS – SUMMARY

☐ Combining the sixth note of the scale with a triad produces a sixth chord.

☐ The major sixth is useful to conclude a passage of music.

☐ The minor sixth usually leads to a major chord.

☐ Adding the second note of the scale to a triad gives an added ninth chord.

☐ The minor added ninth is usually inverted or extended to make it less dissonant.

☐ Replacing the third note of any three- or four-note chord creates a suspended fourth chord.

☐ The suspended fourth is a chord that sounds unresolved.

☐ Adding notes more than an octave above a chord's root note gives an extended chord.

☐ Ninths are extended chords formed by adding notes to various types of seventh chord.

☐ There are three main types of ninth: ninth, major ninth, and minor ninth.

☐ Elevenths are extended chords formed by adding a note to various types of ninths.

☐ Thirteenths are extended chords formed by adding notes to various types of elevenths.

☐ A chord that is made up of two more simple chords is called a polychord.

☐ A polychord played over a non-related bass note is a bitonal chord.

Every musical note has three essential qualities – its pitch, its duration, and when it is played. So far we have dealt only with the first of these. The other two qualities are treated jointly and the resulting combination gives us what we understand as *rhythm*.

It's quite easy to find the right notes on a keyboard and play them – you just need practice in fingering technique and muscle co-ordination. But getting the right rhythm relies much more on your own inbuilt instincts. Like comedians, all the best musicians have an instinctive feel for timing. The first step toward this mastery is to be able to decipher the rhythmic quality of music from a score. This is not only essential for effective keyboard playing. It is also vital if you want to program your own rhythm tracks on a drum machine or on your synthesizer's built-in rhythm unit.

Rhythm notation

The pitch of a note is represented by where the note falls vertically on the staff. Rhythm notation works horizontally – you can tell when a note occurs by where it falls along the length of the staff. The duration of each note is shown by its actual form when written down.

One similarity between pitch and rhythm is that both work according to simple mathematical relationships. As with pitch, the number 2 is very important. We have seen that doubling the frequency of a note raises the pitch by one octave, double it again, and you have a note two octaves higher than the original one, and so on.

In rhythm notation, the number 2 again plays a dominant part. The notation used to represent the duration of a note works in factors of 2. So you have whole notes, half notes, quarter notes, and fractions that go right down to sixty-fourth notes. So one whole note (sometimes called a semibreve) lasts the same as two half notes (also known as minims), or as four quarter notes (also called crotchets). But you should remember that a particular type of note does not last a precise and unchangeable length of time – it is the proportions between them that are unvarying.

As well as showing how long a note should sound, you also have to know whether there are any gaps in the music when no note sounds. Symbols called rests, also in proportional time values, are used for this.

Because the notes aren't allotted specific time lengths, you also need to know how fast to play. To do this you only have to define one note value and the others will automatically fall into line. So the quarter note is usually given a time value in the form of a figure. This is the number of quarter notes that, if

▽ **Indicating rhythm** This example shows many of the different musical symbols used to show the rhythm of a piece. Rhythm is shown horizontally along the staff, so notes that are intended to be played at the same time are placed immediately above or below each other. The duration of a particular note is shown by its written form (see below).

played consecutively, would have a duration of one minute.

But precise accuracy of tempo is seldom necessary. Therefore you will find that many scores give an indication in words of approximately how fast you should play the music.

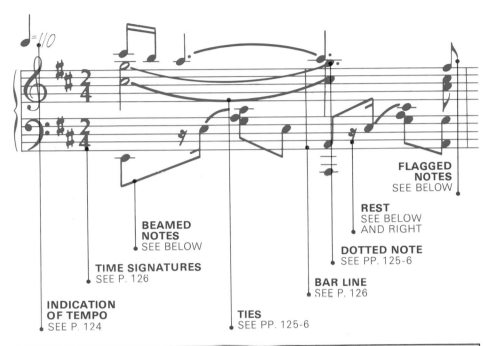

FLAGGED NOTES
SEE BELOW

REST
SEE BELOW
AND RIGHT

DOTTED NOTE
SEE PP. 125-6

BAR LINE
SEE P. 126

BEAMED NOTES
SEE BELOW

TIME SIGNATURES
SEE P. 126

INDICATION OF TEMPO
SEE P. 124

TIES
SEE PP. 125-6

Rests

There are some points in most pieces of music when no note is required to sound. These places are indicated in the score by rests, which have the same range of time values as notes. There is a marked similarity between some of the rests and the corresponding notes, which helps make them easy to read. Because no note is sounding the vertical position of the rest on the staff stays the same at each occurance. Like notes, rests can also be dotted, so that you can increase their time value by half as much again. In pieces of music that are written for several players, one instrument is often silent for long periods of time. To avoid repeating a large number of whole-note rests, a *tacet* rest can be used.

You can also use rests as part of a beamed figure. Again, the rest is treated like a note with a particular time value.

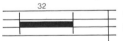

◁ **Tacet rest** This example indicates 32 bars of silence.

Dotted notes and ties

All the basic note types from whole notes to sixty-fourth notes are related to each other by a factor of two. This leaves the problem of representing notes that last a time equivalent to three quarter notes or three eighth notes.

There are two alternative methods of writing down these notes. You can use a device called a tie, which joins two notes together. For example, this allows you to tie together a half note and a quarter note, to

Notes and equivalent rests

The form of the note shows its duration. Notes shorter than a quarter note have flags. These can be replaced by the same number of beams when two notes of the same time value occur together. A dot increases the time value by half.

◁ **Whole note** (or semibreve) and equivalent rest

◁ **Half note** (or minim) and equivalent rest

◁ **Quarter note** (or crotchet) and equivalent rest

◁ **Quarter note** (or crotchet) and alternative rest

◁ **Eighth note** (or quaver) and equivalent rest

◁ **Sixteenth note** (or semiquaver) and equivalent rest

◁ **Thirty-second note** and equivalent rest

◁ **Sixty-fourth note** and rest

▷ **Dotted whole note** and rest

▷ **Dotted half note** and rest

▷ **Dotted quarter note** and rest

▷ **Dotted quarter note** and alternative rest

▷ **Dotted eighth note** and rest

▷ **Dotted sixteenth note** and rest

▷ **Dotted thirty-second note** and rest

▷ **Dotted sixty-fourth note** and rest

produce the equivalent of a "three-quarter" note. The other method is to use dotted notes. A dot after a note means that its time value is half as long again as normal. So you could use a dotted half note to represent the "three-quarter" note.

The advantage of ties is that they can span bar lines, allowing you to hold over a note from one bar to the next. You can also use them to combine notes of widely differing values, such as a half note and a thirty-second note. But dotted notes are easier to read on the page and they are usually preferable unless you want to span a bar line.

You can use dotted rests in a similar way to dotted notes. But there is no need to use ties with rests, since one period of silence runs automatically into another.

Triplets

With note values that are defined in factors of two, there is no obvious way of scoring third, sixth, or ninth notes in time signatures such as 4/4. In this situation you can use triplets – groups of three notes of the same time value that are played in the time normally allocated to two. A small figure 3 is written above or below the notes.

△ **Using triplets** These notes represent a single bar of 4/4 time. This is because the three eighth notes are written as a triplet, so you play them in the time normally taken by two eighth notes. Triplets are useful in time signatures such as 4/4 and 3/4, since they offer the only way of dividing notes by three.

Bars

Most Western music, classical and rock, relies on a basic rhythmic structure. If you listen to a piece of music you can count along with it and you will find that every few beats you feel that a cycle has been completed and that you want to stress the next beat – the first of a new cycle. Each cycle makes up one bar of music.

Bars are vital for both reading music and writing it because they split up the score into small, manageable parts. The end of each bar is marked on the stave by a vertical line. As long as the tempo stays constant, each bar will last the same period of time.

Time signatures

Exactly how many beats of what duration fill each bar is governed by the time signature. This is a label that is placed on the staff immediately to the right of the clef and key signature. It is made up of two figures, one written above the other. The upper number tells you how many beats there are in a bar, while the lower indicates what type of note equals one beat.

The lower figure must therefore be one of the six numbers (2, 4, 8, 16, 32, 64) that are used to define beats. The most common numbers are 2, 4, and 8 (indicating half notes, quarter notes, and eighth notes respectively). The upper figure can have any value at all, but again certain ones are predominant. The most frequently used time signature is 4/4.

Bars containing two, three, or four beats have what are called regular time signatures. Bars with five or more beats have an irregular time signature. You will sometimes also see certain time signatures given names. Signatures with two beats to the bar are called duple meters, those with three beats to the bar are known as triple meters, and

signatures with four beats are called quadruple.

Once you have marked a staff with a time signature, every bar must be filled with notes that add up to the correct number. If you need to change the number of beats, you should introduce a new time signature.

Compound time signatures

If a time signature has more than four beats to the bar, the rhythm pattern splits into smaller units of two, three, four, or occasionally more beats. Time signatures in which this happens are called *compound* time signatures. So simple time has upper figures of 2, 3, or 4, and compound time has upper figures such as 6 or 9.

For example, if a piece of music is written in 9/8 time, each bar will contain the equivalent of nine eighth notes. But when actually playing the music, you would probably emphasize every third note so that the rhythm would be divided up into three groups.

If the number of beats in the bar is not a simple multiple of 2 or 3, then the rhythm is called *asymmetrical*.

Beat structure

The beats in a bar of music are not necessarily stressed equally. For example, in common time (4/4) there are four quarter-note beats in each bar. The first is always the most important, and is usually stressed the most. But there is also a tendency to stress the third beat. The resulting pattern of stresses is known as the macro beat structure.

If there are any groupings of smaller note values within a beat, then they too will exhibit a secondary (or micro) beat structure that follows a pattern similar to the macro structure. A micro beat will be far weaker in terms of stress than even the weak beats of the macro pattern.

Types of time signature

It is easy to see the difference between simple and compound time signatures if you look at the number of stressed beats in each bar. In simple time, each bar has one stressed beat only.

In compound time, each bar has several groups of beats, each starting with a stress. In the diagram below, a tinted circle represents an accented beat.

▽ **Simple time**

2/4 Two quarter note beats per bar; one stressed beat.

3/4 Three beats per bar; one stressed. Each is one quarter note.

4/4 Four beats per bar; one stressed. Each beat is one quarter note.

2/4 has the same rhythm as 4/4, but has twice as many bars.

Two bars of 3/4 give the same pattern as one bar of 6/8.

4/4 is often called common time, with the time signature written as "C".

▽ **Compound time**

6/8 Six beats per bar; two stressed. Each is one eighth note.

5/4 Five beats per bar; two stressed beats. Each beat is one quarter note.

One bar of 6/8 gives the same pattern as two bars of 3/4.

In time signatures with an irregular number of beats in the bar, you have a choice over where to place the stressed beats.

Syncopation

Not all rhythms fall within the neat macro and micro beat structures. A rhythm that has accents that do not fall in the expected places is called a syncopated rhythm.

Syncopation is useful because if you construct a rhythm that doesn't conform to the basic structure, you introduce an element of tension into the pattern. The rhythm seems to require resolution.

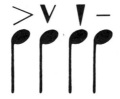

◁ **Accent signs** You will encounter several different accent signs all of which tell you to play the note below with a stronger stress than normal.

▽ **Syncopated rhythm** In this example, from a piece by Beethoven, the stress falls on the third and sixth notes in each bar, which are marked with accents. The natural stress, if no accents had been written in, would have been on the first and fourth notes in the bar.

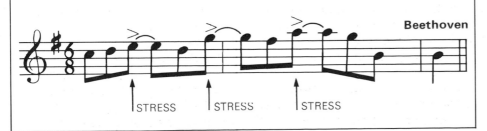

Beethoven

STRESS   STRESS   STRESS

Other aspects of rhythm notation

When you are reading a bar of music, the shape of the notes tells you that each is assigned to a particular length of time. For example, a quarter note in common time (4/4), has a "time slot" equivalent to one quarter of the bar. But this doesn't necessarily mean that you have to sustain the note for that whole period. In fact, unless there is a specific instruction in the score, it should not take up the whole time, because it would slur into the next note. When playing, you are given an element of discretion about exactly how long you should play and how much silence there should be between notes. But there are a number of ways in which the duration of the notes can be specified in the written score.

If a dot is placed above or below a note (usually on the opposite side to the note's tail), you should play the note shorter than normal, or in a *staccato* manner. You should play it for only half as long as it is written, and make sure that you keep it completely separate from the following note. A staccato quarter note could be written as an eighth note followed by an eighth-note rest, but the dot system is clearer to follow when you are actually playing.

An alternative to staccato is *portato*. It is depicted by a short dash, above or below the note, again on the side opposite to the tail. You should hold the note for virtually its full time value, leaving as small a gap as possible between it and the next note.

△ **Staccato and portato** Staccato is is usually shown with a dot, while portato is indicated in musical scores by placing a dash above or below the relevant note.

Reading rhythm

The way in which music is written down is designed to help you "see" the beat structure within the bar. But in many cases the rhythm is quite complex and you have to take it slowly, analyzing the micro beat in detail.

Counting out rhythms

There are various methods of counting beats that help you find out how a particular rhythm should sound. At first you will find it easiest to split the score into small sections – perhaps even into single bars if the rhythm pattern looks particularly complicated.

The first thing to do when you are looking at a bar or phrase is to find the shortest note. If this is an eighth note in 4/4 time, split the bar into eight steps. The most effective counting method is to count "1-and-2-and-3-and-4-and-off", emphasizing each number and the "off". It is important to include "off". If you do not, your rhythm will end before it should: it represents the first beat of the next bar. To help you emphasize the numbered beats, you may find it helpful at first to tap your foot as you count them, or to use a metronome. When you have mastered the rhythm you can speed it up until you are happy with it. You should not try to rush this process, since failure will only lead to frustration.

When you are dealing with patterns that use smaller note values, you should adjust your count accordingly. So if the pattern uses sixteenth notes, you should split your bar into sixteen steps. Probably the simplest way to do this is to count four groups of four in each bar. You can handle other time signatures in a similar way.

Rhythm shorthand

From time to time all players need to write down a rhythm for future reference. This is often useful to show what pattern a chord accompaniment should have. A rhythm shorthand has developed to make this easier.

The system uses the basic staff and bar structure of the score, but employs only the notes' stems and flags.

△ **Rhythm shorthand system** The simplest and quickest way of writing down a rhythm pattern is to replace the notes with their stems, flags, and beams, as in this bar of 2/4 time. You can tie these symbols together to indicate whole and half notes.

Amplitude

As well as the beat structure and accents you need to know the relative volume level at which you should be playing. There are two elements to this: the level at which you start (the *static* level), and the way in which the level varies.

Instructions about the static level usually appear at the beginning of the piece, and further static instructions can occur throughout. The usual way to express these instructions is to use abbreviations based on the Italian words for loud and soft (see right).

Two hairpin-like symbols are used to represent the dynamic levels. One represents *crescendo* (a gradual increase in the loudness), and the other represents *diminuendo* (a gradual decrease in the level). These symbols are positioned within each clef system and span those notes where the dynamic change takes place.

RHYTHM – SUMMARY

☐ You can tell when a note occurs by its horizontal position on the staff.
☐ You can tell the duration of a note by its form when it is written down.
☐ Rests tell you when there are silences in the music.
☐ Ties join notes together; dotted notes sound half as long again as normal.

Static amplitude changes	
Italian	English
Pianissimo (pp)	Very soft
Piano (p)	Soft
Mezzo piano (mp)	Moderately soft
Mezzo forte (mf)	Moderately loud
Forte (f)	Loud
Fortissimo (ff)	Very loud

Dynamic amplitude changes	
Italian	English
Crescendo (Cresc)	Becoming gradually louder
Decrescendo (Decresc) Diminuendo (Dim)	Becoming gradually softer

☐ Music is split into rhythmic units called bars; the number of notes in each bar is shown in the time signature.
☐ The first beat of a bar is usually stressed the most.
☐ A rhythm in which the stresses do not fall in the expected places is known as a syncopated rhythm.
☐ An accent tells you to stress the note immediately below.

Amplification and recording

Nearly all keyboard players are concerned in some way with amplifying the sound made by their instrument. Separate amplification equipment is essential for most synthesizers and you must choose the right type for your instrument and the place where you want to play. Even if you have a portable keyboard with its own built-in amplifier and loudspeaker, you should try using it with an external amplifier and speaker – you may be agreeably surprised at the improvement in sound quality. Another way you can enhance your instrument's sound is to use signal processing devices (effects pedals and similar units), which are also covered in this part of the book.

Recording can be much more than making a permanent record of the music you play. Used creatively, a tape recorder enables you to multiply your musical resources by building up songs track by track. There are various ways of doing this and, thanks to modern microchip technology, the equipment required is no longer prohibitively expensive.

For all music involving electronic instruments it is important that all your equipment is compatible, so that you can connect it together as you wish. This is particularly true in recording. For this reason instrument manufacturers have got together to create an industry standard for connections, known as MIDI. The way the system works is explained at the end of this section of the book.

Amplifiers and loudspeakers

All electric and electronic musical instruments require some form of amplification. Some keyboards, especially those designed for home use, have their own internal amplification system, but virtually no synthesizers (except inexpensive portables) have any built-in amplification.

The human ear responds to changes in the density of air particles (see p. 24), so a loudspeaker must be used to compress and rarefy the air particles in a way that corresponds directly to the changes in the electrical signal created by your instrument.

To get the loudspeaker cone to move, you need a more powerful signal than the one produced by the instrument itself (the *line output*). So you have to amplify this signal to a level at which it can drive the speaker. The signal must also be turned into another form of energy (or *transduced*) so that it can move the air particles.

You can think of headphones as a pair of very low-power loudspeakers. Again the line output has to be amplified to drive them, but most electronic instruments have a headphone amplifier built in. So you can plug the headphones directly into the instrument at the appropriate socket. Electric instruments usually have no provision for headphones, so a separate headphone amplifier is required.

Amplification systems

Apart from hybrid systems such as rotary speakers (see pp. 138-9) there are four types of amplification systems: integral systems, combo amplifiers, systems using a separate amplifier and speakers, and set-ups combining mixer with pre-amp, power amp, and speakers.

Your choice of system will be dictated by the place where you are playing and what equipment you are using. In your home you will need only a low-powered amplifier and speaker, but in a large hall the demands become much more exacting, making bigger speaker systems and high-powered amplifiers necessary.

Integral amplifiers and speakers

Most home keyboard instruments have one or two small built-in monitor loudspeakers. These speakers are usually between 3 and 5 ins (7.5 and 12.5 cm) in diameter and are mounted on the top or underside of the unit. They are driven by small amplifiers (usually giving about 5 watts of power) inside the instrument.

The quality of these devices is not usually very good, although on some electronic pianos fitted with stereo chorus circuits, the quality is better. Tone controls are not usually provided, and you can generally only adjust the volume. The way the integral speakers are mounted usually gives a finite-baffle effect (see p. 138).

But if you have a keyboard with this type of amplification you need not be limited by it. You can nearly always take a line output from the rear panel of the instrument and use a better amplification system. With some keyboards this does not automatically switch off the internal speakers, but you can do this by inserting a jack plug with no lead attached into the headphone socket of the instrument.

Built-in monitor speakers are useful, especially on portable machines. But if you are running your instrument on batteries, the monitors will use them up at a far faster rate than if the instrument's output was fed to an external amplifier.

Combo amplifiers

The combination, or *combo*, amplifier provides an amplifier and speaker in the same housing. You can use it either for instruments without built-in monitors, or in situations where built-in amplification would not be powerful enough or give you good enough sound quality.

Combo amplifiers are usually portable, offer between 10 and 100 watts of power, and incorporate a single speaker between 5 and 12 ins (12.5 and 30.5 cm) in diameter. Sometimes there are two speakers, one for the low frequencies, the other for the high ones. Combos were originally used mainly by guitarists, but with different approaches to the problems of amplification, keyboard and bass combos are becoming more and more common.

Separate amplifiers and speakers

Like guitarists and bassists, professional keyboard players used to employ an amplification stack. This would serve both to project the sound out to the audience, and to enable the player to hear the keyboard's sound. The stack would consist of speaker cabinets, typically containing four speakers 12 ins (30.5 cm) in diameter or a single unit 15 ins (38 cm) across, and separate amplifiers either on top of the cabinets or next to the player.

But this system of amplification is becoming less popular. The reason is that most keyboard players use several instruments together with effects and such a system requires a more flexible amplification set-up. In addition, playing levels, especially in rock bands, have increased so much that it is best to feed the signals from all the keyboards directly into the main PA system. You can then use monitors to send a small amount of this signal back to you, so that you can hear what you are playing at a comfortable listening level.

An advantage of this type of arrangement is that you can split the signal into high- and low-frequency elements before it reaches the main amplification stage. In this way you can use different amplifiers and loudspeakers for high and low frequencies. This helps to reduce distortion, producing a much better sound.

Mixers, power amplifiers and loudspeakers

A more efficient set-up provides you with an audio mixer, so that you can control the complete sound accurately. If you are using several keyboards, together with effects units and signal processors it is worth using a mixer to ensure that these devices are used in the right proportions before amplifying the combined signal. A mixer also allows you to combine and amplify signals from other instruments and vocalists.

Types of amplification system For home performance and use in fairly small rooms, a combo amp (below) is useful. This contains both amplifier and loudspeaker and should give you controls for volume, treble, mid-range, and bass. When playing in large halls a system with speakers and separate amplifier, and mixer (right) is best. A mixer (above) can form the heart of a complete power amplification system for several different instruments. With a powerful system of this sort, you also require on-stage monitors. These are high-quality speakers that allow you to hear your own sound.

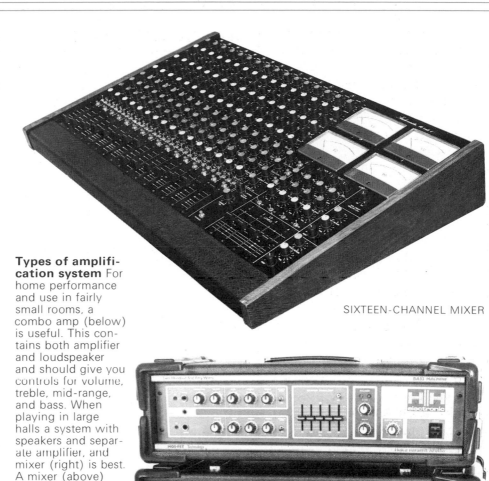

SIXTEEN-CHANNEL MIXER

KEYBOARD COMBO AMPLIFIERS

SEPARATE AMPLIFIER AND SPEAKERS

How amplifiers work

An amplifier has two kinds of input and one output. You feed into it both the signal that you want to amplify and AC power. As a result, you get a more powerful version of the original signal at the output.

In simple terms, an amplifier consists of three sections. The *buffer* section ensures that the incoming signal itself is not affected by the way you set the controls. The *pre-amp* stage increases the signal's amplitude enough to drive the *power amplification* stage. The pre-amp also often has tone controls that enable you to enhance or cut the bass or treble frequencies. The power amp itself turns the low-level output from the pre-amp into an alternating current powerful enough to make the loudspeaker diaphragms move.

◁ **Outdoor playing** Playing outside like Elton John, you have to be just as careful to get the correct amplification as you do in a hall. Many bands use a large PA system with stacks of speakers.

Amplifier specifications

If you are thinking of buying an amplifier, it is important to understand exactly what the device can do. To help you, it is worth getting to know the meaning of the technical specifications that the manufacturers give their amplifiers.

Power

The power of an amplifier is measured in watts. A watt is a unit of electrical power and is calculated by multiplying the voltage by the amount of current in the circuit. So a light bulb running from a 240 volt supply and with 1/6 of an amp (the amount of electricity) flowing through the filament is rated as a 40 watt bulb (240 ×1/6=40). But the power of an amplifier cannot be expressed as a simple value in watts because amplifiers deal with an alternating signal. So the concept of the root mean squared (RMS) watt has evolved. An amplifier with a power of 50 watts RMS can handle 50 watts over a continuous period and

over a wide range of frequencies without serious distortion. Another method of quoting the wattage is in terms of "watts music power" or "watts peak to peak". Both of these give an inflated value of the amplifier's power and can be very misleading. As a rough rule a 50 watts RMS amplifier is equivalent to one of 100 watts peak to peak. So if an amplifier's power specification is quoted in watts alone, find out which system is being used.

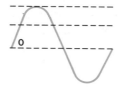

PEAK POWER
RMS POWER

0

◁ **Power ratings**
The RMS level gives the most accurate figure.

Gain

The gain of an amplifier is the amount by which it increases the power of the signal fed to it. The unit for measuring gain is the decibel (see p. 29). The decibel is a ratio and, in the case of an amplifier, this ratio is between

the input and the output. But gain figures alone can tell you little. You need to know more about an amplifier's performance characteristics in different circumstances.

Frequency response

Amplifiers do not have the same gain characteristics for signals of all frequencies. An audio amplifier should be able to amplify signals over the entire audio spectrum, especially if you are using it to amplify keyboard instruments. But it is difficult and expensive to produce an amplifier that will amplify every frequency over this range by the same amount.

Most units will amplify a certain range of frequencies by a fairly constant gain factor. This span of frequencies is known as the amplifier's *bandwidth*. An amplifier's specification might read "25 to 20,000 Hz ± 3 dB", which means that all signals within this frequency range will be amplified by a gain factor that varies less than 3 dB either way. Frequencies below 25 Hz and above 20,000 Hz will suffer from a poorer gain factor. You will sometimes see the performance of an amplifier at different frequencies shown on a graph. This is known as a *frequency response curve.*

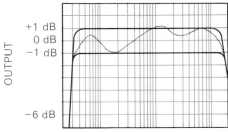

FREQUENCY
100 Hz   1,000 Hz   10,000 Hz

+1 dB
0 dB
−1 dB

−6 dB

OUTPUT

△ **Frequency response curve** This is a graph that shows the way an amplifier's output can vary at different frequencies. The upper and lower curves show the extremes of the gain factor, while the center line shows one possible response curve within these extremes.

Input sensitivity

There is a minimum input signal that allows an amplifier to run at its maximum specified output. The input sensitivity is the value of this minimum input level.

Signal-to-noise factors

Noise is a hissing sound, made up of random pitches at all frequencies. You get a certain amount of noise with any audio electronic circuit. On some synthesizer voice modules you will find a noise control that allows you to use noise as an audio source. But on an amplifier noise is considered to be something to avoid. The specifications of amplifiers quote the signal-to-noise ratio as a decibel value. An amplifier with a signal-to-noise figure lower than −60 dB (for example −50 dB) is extremely noisy and worth avoiding.

Power rails

An amplifier's working power is taken from a constant direct current voltage called a *power rail.* A power rail has to be able to supply a lot of current, which must not fluctuate in level. So a power rail is set up by transforming the AC current to DC and making sure that there are no fluctuations in the current.

Valve and transistor amplifiers

There are two distinct types of amplifier – those using valves and those employing transistors. There is a difference in the sound quality between signals amplified by the two types so you can't make exact comparisons between valve and transistor models. The basic working principles of valve and transistor amplifiers are similar, although the two types look very different and transistor models are smaller than valve types.

Valve amplifiers

A valve looks rather like a small light bulb, and incorporates two metallic plates (the *anode* and the *cathode*) in a gas-filled container. External connections are made to these plates so that the valve can be connected in a circuit. A small heater element is positioned close to the cathode and as this heats up electrons are freed and can flow over to the anode. A metal grid is located across the flow of the electrons and by altering the electrical potential of this grid the flow of electrons between the anode and the cathode can be controlled. As this controlling voltage rises and falls, the current flow also rises and falls. Because the circuitry allows the amplifier to make the voltage move between the levels of the power rails, the input signal is amplified considerably. In a complete amplifier this would only serve as one stage of the entire circuit, and in

The resulting current is called a *regulated power supply.*

Once an amplifier has steady power rails, it is possible to swing the output voltage almost as far as each rail. So if you had a rail of +50 volts and one of −50 volts, the peak-to-peak output voltage of the amplification system could be almost 100 volts.

order to get a stable, low-distortion, high-gain performance, up to six or eight valves can be used.

Valve amplifiers have certain drawbacks. Because they employ glass "bulbs", they are fairly fragile. They are also rather large and bulky. Valves run at a fairly high voltage level (over 300 volts), so household electricity has to be transformed up;

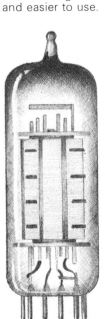

△ ▽ **Valves and transistors**
Valves (right and below) are large and made from glass. Transistors (above) are much smaller, tougher, and easier to use.

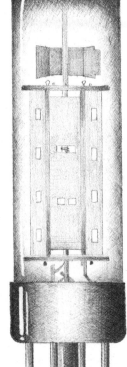

and because each valve has a heater element, it is important that you keep valve amplifiers adequately ventilated. Another problem with valves is that even if you take care of them they occasionally fail (usually because the heater filament has burned out) and you have to replace them. The frequency with which this happens depends on how much you use the amplifier.

Transistor amplifiers

A transistor consists of layers of conducting material sandwiched together. The material (usually silicon) is treated to allow electrons to flow across the junctions between the layers in a controlled way.

The actual amplification circuit is very similar to that of a valve amplifier, except that it doesn't need to run at high voltage levels. There are various different types of transistors. Smaller ones, often only a few millimeters across, are used at the low-power stages of amplification, while larger transistors, usually requiring *heat sinks* to keep them cool, are employed at the final output stage.

The components of a transistor amplifier that do the actual amplification take up very little

space. It is usually the power circuitry, which transforms the alternating current into two steady power rails, that takes up most of the space. Transistors are far more reliable components than valves.

Transistors versus valves

There are no hard-and-fast rules governing when you should use a transistor amplifier and when you should use a valve one. The valve amplifier's much warmer, richer sound is produced because when it is driven at high levels, the even harmonics tend to get distorted. On the other hand, when a transistor amplifier distorts, it is the odd harmonics that are most affected, and this causes a rather unpleasant sound. Nevertheless transistor amplifiers give a considerably cleaner and more faithful rendition of the sound, and the technical specifications of transistor models are correspondingly better. Another advantage of transistor types is their smaller size and lighter weight.

Deciding which type to use

But sound quality is the most important thing, and a transistor

amplifier is not always ideal. It is generally best to use valve amplification for electric instruments and transistors for electronic keyboards.

The vibrations that are used to create the sound of an electric instrument (such as a Fender Rhodes piano, a Clavinet, an electric grand, or a Hammond organ) come from a mechanical source and are transduced into electrical signals via pick-ups. As a result, what is produced is more like an acoustic signal and the valve amplifier is more suited to this type of signal. For this reason, and because valve amplifiers were the only types available when instruments such as the Hammond organ first appeared, it has become traditional to use valve amplifiers most often with electric keyboards.

On an electronic instrument, the output signal is constructed by electronic oscillations alone, with transistor amplification and processing used inside the instrument. So the clean, bright sound of a transistor amplifier is more appropriate for these keyboards. But there are no hard-and-fast rules about this. You should use the type that gives you the best sound.

Using distortion

Distortion is not always an evil. In fact, in the rock world, the smooth sound of a Hammond organ being distorted by a valve amplifier is the trademark of some players. This kind of sound is almost impossible to achieve with a transistor amplifier, although Korg incorporate a control that gives an electronic simulation of the sound on their tone-wheel copy organs (right).

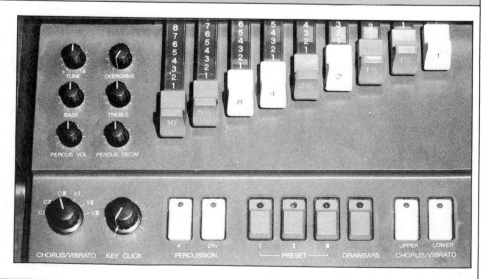

Loudspeakers

The loudspeaker is the link between player and listener. It
forms the last stage in the sound-
production process of an
electric or electronic musical instrument. It changes an electric
signal to a physical movement
that makes the air particles
vibrate so that you can hear a
sound (see p. 24). There are
many different types of loudspeakers (see pp. 136-8), but
they all use the same basic
operating principles.

How loudspeakers work

A loudspeaker contains a paper
or plastic cone positioned so that
it is free to move back and forward on a flexible mounting. The
speaker's mechanism ensures
that the cone will move in a way
that directly corresponds to the
actual movement of the electric
current which is produced by
the amplifier.

The principle used involves
two magnets. If a permanent
magnet is placed in a magnetic
field, it is either attracted or
repelled, according to the
polarity of the magnetic field. So
a large fixed permanent magnet
is mounted on the speaker's
chassis. Around the apex of the
speaker cone is a coil of wire
(the *voice coil*) which is placed
so that it falls within the magnetic
field of the permanent magnet.
When an electric current flows
round the coil, it becomes magnetized and a force of attraction
or repulsion is set up depending
on the direction of the current.
As this current is an alternating
one, the cone will move back
and forward according to the
powers of attraction and repulsion set up between the coil and
the permanent magnet.

The way in which the speaker
is constructed affects the way in
which it responds and moves the
air particles. The size of the
cone itself is very important –
usually, the larger the cone, the

better the low-frequency
response. The bigger the voice
coil and the larger the permanent magnet, the more efficient
and powerful the speaker. And
factors such as the way the cone
is suspended and the materials
from which the chassis and cone
are made also influence the
sound quality.

▽ ▷ **Inside a loudspeaker** The voice
coil is positioned within the magnetic
field of the speaker magnet and at the
apex of the cone. This speaker has two
cones (the smaller one is for the treble
frequencies) but the operating principle
is the same. The transparent speaker
cabinet (below) shows how the chassis
speaker is placed inside its housing.

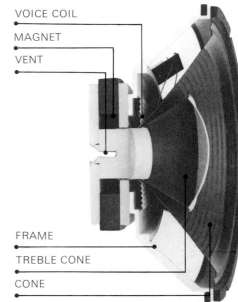

VOICE COIL
MAGNET
VENT
FRAME
TREBLE CONE
CONE

Choosing loudspeakers

There are countless different loudspeakers available, all with different qualities. There are several things to consider when you are looking for loud-speakers – their efficiency, power handling, frequency response, and impedance. You should also consider the type of speaker cabinet and whether you are going to use a multiple speaker system (see pp. 137-8).

Efficiency

The more efficient a loudspeaker is, the more sound it will produce from a given signal. All loudspeakers are in fact surprisingly inefficient. Only under ideal circumstances will any speaker turn into sound 50 per cent of the energy fed into it. The remaining 50 percent or so is lost in heat.

The efficiency of a speaker is dictated both by its design and by the cabinet in which it is housed (see p. 137). An inefficient speaker has two major drawbacks – first, it wastes power on generating unwanted heat, and second, if the heat builds up too much it can actually destroy the loudspeaker.

Power handling

The power that a speaker or combination of speakers can handle should be at least twice that of the amplifier you are using. Failure to use speakers of the correct rating can mean that they are unable to dissipate the heat produced when you run your amplifier at peak levels. Again, this can result in too much heat building up and the speakers being destroyed.

Frequency response

Every speaker has its own characteristic frequency response, measured in much the same way as that of an amplifier (see pp. 132-3). Poor frequency response is the most common failing of amplification systems. It is pointless spending a lot of money on a high-quality synthesizer if you are unable to realize the instrument's full potential because the amplification system can't handle the low and high frequencies correctly.

In general, because electronic keyboards have such a wide range of frequencies, a single loudspeaker cannot handle the entire signal effectively. So multiple speaker set-ups are used, much like the two- and three-way systems in many hi-fi cabinets.

Impedance

When an amplifier is driving a speaker, the speaker needs to take energy from the circuit in order to make its cone move back and forward. This in turn restricts the flow of the current round the circuit – in fact the speaker acts like a *resistance* in the circuit.

Electric resistance is measured in units called ohms. There is a simple formula for calculating resistance: resistance = voltage ÷ current. But working out the resistance of a loudspeaker isn't as simple as this, because the figure depends on the alternating current. For example if an AC signal oscillating at 1,000 Hz were being fed to a speaker, the resistance would be different to that if the signal was oscillating at 50 Hz. So the term *impedance* is used to express the resistance of a speaker – and this is also measured in ohms. Impedance is particularly important when you are using more than one speaker in a system (see p. 137). This is because you have to work out the combined impedance for the whole system.

◁ **Jerry Lee Lewis** Lewis is playing live. In the background is amplification equipment made by Marshall.

Using multiple speakers

To match the power output of your amplifier and to get a better frequency response, it is often worth using a multiple system that consists of several loudspeaker units.

Connecting together speakers can cause problems, especially if you want to use three or four different speakers with varying impedance ratings. If you look at the rear panel of your amplifier, you will see two terminals for connecting speakers and the rating of the required speaker impedance. (This information will be in the owner's manual if it is not printed on the amplifier.) The figure is usually 4, 8, or 16 ohms. This means that you should use a total load of no less than the stated figure. If you connect an 8 ohm load to an ampli-

fier on which 4 ohms is the stated load you can do no damage (although you will lose efficiency). But if you connect 4 ohms to an 8 ohm output, you run the risk of destroying the output stages of your amplifier, especially if you are running it at high levels.

So if you are using more than one speaker you should arrange them so that they present the right load to the amplifier. If you use two loudspeakers you can connect them either in series or in parallel. If you use series connection the overall load (R) is found by adding together the two impedances ($R = R1 + R2$). If you use parallel connections, the formula is more complex ($R = 1 \div R1 + 1 \div R2$).

If you want to improve the frequency response of a speaker system, you should use

speakers for different frequency bands. This is especially true if you are amplifying a synthesizer. There are two systems, both of which include devices called *crossovers*. A crossover is a kind of filter that accepts a full-frequency signal and splits it into two or three frequency bands. The points at which the bands cross are known as the *crossover frequencies*. In a three-way system you could have one crossover frequency set at 200 Hz and the other at 2,000 Hz. Frequencies below 200 Hz would then be sent to a low-range speaker; those between 200 Hz and 2,000 Hz would go to a mid-range speaker; and those above 2,000 Hz would pass to a high-frequency unit. This type of system gives an enhanced frequency response.

Loudspeaker cabinets

If you simply propped a chassis loudspeaker against a wall and fed an amplified signal to it, the resulting sound quality would be poor. This is because the air that was being compressed at the front of the cone would start to react with the air behind the cone that was being rarefied, and the two would start to cancel each other out. As a result there would be a dramatic drop in speaker efficiency and you would almost immediately notice that the sound was lacking in bass frequencies. This is why the speaker cabinet is so important. It gives the speaker its most efficient "interface" with the surrounding air.

Speaker cabinets should be made of tough, sturdy material that is fairly dense and will eliminate vibrations. This is especially true with high-power bass speakers. One of the best materials for speaker cabinets is reinforced concrete, but this is impractical. Plywood is most commonly used. There are four

INFINITE-BAFFLE SPEAKER CABINET

FINITE-BAFFLE SPEAKER CABINET

BASS REFLEX SPEAKER CABINET

HORN-LOADING SPEAKER CABINET

basic types of speaker cabinets: infinite baffle, horn loading, finite baffle, and bass reflex.

Infinite-baffle speakers

This type of speaker is suspended in an airtight box. Because no air can escape, there is little interference between the compressed and rarefied air masses in front of and behind the

speaker. But this system is not very efficient – partly because the speaker has to work harder to move against the fixed mass of air sealed in the cabinet. This fixed volume of air is much harder to move than air that is "free".

Horn-loading speakers

This is a variation on the infinite baffle type, but with a special front section or "throat". The efficiency of this type is dramatically increased because there is a flared horn mounted on the front. This is rather like putting a conical loud-hailer on the front of the speaker cone. But the shape of the horn is precisely calculated, to perfect the sound. Unfortunately horn-loaded speakers are usually very large and expensive, so they are generally used only for bigger rigs and PA systems.

Finite-baffle speakers

If the speaker cabinet is not airtight, but left open at the back, air can move freely behind the speaker. This makes it more efficient in some ways, but sound is emitted at the back of the cabinet. This means that sound with frequencies of wavelengths greater than or equal to the depth of the cabinet suffer interference. This type of enclosure is therefore not very good for bass systems.

Instruments with built-in amplifiers and speakers usually use a finite baffle arrangement. The speaker is mounted inside the instrument with no special cabinet. This is the main reason why most of these keyboards have a poor bass response.

Bass reflex

A good variation on the finite baffle system is the bass reflex cabinet. The principle is to take the "out-of-phase" rear element of the speaker's movement, turn it round to make it in phase, and feed it out of the front of the cabinet to enhance the sound already coming out of the front of the speaker. To escape the cabinet, the sound has to travel down a passage of baffle boards to ensure that its phase has been inverted before escaping through the bass port. The length of the passage should be more than that of the wavelength of the lowest frequency the cabinet is expected to handle.

Virtual bass

When you are using instruments with a particularly deep bass response, the phenomenon called *virtual bass* can be useful. Virtual bass saves sounds from being lost to us, even if we can't actually hear them.

When you listen to someone speaking, you can usually tell, from the context and the first syllable, what each word is going to be. In a similar way the ear can hear a set of harmonics and from them your brain will automatically work out the fundamental frequency of the note.

Unless you had very good speakers, the fundamental pitch of a sawtooth bass note down in the 64' register will not sound as strongly as it should – the speaker's frequency response will not be good enough to reproduce it faithfully. The brain, however, knowing the harmonics that make up the waveform, will be able to work out the fundamental pitch. Of course, the note will not sound exactly as it should, but the effect of virtual bass means that this information isn't totally lost.

The Leslie loudspeaker

One of the most interesting amplification developments for use with keyboard instruments is the Leslie rotating loudspeaker. This was developed in the US by Don Leslie of Electro Music and makes use of the principle of the Doppler effect (see p. 31). This is the effect that makes sound coming from a moving source seem to change in frequency. The most familiar example is the siren of a passing fire engine. or ambulance.

Leslie realized that this could be used to introduce a real pitch shift in musical tones. He saw that by rotating a loudspeaker he could create a continuously changing Doppler effect, and that the pitch would vary as if the speaker was moving toward and away from the listener.

It proved difficult to construct a mechanism that could rotate a heavy-duty loudspeaker, so instead Leslie mounted a bass speaker facing downward so that it projected its sound on to a spinning drum with an angled board attached. This sent the sound out to the listener, and it seemed as if the speaker itself was turning. A similar unit was built to handle the treble frequencies, but this device had a twin spinning horn (the second horn being a dummy to balance the first).

You can set the treble and bass units to spin at different speeds and in different directions. A rate of one revolution every 1.3 seconds produces a chorale effect, while a tremolo effect can be achieved with the units spinning at about 7 rotations per second.

In the jazz and rock worlds, the Hammond organ and Leslie speaker have often been used together. A common effect is to hold down a chord and then switch between chorale and tremolo. You can hear the speaker speeding up and slowing down, and the effect is both dramatic and very pleasing to the ear.

As an amplification system, the Leslie is highly inefficient. This is because it projects its sound in every direction. So even in a small room a 100 watt Leslie system doesn't sound very powerful. But it does have one other interesting effect. It is very difficult to pinpoint exactly where the sound is coming from – the sound seems to fill the whole room, surrounding you completely.

Some current electronic keyboards have built-in circuitry that is designed to simulate the tremolo effect of the Leslie. But this is not as good as a true Leslie speaker since the resulting sound does not have the same presence.

▷ **Rotating loudspeaker** This recent Leslie loudspeaker is a bass-reflex type with four built-in amplifiers that cover a very wide range of frequencies. As well as conventional speakers for bass, mid-range, and treble frequencies, the cabinet contains a rotary speaker and a rotating horn, which give the characteristic changing frequencies for which the Leslie system is best known.

Mixers

A mixer takes two or more signals and allows you to combine them into a single composite signal that you can feed into an amplifier. For most keyboard players with two or more instruments, even when playing live, a mixer is an essential tool.

A typical keyboard set-up might include an electric piano, a monophonic synthesizer, and a rhythm unit. You might also have a stereo chorus unit and a microphone so that you can add vocals. This gives you a collection of separate audio sources requiring amplification.

The solution to this problem is a simple "Six into two" mixer with an *effects send and return*

Signal processing

You can create a wide range of extra sounds, produce interesting special effects, and enhance the sound quality of your instruments by using special signal processing devices. These are relatively cheap and often come as small units operated by a foot pedal. For example, you can

facility. The advantage of a mixer is that you can use one amplifier for several different instruments. It also means that you do not have to keep adjusting different volume controls on pieces of equipment that may be quite far apart.

Using mixers

You plug the instruments and the microphone directly into the mixer, and connect its two stereo outputs to your amplifier. You can then adjust the input levels on the mixer to get a balanced sound. If you leave the channel volume controls set at about six tenths of their maximum setting, it will give you room to boost individual signals

make an inexpensive keyboard sound very impressive simply by feeding its output through a chorus unit and some form of spatial effect generator such as a reverberation unit. Many successful recordings use inexpensive portable keyboards processed by various studio effects to give the required sound.

if required. *Pan* controls on the mixer allow you to position each channel anywhere in the stereo image from far left to far right.

Mixers can also provide equalization controls. These allow you to filter out unwanted frequencies from the sound of each channel.

You can connect the chorus unit to the effects send and return sockets on the mixer. A separate control for each channel allows you to send any amount of the signal through the effects send output. The processed signal, returning from the chorus unit, is fed back into the mixer via the effects return socket, and mixed in with the signals from the other channels.

Effects pedals started life as electric guitar accessories. In the late fifties and sixties, when players were striving to get their own individual guitar sound, adding an effects pedal was one way of achieving this. Now keyboard players can benefit from the same technology. There are many different types. Some come in the form of pedals, while others are designed for rack mounting. The types most used by keyboard players range from simple expression pedals, which are little more than foot-operated volume controls, to large, rack-mounted graphic equalizers, which offer a great deal of control over different frequencies. Some effects units are very versatile – delay units can incorporate flanging and chorus facilties.

Expression

The simplest effects unit is the *expression* (or *swell*) pedal. This is connected between the instrument and speaker. It consists of a volume control that you regulate with the rocker foot-plate. This unit can be particularly useful because the first section of a sound is so important to its overall effect. By introducing slowly an organ or electric piano note and using the expression pedal, you can change the whole character of the sound.

Wah-wah

One of the first active effects pedals, this was developed mainly for the use of guitarists. It is simply a band-pass filter on which you can alter the cut-off frequency by using the foot pedal. Originally the wah-wah pedal provided one of the few ways of changing timbre while playing. Now that keyboards are more versatile, this pedal has become largely redundant.

Distortion and fuzz

These signal processors boost the output level so that the signal clips, producing a square or rectangular wave. This form of distortion can sound pleasing, especially when an electronic organ is playing a simple, single-note melody.

Phasers

These devices change the phase relationships of different parts of a signal, to add and cancel out harmonics. The result is a rather lush swirling effect that can considerably enhance the sound being processed.

Delay and echo

These effects accept a signal and then play it back a short time later. Originally analog delay units were used. But these systems introduce a lot of noise and current quality delay units have digital circuitry. You can use delay units in several different ways. If you send some of the delayed output signal back to the input, you can create an echo effect. You control the period between each echo by setting the delay time, while the echo's delay rate is set by the amount of signal fed back to the input. If you send 100 percent of the signal back, the effect becomes a repeat of the original.

Chorus

Most delay line units have a built-in low-frequency oscillator. You can use this to vary the delay time continuously. By setting the initial delay time to around 1/40 sec and then varying the delay with the LFO you can produce a chorus effect. Separate chorus units are also available as pedals.

Flanging

This whoosing and whining effect can be achieved with a digital delay unit. You use the same method as for the chorus effect, with the addition of feedback (see p. 28).

Equalization

Equalization involves amplifying or attenuating an audio signal in various frequency bands. A graphic equalizer has several controls, usually sliders, each of which represents a fixed frequency band. When a control is in its mid position the signal is unaffected. Increasing the setting boosts any part of the sound that falls in the frequency band. The more bands that are covered, the more flexible the equalizer. The frequency bands of a graphic equalizer are fixed. An equalizer with variable frequency bands is called a parametric equalizer.

△ **Equalizer** This graphic equalizer is designed for use in a rack system.

△ **Delay** This digital delay unit features options for flanging and delay.

△ **Flanger** This pedal operated effects unit gives you a whoosing and whining sound.

△ **Chorus** This pedal gives a rich, full sound quality with control over both rate and depth.

△ **Noise gate** This pedal is useful for removing unwanted noise or hum from a signal.

Recording

Most people begin by playing live, but you may want to record what you play. This will not only enable you to keep a record of your music – you can also use the tape recorder creatively to build up songs track by track. The sounds offered by electronic keyboards lend themselves especially well to building up different tracks. In addition, if you have a rhythm unit – either built in to your instrument or as a separate add-on, you can provide a rhythm section on a separate track.

Over the last few years, tape recorder manufacturers have started to produce low-cost, semi-professional multi-track tape recorders that allow musicians to have their own studio at a fraction of the cost of a professional one. In fact you can now buy a good multi-track tape recorder for less than the cost of a good polyphonic synthesizer.

It was the Teac Portastudio 144, introduced in the late seventies, which showed that you could get good results from a cassette recorder. It features all the basic facilities that are required to build up a complete recording and it forms a compact, portable unit that set the trend for a generation of tape recorders.

Recording tape

Magnetic tape is at present the best material on which to record sound. This will remain true until electronic memories become far less expensive or until a whole new recording technology evolves. This tape is cheap, easy to work with, and gives good results if used correctly. (The compact disk provides an efficient high-fidelity sound-storage system, but the process of getting sounds on to the disk is too expensive for this to be a practical record-and-replay system.)

Magnetic recording tape consists simply of a thin plastic base coated with a layer of metal oxide. This metal oxide contains millions of magnetic particles or *dipoles*, which are like small magnets, each about a millionth of an inch long. A magnet exerts a magnetic field with north and south poles. A north pole attracts a south pole, while two north or two south poles will repel each other. On a blank tape, the dipoles are arranged in a random order and no magnetic field is exerted by any of the dipoles lining up. But sound can be stored on the tape by arranging the dipoles in a particular way. This is done by generating a magnetic field at the recording head of a tape machine. The dipoles respond to this field and are rearranged accordingly.

△ **Recording heads** Teac's Model 144 Portastudio features a dual-purpose four-track record and playback head (top) and a four-track erase head.

The tape recorder

The component that puts sound on to the magnetic tape is called the *recording head*. In a recording head, the coils of an electromagnet are wrapped around a specially shaped magnet. At one end there is a small gap where a very strong magnetic field is created. When you pass tape over this gap, the dipoles on the tape rearrange themselves in a way that corresponds to the current applied to the recording head – and this is how your sound is recorded.

To play the sound back, the tape recorder has a replay head. This is identical in design to the recording head. The realigned magnetic dipoles are passed over the gap and create a magnetic field. This induces a very small amount of electric current in the electromagnet's coil on the replay head and this signal has to be amplified to make the sound audible.

The third head in a tape recorder is the erase head. When you are making a recording, you want to be sure that all the dipoles on the tape are randomly arranged before you start aligning them, so the erase head restores this randomness (getting rid of any previous recording) before the tape passes to the recording head. The erase head is brought into play automatically whenever you are recording, so there is not normally any need to erase before you start taping.

Some tape recorders (including almost all cassette units) have only two heads. With these machines, the recording head doubles as the replay head. If you have a three-head machine and you listen to the replay head's output while recording, you will notice a short time delay between the live signal and the one being played back. This is because of the time it takes the tape to travel between the heads.

Tape-head designs

Originally, all tape recorders were monaural, the recording head was as wide as the tape, and any recording used up the tape's entire width. Soon savings were made by dividing the tape's width in two, so you could make two recordings on the same length of tape. Naturally the number of dipoles passing under the head was reduced. But with better equipment, the signal loss was hardly noticeable. One disadvantage of this half-track mono system was that it was impossible to edit one track by cutting up the tape without affecting what was on the other. The next development was to put two tracks side-by-side and use them for stereo recording to give a half-track stereo machine. Quarter-track stereo, allowing a stereo program to be recorded on both "sides" of the tape, followed this.

The most recent development is the eight-track recorder, which enables you to put down eight different parallel tracks on quarter-inch tape. This makes each track less than 1/32 in. wide, so to keep up quality the tape normally runs at 15 ins per second.

The Teac Portastudio and the cassette-based models that have followed it use four tracks. The Portastudio runs the tapes at $3\frac{3}{4}$ ins per second, though some four-track machines run at $1\frac{7}{8}$ ins per second and give surprisingly good results at this slow speed.

Getting the best out of your tape recorder

The more magnetic dipoles that pass under the tape recorder's head in a given amount of time, the better the sound quality is likely to be. More dipoles give the sound better resolution, in the same way that more lines on a TV give a better picture.

There are three ways in which you can make more dipoles pass under the head. You can increase the speed at which the tape travels; you can increase the width of the head itself; and you can use tape that has more dipoles on it in the first place. This is why cassette recorders designed for multitracking have higher tape speeds than those intended to form part of a regular hi-fi system, and why you will get better results if you use better quality tape.

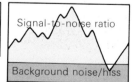

Signal-to-noise ratio

Background noise/hiss

△ **Setting levels** When recording, set the levels as close to zero as possible to make best use of the signal-to-noise ratio. At lower levels, there will be more noise in the recording.

Eliminating noise

All forms of magnetic tape produce the characteristic hissing sound called noise. Play back a blank tape and you will hear this clearly. The better the tape, the less hiss it will produce, but you will never eliminate it completely. A faster tape speed, top-quality tape, and a broad head will help, but there are other steps you can take to reduce it and improve the signal-to-noise ratio (see p. 133).

The most important thing is to record at the highest possible level. If you can keep the signal just below the maximum handling level of the tape, you will keep the noise to a minimum. But if you record your signal inefficiently by using a lower level, you will find that the noise level is too high.

Noise reduction

Other ways to improve the signal-to-noise ratio require the audio signal to be processed to make better use of the tape's dynamic range. The Dolby System takes the signal to be recorded, detects frequencies below a certain audio level and boosts the higher-frequency elements of the signal. On replay these signals are processed in reverse to restore the original format. When you are in replay mode, as the circuitry restores the audio signal to its original format, the background noise from the tape is also reduced in the damaging high-frequency area, improving the overall quality of the recording.

With dbx noise reduction the audio track is compressed so that loud sounds appear quieter and soft sounds louder than normal. When there is less variation in levels, the tape recorder can be used much more efficiently, since the recording levels do not have to be set to allow for wide variations in signal strength.

Using the bias oscillator

This provides an inaudible, very-high-frequency signal that is recorded along with your program signal. Its purpose is to make sure that the tape performs to its best level, and it acts to reduce noise and distortion while enhancing frequency response. Different types of tape require different bias settings, and most good quality recorders have switchable bias frequencies. Recording tape normally has the required setting printed on the label.

Cleaning your recorder

Another thing that affects the performance of a tape recorder is cleanliness. Today's tapes are very good, but even so, particles of loose oxide do get on to the recording heads, and it is vital to keep the heads clean at all times. Any oxide build-up will result in the tape not making proper contact with the heads, and there will be a loss of the high-frequency part of the signal.

You should use your manufacturer's recommended cleaning fluid to clean the heads. Apply this to the heads and capstans (not to the rubber roller), using a Q-tip. If the head is dirty, the Q-tip will look brown. When you have finished, dry the heads using a fresh Q-tip. Make sure they are properly dry before you start to record again.

If you think the rubber roller needs cleaning, you should use a Q-tip dipped in warm water, not in head-cleaning fluid.

Tape heads can also suffer from stray magnetic fields, which cause signal loss, especially over the high frequencies. To get the best results you should demagnetize the head occasionally. You can buy head demagnetizers for this purpose. Follow the instructions carefully, otherwise you may end up with a head that is more severely magnetized than when you started.

Head alignment

If your tape heads go out of alignment, the output levels may drop. To test this it is worth making a test tape when you first buy your recorder (the heads should be perfectly aligned). If you record a tone at a fixed level, you can play it back later to see if the level is the same. If you think the heads have gone out of alignment, you should consult your owner's manual. Sometimes you can realign the heads yourself, though often it is best to return the machine to your dealer for this.

Multi-tracking

If you have tried basic recording and enjoyed creating your own arrangements, it is worth considering buying a multi-track machine to give you a separate track for each line and setting up a small home studio. Most home recordists find that a cassette-based system is sufficient. But if you want to make tapes of broadcast quality, you will have to use reel-to-reel.

But whichever system you choose, being an electronic keyboard player gives you an important advantage – you don't have to go to the expense of setting up an acoustically engineered studio because most of the sounds you are using are electrically or electronically generated.

There are three essential elements in this type of home studio: a multi-track tape machine, a mixer (sometimes this is a built-in feature of the recorder), and a pair of speakers or headphones for monitoring. The mixer makes it much easier to monitor what has gone on to the tape when you are recording individual lines, and is vital when you want to make a stereo mixdown from the completed multi-track channels. A stereo tape recorder is also useful for making a final version of your music.

The multi-track machine

A multi-track tape recorder has four or more parallel channels that can be recorded one at a time or in groups. In a conventional, three-head tape recorder there are separate recording and play-back heads, making it impossible to monitor previously recorded tracks so that you can synchronize further material. In a multi-track machine recording

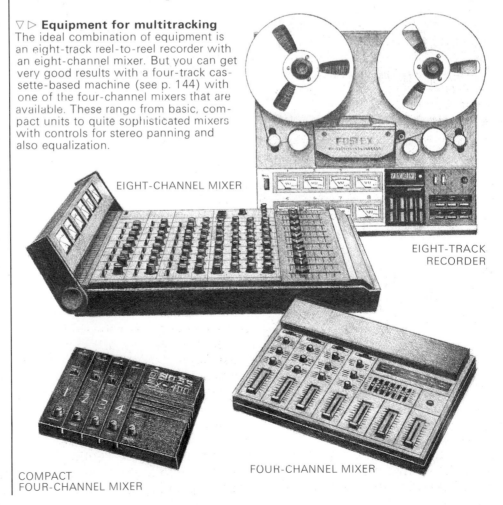

▽ ▷ **Equipment for multitracking**
The ideal combination of equipment is an eight-track reel-to-reel recorder with an eight-channel mixer. But you can get very good results with a four-track cassette-based machine (see p. 144) with one of the four-channel mixers that are available. These range from basic, compact units to quite sophisticated mixers with controls for stereo panning and also equalization.

EIGHT-CHANNEL MIXER

EIGHT-TRACK RECORDER

COMPACT FOUR-CHANNEL MIXER

FOUR-CHANNEL MIXER

and replay are done by the same head, so you can monitor whichever tracks you like, while recording on any others. This ensures that all the tracks are synchronized.

Making changes

The multi-track recorder is a very flexible machine to work with because you can keep re-recording the same track until you get it right. Another advantage is that if you make one mistake in the middle of a track, you can, in many cases, go straight to the middle of the piece and re-record one section.

This process is called dropping in. You do it by simply playing back the tape to a convenient point before the phrase you want to change and switching the machine to record mode. You can then play over the track that you weren't happy with before switching back to play mode at the next conveni-

ent break in the music.

It may take a while to get the timing exactly right, and if there are no convenient breaks in the music it may be impossible to drop in. But often this process can save you a lot of time.

Channel separation

For a "live" recording, you should place all the acoustic instruments as far apart as possible, so that the sound of each instrument is picked up only by the microphone it is intended for. If a microphone does pick up sound from an adjacent instrument you cannot mix out any particular signal completely. This could be a problem if you wanted to re-record part of a track.

If you are overdubbing one instrument at a time, there will be no acoustic spillage. But there may be another problem. Cassette recorders have very narrow tracks and the gaps

between them are narrower still. So there is a risk of a recording made on one track being picked up by the head of another track. This is known as *crosstalk*.

If you look at the specifications of a multi-track tape machine you will see that there is a figure for crosstalk characteristics. It is measured in decibels and quoted at a certain frequency, for example 60 dB at 1 kHz. This particular figure means that if you record a tone of 1 kHz on one channel you will hear one-thousandth of the signal from the adjacent channels. This is quite a good figure for a home recorder, but even this amount of crosstalk can pose problems.

Drums usually give the worst crosstalk. But if you are overdubbing you usually record these first, so you can make sure they are correct before moving on. It can help to keep the drums

---

Making a four-track recording

▽ **1 Rhythm** First record the rhythm track. Using one of the outer tracks of the tape should help you to keep this channel separate from the others by cutting down crosstalk.

◁ **2 Keyboard** You can use the next track of the tape to record the keyboard part, which can be made up of melody and chords as you wish.

◁ **3 Bass** Add the bass using keyboard, bass guitar, or any other suitable instrument. Do this while listening to the rhythm track, which you can play back through headphones using the monitor mix facility on the tape machine. Use the tape's second track.

◁ **4 Vocals** Finally, add the vocals. Try listening to the backing through one of the stereo headphones while listening to your own voice through the other ear.

5 Mixing Start with a static mix (see opposite) and then listen to each track in turn, making adjustments. Then try another mix with the adjustments incorporated, and keep remixing until you are satisfied.

on one of the outside tracks on the tape. If you do this the crosstalk can only affect one channel.

Click tracks

An often-used aid to putting together a recording is a *click track*. Originally this consisted of a metronome's steady beat and served as an acoustic guide to ensure that each track was in time. But with improvements in electronics, you can now use a click track as a synchronizing pulse for other electronic devices.

If you are using a rhythm unit and sequencers as a basis for your composition, work out the rhythm pattern first, and program the unit to provide a pulse output for every step of the pattern (see pp. 78-9). You can link the rhythm unit to the sequencer to provide a complete rhythm track and then record the sync pulses on one of the outside tracks of the multi-track tape. When you play back the click track, you feed it into the rhythm unit to trigger it and the sequencer in sync with the tape machine.

While monitoring your rhythm unit you can use the other tracks of the tape to record other instruments as normal. Only when you come to the mixdown stage do you actually record the output of the sequencer and rhythm unit – these go straight into the mixer and on to the master tape. This gives you greater sound flexibility and, if you are using a stereo rhythm unit and a sequencer driving a stereo instrument, it is equivalent to adding three extra tracks to your tape machine.

Bouncing

Multi-track recording is very like sound-on-sound (see below) except that you have a separate track for each line. It is best to start with the rhythm track, then add the other parts on to the tape's other three tracks, next mixing them down into a stereo image which you record on your two-track stereo recorder.

This will give a high-quality result, but you still only have four tracks. To get over this restriction you can use a technique called *bouncing*. You start

Mixing

This is the process of making a master stereo recording of all the tracks, with all the instruments correctly balanced and panned, and the desired effects and equalization applied. To make this master recording you have to take signals from the individual outputs of your recorder to a suitable mixer, with at least one channel per track, and then feed the output to a monitor amplifier and speakers and to a master tape recorder. This can be a long process, and you should take care to ensure you get exactly the result you want.

You should start by listening to a very rough *static mix* of the entire recording. This is a mix in which you do not adjust any of the levels during playback. Make notes as you go about how and when you want each track to come through, and then listen in

Using sound on sound

If you do not have a multi-track tape recorder, you can still build up a recording one track at a time. To do this you use a technique called *sound on sound*. You require two tape machines and a simple mixer. Alternatively you can use a single three-head tape recorder if it has a sound-on-sound facility.

The main problem with this

by recording three of the tracks and then mix these together and record the composite signal on track four. This frees the first three tracks for more instruments or vocals. If you repeat this process it is possible to add a further set of tracks. Any more bouncing may lead to an unacceptable amount of tape hiss. The main problem with this method is that you cannot individually change tracks once they have been combined and bounced – they are permanently grouped together.

turn to each track, adjusting its equalization, noting what effects you want to add, when to fade up and down the level of the signal, and if you want to pan.

When you know exactly what you want, try a *dynamic mix*. Record this on the master tape machine, then listen to it, again making notes of everything you do wrong. Then go back and try again, repeating the process until you are satisfied with the result. But do not spend very long periods of time repeatedly remixing – you will only cloud your judgment. If you are having problems, it is best to leave it for a while.

When you've got a good take, leave it again and listen to it the next day, when you will be more critical. If you're still satisfied, play it to a friend. If you do not feel the need to make excuses for technical faults at this stage, you have a successful mix.

method is that you cannot remix at the end. If the drums are too soft at the beginning you can't go back and turn them up. But it is an inexpensive system and a good way to start recording.

The first thing to do if you are using one tape machine is to record the rhythm track on to channel A. You should use a lead-in count that you can employ throughout the process.

The first track should include drums if you are using them, since it is almost impossible to put these on afterward. It is best to record this track with some extra treble, since the upper frequencies will suffer as you layer extra sounds on top. If you are satisfied with the recording and playing, move on. If not, repeat the process – you will not get another chance.

The second stage is to replay the first track into the mixer and add the next instrument or vocal, so that a balanced mix of both is fed into the input of channel B. When you are happy that you know what you are going to play, record this mixed signal on channel B.

You can now repeat the second stage, but this time use the combined recording on channel B with another source and record it on channel A. You will be recording over the initial rhythm track. For every step (or generation) of recording, more noise and distortion will be added and the early tracks will suffer as a result. But if you keep the levels as near to the maximum as possible, you should be able to record four tracks without too much difficulty. You use almost the same technique if you have two tape recorders, except that you are bouncing between tape machines rather than between tracks.

Microphones

Although you don't require microphones to record electronic instruments, you may want to add some acoustic sounds such as vocals, piano, or sound effects. Several types of microphone are available.

Dynamic microphones are sturdy, and not prone to distortion at high levels. They are excellent all-purpose microphones and are useful for any acoustic or amplified instrument. Their only drawback is their relatively poor frequency response at both ends of the audio spectrum.

Ribbon microphones (sometimes called *velocity microphones*) have a good low-frequency response and are especially useful for speech and for acoustic stringed instruments. Unfortunately they are rather fragile, susceptible to vibration, and have quite low signal-output strength. They are also quite costly.

Condenser microphones require their own power source. Their quality is superb, but their output is very low and a pre-amp is required to boost the signal, inevitably adding a little extra noise. In addition these microphones are very fragile and cannot handle signals that vary widely in amplitude. They are useful for acoustic guitars, drums, and vocals. *Electret microphones* are very similar to

▷ **Microphone types** For the keyboard player, a headset microphone (**1**) is useful – it allows you mobility while keeping your hands free. Superdirectional microphones (**3**) are selective, while omnidirectional types (**4**) enable you to cover a wide zone. Cardoid types (**2 and 5**) have a heart-shaped response area.

condenser types but they do not require their own separate power source.

Signal directions

Microphones also vary in their response to signals coming from different directions. It is especially important to be aware of this in a small studio, because you have to get the complete sound from each instrument, while keeping out as much extraneous sound as possible while you are recording.

Omnidirectional microphones will pick up sound coming from all directions. They are useful if you want to cover a wide area. *Bidirectional microphones* pick up sounds coming from the front and rear only. *Cardoid microphones* have a response shaped rather like a heart. They pick up sound from in front and some sound from the sides. *Superdirectional microphones* pick up only sounds that come from a very narrow area in front. You have to aim this type

of microphone directly at the source to get the best signal. This can be useful for detecting and isolating sounds from a long distance away. This is ideal when there is a lot of background noise.

▽ **Professional studio** London's Abbey Road studios are equipped with a 48 track Solid State Logic mixing desk. This is a modular system in which the number of tracks is governed by the number of input-output modules. Each module includes an impressive range of controls, and the whole mixing desk is computerized.

The MIDI system

It is very useful to be able to connect electronic musical instruments together. If you can combine a sequencer, a rhythm machine, and a keyboard so that they have certain common control settings you can use the set-up to produce complete electronic compositions very easily. You can program the melody and bass line into the sequencer, so that it plays back the data using the voice circuitry of the keyboard while synchronizing itself to the rhythm pattern from the drum machine.

Originally not all synthesizers, drum machines, and sequencers were compatible. Most used the relationship of one volt per octave for determining the pitch of the oscillators, but all sorts of different trigger pulses were used to fire the envelope generators and synchronization between rhythm units and sequencers usually worked only with products from the same company.

In 1982 many of the top companies met to discuss the formation of a new industry standard that would overcome this difficulty. The next year a final specification was agreed on. This is called the Musical Instrument Digital Interface, or MIDI.

MIDI connections

The MIDI connectors on instruments usually take the form of three 180° five-pin DIN sockets marked "MIDI in", "MIDI out", and "MIDI thru". Some instruments do not have the latter, and some others use XLR connectors, which are thought to be better for touring.

Five-pin plugs are used to connect these ports, though only three of the pins are actually used. The cable, which should be no longer than 50 feet (15 meters), should consist of a screened pair of twisted conductors. The screen should be connected to pin 2, and the conductors to pins 4 and 5. You can connect rhythm units, keyboards, and sequencers using MIDI in different combinations.

Linking keyboards

The simplest MIDI application is to connect two keyboards, feeding the MIDI output of one to the MIDI input of the other. This will give you a way of layering or coupling the sounds of two MIDI-equipped instruments. When you play a note or chord on the first keyboard, the same note or chord will sound on the second. If both keyboards are touch-sensitive both will respond to your touch in the same way. If you change the program number of the first instrument, the second will follow suit. But if you try to do the same on the second instrument, this will not happen – data can only be sent one way.

An expander unit is a valuable extra for use with your MIDI keyboard. This is a MIDI instrument with voice circuitry but no keyboard. You use it as an extra voice that you can layer on top of your keyboard's sound.

Linking drum machines

You can send MIDI data from a keyboard to a drum machine or vice versa. The former system allows you to trigger the drum machine's voices using the bottom octave of the keyboard. So if you have a touch-sensitive keyboard it is possible to play the drum voices dynamically. With some units you can program the dynamics of the drum pattern directly from the keyboard.

Sending data from a drum machine to a keyboard is only useful if the keyboard is equipped with a built-in sequencer or arpeggiator. In this case the tempo control of the rhythm unit will also determine the playback rate of the sequencer or the arpeggiator.

Linking a sequencer or computer

This is one of the most useful applications of MIDI. The system is usually connected up with the MIDI outputs and inputs used for both devices. You can play a sequence of notes and chords on the keyboard and this will be

▷△ **A MIDI system** This group of instruments — keyboards, drum machine, sequencer, and computer — shows the range and type of hardware you can connect together using the MIDI interface.

stored in the sequencer or computer memory. On playback the data is fed back into the instrument and the music recreated. You can use the sequencer to store many different playback settings, including those of performance controls and program data. You can adjust the tempo and play on top of the sequence.

Linking rhythm unit, keyboard, and sequencer

This combination enables you to synchronize a programmed rhythm track to a programmed sequence and play everything back at a tempo set by one unit – usually the rhythm unit. The MIDI link will also send start and stop data so you need only press one button to start the process.

MIDI commands

Commands transmitted along the MIDI line fall into two categories: channel commands and system commands. Most MIDI instruments can receive data along one of 16 different channels. So if you recorded a sequence on a sequencer and assigned it to channel 7, only an instrument set up to receive data on channel 7 would respond. These channel commands transmit note data and data relating to keyboard sensing.

System common commands are used for all units connected through the MIDI system and transmit information such as program selections. System real-time commands are used to send clock rates and start-stop information to all units in the system. System exclusive commands are used for particular manufacturer's products.

Wiring and soldering

Everyone involved in the use of electronic musical instruments has to deal with several different types of electrical energy. Each type requires different cords and connectors. The most common forms you will encounter are cords carrying AC power, and the different types of audio connections that link your instrument to its amplifier and the amplifier to the loudspeakers.

Soldering

In order to wire the plugs used for audio connections, you need to be able to solder. Solder is simply a metal alloy that melts when you heat it with a soldering iron. If you apply it to two metallic surfaces it will bond them together as it cools. The resulting joint is very efficient electrically. For soldering plugs an iron of 15 to 25 watts with a tip of 1/8 in. is usually sufficient.

The key to successful soldering is moderation. Do not use too much heat – just enough to melt the solder and get it flowing. Large blobs of solder usually make poor joints. Solder carefully, and if you are in doubt about a joint, solder it again.

Cords and connections

In many countries the power plug is pre-fitted and permanently attached to the cord. But if you need to fit a plug, be sure to follow the manufacturer's instructions carefully.

Cord for musical instruments is usually rated at 3 or 5 amps. In other words it is capable of carrying 3 to 5 amps of electrical energy. Occasionally, for items such as Leslie loudspeakers and early tone-wheel organs, a higher-rated cable is necessary.

Always use double-insulated cable and if a fuse is required, fit one of the correct value. (This will be specified in the owner's manual of your instrument.) Never use a fuse of a higher rating then the one recommended.

In countries that use power cords with only two wires you do not need to make an earth connection. But in the UK and many European countries the cord incorporates an earth wire. Consult your owner's manual if you are unsure how to make the connections.

Power adaptors

Battery-powered keyboards can often be used with an AC adaptor. This simply takes the higher voltage AC mains current and turns it into a smooth low-level DC voltage that corresponds to the voltage put out by the batteries.

There are several important things you should look for when choosing and using an adaptor. First of all, it must produce the correct voltage and its plug must fit your instrument. It must also have the correct polarity. The output plug can be either positively or negatively wired and it is important that this corresponds to the demands of your instrument. If you get the polarity the wrong way round this can cause serious damage.

The adaptor must be capable of producing enough current. An instrument needs a certain amount of power to run properly. You will find the correct current given in your owner's manual. If the manual states that your instrument draws 300 milliamps at 9 volts, then you require a 9 volt adaptor rated at 300 milliamps at least. Any value over 300 milliamps will be fine, but if the value is less you will probably hear a hum if you try to connect it to the instrument.

The adaptor should also produce a DC voltage that is smooth enough. Not all adaptors are produced specifically for audio equipment and on these adaptors the smoothness of the voltage is not as important. If there is any fluctuation or ripple in the DC output the instrument will produce an audible hum when you use it. So ensure that you use an adaptor that has a specification of at least ±3 millivolts minimum ripple.

As you can see, there are a lot of factors that can influence the quality of an adaptor. If you are in any doubt, you should choose the one recommended by the manufacturer of your keyboard. It may be more expensive than the one in your local electrical store, but it will function correctly.

Keyboard-to-amplifier connections

For most of these signals you should use a screened cord. This contains a central insulated conducting wire, which carries the signal. Around this is a screen made up of thin wires that can be either braided together or simply wrapped around the central core. The screen protects the low-level signal in the central wire from any noise, hum, or radio frequencies, and is connected to ground.

Jack plugs are the most common form of audio connector.

These are available in standard or smaller "mini" forms. The screened cord is soldered to the plugs to make a permanent and reliable connection.

RCA phono plugs, which cost less than jack plugs, are increasingly employed for equipment intended for use in the home, but jack plugs are better in situations where strength and reliability are important. Professional touring musicians use XLR connectors, which are even stronger.

Amplifier-to-speaker connections

Many amplifier-to-speaker connections employ jack plugs but screened cable is not suitable except for very low-level signals. Because the power produced by the amplifier is quite high, you need a good conducting cord to ensure that no signal is lost. Twin-core mains cord is often a good choice. This should be wired so that the tips and shields of both connectors correspond. You should never use loudspeaker cord in place of screened cord for connecting instruments to an amplifier.

Data connections

Control data is often transmitted via screened cords. This applies especially to trigger and control voltage information. But when using high-speed data communication systems such as the MIDI, you should take care that the cord you use is suitable. Twin-screened cord can be used for the MIDI system (see pp. 148-9). For other systems, you will usually find that special cord is supplied with the equipment.

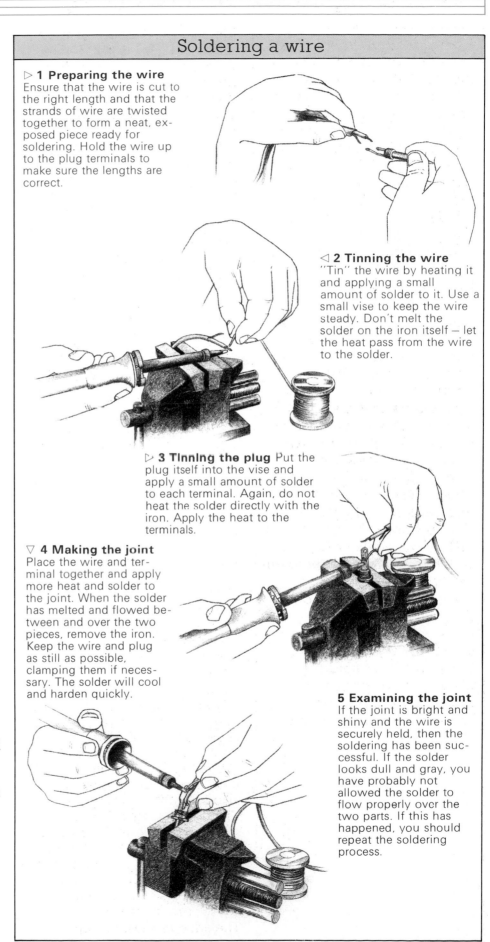

Soldering a wire

▷ **1 Preparing the wire**
Ensure that the wire is cut to the right length and that the strands of wire are twisted together to form a neat, exposed piece ready for soldering. Hold the wire up to the plug terminals to make sure the lengths are correct.

◁ **2 Tinning the wire**
"Tin" the wire by heating it and applying a small amount of solder to it. Use a small vise to keep the wire steady. Don't melt the solder on the iron itself — let the heat pass from the wire to the solder.

▷ **3 Tinning the plug** Put the plug itself into the vise and apply a small amount of solder to each terminal. Again, do not heat the solder directly with the iron. Apply the heat to the terminals.

▽ **4 Making the joint**
Place the wire and terminal together and apply more heat and solder to the joint. When the solder has melted and flowed between and over the two pieces, remove the iron. Keep the wire and plug as still as possible, clamping them if necessary. The solder will cool and harden quickly.

5 Examining the joint
If the joint is bright and shiny and the wire is securely held, then the soldering has been successful. If the solder looks dull and gray, you have probably not allowed the solder to flow properly over the two parts. If this has happened, you should repeat the soldering process.

GLOSSARY

Accent Emphasis put on a note or drum beat to make it stand out against the surrounding notes.

AD Attack-delay. A simple form of envelope generator.

Additive synthesis Creation of a waveform by adding together sine waves of different pitches and amplitudes.

ADSR Attack-decay-sustain-release. The most common type of envelope generator.

Algorithm In computing, a diagram representing a computer program. In FM synthesis, the order and shape in which the operators are arranged.

Amplitude The size of a signal. This usually corresponds to the volume.

Amplitude modulation The automatic control of one signal's amplitude by another signal.

Analog Continuously variable. An analog waveform in an electronic circuit corresponds to the actual changes in air density that the sound would make.

Analog sequencer Device, usually used in conjunction with modular synthesizers, that enables you to define two or three control voltages for each step of a sequence.

Aperiodic waveform Wave, such as an envelope, that does not repeat itself and that must be triggered every time it is required.

AR Attack-release. A simple envelope waveform.

Assignment Way in which data is sent to a particular voice module when a note is pressed on a synthesizer keyboard.

Attack The first phase of a control envelope. The time it takes for the envelope to rise from its initial level to its maximum level.

Auto correct Facility enabling the timing of a sequence or rhythm track to be automatically corrected to the nearest fraction of a beat.

Band-pass filter Filter that allows only those frequencies around the cut-off frequency to pass, attenuating those above or below this point.

Bandwidth The useful frequency response of a system. Generally used as part of an amplification specification.

BASIC The programming language used by most personal computers.

Bending Raising or lowering the pitch of a note.

Bit In computing, a single binary character that can exist as either ''0'' or ''1''.

Byte In computing, the equivalent of a word. It is made up of eight bits.

Carrier A waveform that is modulated by another signal. With Yamaha's FM synthesizers it is the waveform from the carrier operators that are actually heard.

Cartridge memory Plug-in electronic memory pack performing similar function to a cassette memory.

Cassette memory Facility that enables digital information to be stored on a standard audio cassette, so that you can keep a permanent record of programming data.

Center dente Mechanism that enables a pitchbender to be returned to its initial position after use. Without such a facility, it would be impossible to keep the instrument in tune.

Chorus Processing circuit that mixes an original signal with a continually varying delayed version of the same signal. This makes the sound seem fuller.

Click track Track used to synchronize various devices during recording.

Clock Rate that controls the playback speed of a sequencer or rhythm unit. In a complete system where sequencer, synthesizer, and rhythm unit are all synchronized together, everything should be related to a single clock rate.

Contour amount See Envelope amount.

Controller Device that gives you musical control over a synthesizer. The keyboard is the controller for most synthesizers.

Control voltage Signal used to alter a control element on a voltage-controlled device. For example, a voltage-controlled amplifier receives a control voltage from the envelope generator.

CPU Central processing unit. The heart of a computer microprocessor.

Cut-off frequency The frequency around which a filter operates.

DADSR Delay-attack-decay-sustain-release. Hybrid envelope generator, which waits for a certain period (the delay time) before producing the usual ADSR waveform.

Data Information

Decay The second stage in the ADSR envelope chain. It is the rate the envelope waveform takes to fall back from its maximum level to the sustain level. The decay rate only applies as long as the note remains held.

Decibel Ratio between the amplitudes of two signals. Abbreviated to dB.

Dedicated Specifically designed for a certain task.

Delay line Unit that accepts an audio signal and outputs the signal a period of time later.

Digital Represented in the form of a number, usually a binary number. Digital information can be manipulated by computers.

Digital sequencer Sequencer that accepts data from a controller and stores that data in a digital memory. The sequence can then be replayed to a synthesizer voice module.

Disk drive Memory storage device used with microcomputers that can be used to dump and load large amounts of digital information in a very short time.

Download To clear the memory bank of a computer-based instrument by feeding the information in its memory on to some external storage device. Downloading is also known as dumping.

Drift Unwanted wandering of a signal's voltage or pitch.

Dump See Download.

Duophonic Having two voice modules. An instrument with two voice modules can produce two notes at once.

Dynamic range The amplitude levels at which an instrument operates. A drum has a virtually infinite dynamic range, since its amplitude can be almost zero when hit gently and extremely loud when hit with severe force.

Dynamics The elements of a sound (usually amplitude and timbre) that change over the course of its duration.

Earth Point of zero potential in an electrical circuit. Any device that is connected to earth cannot become live. Also known as ground.

Echo The distinct repetition of an audio signal.

Edit To alter a programmed group of settings or values.

Emphasis See Feedback.

Envelope Modulating control voltage that can be used to change the timbre and amplitude of a tone while it is sounding. An envelope generator, when instructed to do so (usually by playing a note) produces an aperiodic waveform that can also be used to vary the pitch and pulse width of a signal. The most common type of envelope is the ADSR.

Envelope amount The amount of an envelope signal that is to be applied to modulate a specific control element.

Equalizer Complex tone control that enables the user to control accurately a sound's timbral balance. See also Graphic equalizer and Parametric equalizer.

Equal temperament Keyboard scaling system that divides the octave into 12 equal parts so that the ratio between two adjacent pitches is always the same.

Error correct Facility used with sequencers and rhythm machines that enables the notes fed into the device to be rounded up to the nearest fraction of a beat when entering rhythms or sequences in real time.

Feedback Sending the output of a particular circuit or device back to the input. Feedback can be used to introduce resonance to a filter circuit.

Filter Device that allows only certain frequencies of a signal to pass.

Flanging Effect achieved by introducing a controlled amount of feedback from the output of a delay line back to the input.

Floppy disk Small thin magnetic disk on which large amounts of information can be stored. In musical applications disks are generally used to hold programs, digital sampling data, and sequencing information.

FM synthesis Sound synthesis technique that relies on the waveform produced when one or more sinewaves (modulators) modulates another (the carrier).

Frequency modulation Automatic control of a waveform's frequency by another signal.

Fundamental The basic pitch of a note.

Gain Factor by which a signal is amplified. Gain is normally measured in decibels.

Gate Control signal indicating the time a note is held.

Glide Continuous transition of a note's pitch from a certain fixed value to that at which the note is supposed to sound.

Glissando Transition between one note and another in distinct steps.

Graphic equalizer Hybrid tone control that enables individual frequency bands to be amplified or attenuated.

Ground See Earth.

Hardware The physical equipment (the circuitry, keyboard, etc) used to make a sound.

Harmonics Pitches that are simple multiples of the fundamental frequency. Most sounds are made up of the relative harmonics above it.

Hertz The unit of frequency. One Hertz represents one cycle per second. The unit is abbreviated to Hz.

High-note priority In a voice-assignable instrument, this means that if more notes are played and held than there are voices, the highest pitched notes will be the ones to sound.

High-pass filter Filter that attenuates all frequencies below the cut-off frequency.

Incrementor Multi-purpose control used on some programmable polyphonic synthesizers.

Interface Circuitry that has to be connected between certain devices before they can be connected together.

Interval The musical gap between two pitches.

Joystick Performance control in the form of a movable lever.

Just intonation Keyboard scaling system that divides the octave into twelve unequal steps.

Keyboard priority System that determines which notes sound on a synthesizer when more notes are played than there are voices.

Last-note priority In a voice-assignable instrument, this means that if more notes are played than there are voices, the last ones played will be the ones to sound.

Layering Combining sounds so that pressing a single key introduces two or more distinct sounds to be played on top of one another.

LCD Liquid-crystal display. Visual indicator that can be used to show complex information, such as words, and that is usually black on a gray-green background.

LED Light-emitting diode. Visual indicator, usually red in color.

LFO Low-frequency oscillator. This is used as a modulation source.

Low-note priority In a voice-assignable instrument, this means that if more notes are played than there are voices, the lowest pitched notes will be the ones to sound.

Low-pass filter Filter that attenuates all frequencies above the cut-off frequency.

Memory Circuitry used to store information.

Memory protect Switch that prevents accidental erasure of data stored in a memory.

MIDI Musical instrument digital interface. The most recent industry standard for connecting various computer-based electronic musical instruments.

Mixer Circuit that enables various signals to be combined in different amounts to form a single composite signal.

Modifier Device that acts on a signal and changes its character.

Modular Made of separate, interchangeable units.

Modulation The act of applying a control signal to an audio signal or to another control signal, to change its character.

Module Device that forms part of a modular system. See also Voice module.

Monitor In music, good-quality loudspeaker used while mixing and recording. In computing, a visual-display screen connected to a computer.

Monophonic Capable of producing only one independent note at a time.

Multiple trigger System that produces a pulse every time a new note is played.

Negative feedback Sending an inverted portion of an output signal back to the input. Because it is inverted, the signal damps the resulting output.

Noise generator Circuit that produces a random combination of all frequencies in the audio spectrum, producing a hissing sound with no pitch.

Non-volatile memory Circuitry that stores information even when the power has been turned off.

One-shot Single event, such as the firing of an envelope generator.

Operator In FM synthesizers, the voice element that corresponds to a combination of voltage-controlled sine wave generator, envelope generator, and voltage-controlled amplifier.

Oscillator Circuit that generates a constantly repeating waveform. The rate at which it repeats determines the output's pitch.

Overtones Pure tones that form part of the make-up of a sound, but, unlike harmonics, are not simple multiples of the fundamental.

Parametric equalizer Complex tone control that enables two or three frequency bands to be amplified or attenuated. Unlike a graphic equalizer, this type allows the frequencies and spans of these bands to be varied.

Patch The way in which the elements of a synthesizer (such as the VCO, VCF, and VCA) are connected together.

Patch cords Connecting cables used to link the parts of a modular synthesizer.

Performance controls Conveniently located control mechanisms used to vary certain elements of a sound during performance.

Periodic waveform Wave that continuously repeats itself, and therefore has pitch.

Phase The point in its cycle that a periodic waveform has reached at a particular time.

Phase locked At the same point in a cycle. Two waveforms that reach the same point at the same time are said to be phase locked together.

Phaser Signal processor consisting of a filter that introduces a slow cyclic mellow change to the character of a sound.

Pink noise Noise signal that has been biased so that it contains equal amounts of signal over each octave of the audio spectrum.

Pitchbend See Bending.

Pitch-to-voltage converter Device that produces a voltage proportional to the frequency of the signal applied to it.

Polyphonic Instrument that has more than one voice and so can play more than one note at a time.

Port Input or output socket used to make connections between one device and another.

Portamento Smooth transition of the frequency of a voice between notes.

Positive feedback Sending a portion of the output signal of a device back to the input. This tends to reinforce the signal.

Potentiometer Rotary control.

Preset Value that has been set at an instrument's design stage and therefore cannot be varied. Electronic musical instruments often have preset voicings.

Pressure sensitivity The ability of certain keyboards to respond to the amount of pressure you give in performance. The application of further pressure can be used to introduce an extra degree of control over the sound.

Programmable Allowing the construction of user-defined sounds.

Pulse wave Periodic waveform produced by an oscillator that exists in alternate high and low states.

Pulse width The ratio of the periods that a pulse wave spends in its high and low states.

Pulse-width modulation Varying the pulse width by means of a control signal.

RAM Random access memory. A memory system in which you can store your own sounds.

RAM pack Cartridge, containing a RAM, which plugs directly into an instrument or computer.

Ramp wave Periodic waveform that rises or falls to a certain level before being instantly reset to its original level. A ramp wave has a characteristic brassy timbre.

Real time Method of programming sequencers and rhythm units to give the exact timings required in performance. For example, to program a rhythm unit in real time you play it like a drum kit. It will then replay the data fed to it as it was played.

155

Release The final stage of an ADSR envelope. The time it takes for the envelope to die away and return to its initial minimum position after the note has been released.

Ribbon cable Flat, multistranded cable, usually color-coded, used to send data in parallel between two pieces of digital equipment.

Ribbon control Performance control device that makes the pitch of a note rise or fall depending where on the ribbon you touch your finger.

Roll-off The rate at which a filter attenuates frequencies on either side of its cut-off frequency.

ROM Read-only memory. Memory device with contents that are preprogrammed at the manufacturing stage. You cannot write your own information into a ROM.

ROM pack Plug-in cartridge used to send control data to an instrument or computer.

Sampling keyboard Instrument that can "record" any sound fed to it and then reproduce that sound at any pitch over the complete range of the musical keyboard.

Sequencer Device that can memorize and play back a predetermined string of pitch, voltage, and timing information. This information can be sent to an instrument which will then be played automatically.

Sine wave A smooth, continually varying waveform that contains no overtones or harmonics. This is the basic tone in sound synthesis.

Software Set of instructions, or program, used to tell a computer or microprocessor what to do with the information presented to it.

Split keyboard Single keyboard that can be divided in two, allowing different sounds to be assigned to either end.

Square wave Periodic waveform that exists in alternate high and low states. Unlike a pulse wave, it exists in its high and low states for equal periods of time.

Static filter Filter with characteristics that are set only by the control panel. It is not possible to modulate a static filter.

Step time The division of timing events into equal lengths. Step time is often used to program rhythm units and sequencers. To play notes of different durations, it is necessary to assign the required number of steps for each note.

Sub-audio Frequency that falls below the threshold of human hearing.

Subtractive synthesis Method of sound synthesis in which oscillators produce a harmonically rich waveform, and the required sound is produced by removing the unwanted frequencies by filtering. This is the most common method of sound synthesis.

Sustain The third phase of an ADSR envelope. The level the envelope maintains while the note is held.

Touch sensitive Responsive to touch. This term is used to describe keyboards that respond to the way they are pressed during performance.

Triangle wave Periodic waveform that rises at a constant rate and then falls at the same rate.

Trigger One-shot waveform that indicates when a note has been played.

VCA Voltage-controlled amplifier. Device that determines the gain or attenuation of the signal applied to it. The more voltage applied, the greater the gain.

VCF Voltage-controlled filter. Device that determines the timbre of a sound. The voltage applied to the VCF governs the value of the filter's cut-off frequency.

VCO Voltage-controlled oscillator. Device that produces a note of a defined pitch. The greater the voltage applied the higher the pitch of the note.

VDU Visual display unit. Screen used in conjunction with a computer to display information.

Voice module Complete set of circuits in a synthesizer used to produce a sound. In subtractive synthesis a simple voice module can consist of VCO, VCF, VCA, and envelope generator.

Volatile memory Memory system that requires power for the contents to be retained. When the power is switched off the data is lost.

Voltage control The basic principle used in subtractive synthesis. The various circuit elements control one another by voltages.

White noise Random combination of all frequencies throughout the audio spectrum.

INDEX

ACKNOWLEDGMENTS

Dorling Kindersley Limited would like to thank Debbie Rhodes and Steve Wilson for additional design work, Angela Murphy for picture research, and the following individuals and organizations for their help in preparing this book: Hilary and Richard Bird, Martin Brady, Vic Chambers, Paul Colbert, Andy Ferguson, Fred and Cathy Gill, Nancy at Cracks 90, Ann Osborne, Frances Palmer at the Horniman Museum, Tony Wallace. Casio (UK) Ltd, Fostex Corporation, Keyboard Hire, Moog Music (UK) Ltd, National Panasonic (UK) Ltd, Oxford Synthesizer Co, Roland (UK) Ltd, Rose Morris Co, Sequential Circuits Inc, Syco Systems, Tickle Them Ivories, Yamaha (UK) Ltd, Terminal Studios.

David Crombie would like to thank Howard Brain and Gary Masters (Chromatix Ealing), Brian Nunney, Fred Mead (Roland (UK) Ltd), Martin Brady (Casio Electronics Company Ltd), David Seville, Mike Ketley, Gerry Uwins (Yamaha-Kemble Ltd), John Dixon (National Panasonic (UK) Ltd), Tim Oakes (Sequential Circuits Inc Europe), Doug Ellis (Rosetti Ltd), Rob Castle (Rose Morris Ltd), Chris Huggett (Oxford Synthesizer Company), David Caulfield, Gwen Alexander (Alexander Caulfield PR), Tim Salthouse (Tradewinds Promotions), Tony Bacon (*1, 2, Testing* Magazine), Mike Beecher (Electro-Music Research), Sarah Thurley (Charing Cross Hospital), David Sinclair, Jill Sinclair, Paul Henderson, Peter Lavender, Dene Sinclair.

Reproduction by F. E. Burman Limited, London
Typesetting by Chambers Wallace Limited, London

Photographic credits
B=bottom, C=center, L=left, R=right, T=top
2 Martin Dohrn
5 Cracks 90
6 Michael Brown (BL), BBC/LFI (BC)
6-7 Peter Mazel/LFI
7 Sam Emerson/LFI (T), Arnold Williams (B)
8 The Bettman Archive
9 SKR Photos/LFI
10 SKR Photos/LFI (T), Frank Griffin/LFI (B)
11 Michael Putland/LFI
12 Gary Merrin/LFI
13 Paul Cox/LFI (T), Paul Canty/LFI (B)
14 Peter Mazel/LFI (T), Gary Merrin/LFI (B)
15-16 Arnold Williams/LFI
17 Michael Putland/LFI
18 Paul Canty/LFI
19 SKR Photos/LFI
20 Photo-Selection/LFI (T), Paul Cox/LFI (B)
21 Paul Cox/LFI (T), Adrian Boot/LFI (B)
22 Paul Cox/LFI (T), Arnold Williams (B)
23 Syco Systems
33 Sequential Circuits/Syco Systems
34 The Horniman Museum and Library
36 Martin Dohrn
38 Adrian Boot/LFI
40 Hammond Organs
41 SKR Photos/LFI (T), Chris Walter/LFI (B)
42-3 Technics/Lippa, Newton, Nokes
46 SKR Photos/LFI
49 Moog
50-57 Martin Dohrn
58-9 Tony Hutchings
60 Oxford Synthesizer Company (T), Roland (UK) Ltd (TL, B), Korg (BL)
62-3 Roland (UK) Ltd
64-5 Yamaha
67 Syco Systems/Zefa Picture Library (T)
68-9 Andrew Catlin (T), Syco Systems/Zefa Picture Library (B)
72 Roland (UK) Ltd
73 Roland (UK) Ltd (T, R), Sequential Circuits (BL)
74-5 Casio
75 Tony Hutchings (T)
76 Tony Huthchings
77 Yamaha (T), Tony Hutchings (B)
78 Syco Systems/Zefa Picture Library (T), Simmons (B)
79 Roland (UK) Ltd/Turnkey
81 Martin Dohrn
82 Paul Cox/LFI
83 Adrian Boot/LFI
89 Peter Mazel/LFI
90 Barry Wentzel/LFI (T), Roland (UK) Ltd (B)
91 Miles Copeland/LFI
101 David Redfern
102 John Bellissimo/LFI
107 Frank Griffin/LFI (TL), Sam Emerson/LFI (C)
108 David Redfern (T), LFI (B)
109-15 Martin Dohrn
116 John Bellissimo/LFI
117-20 Martin Dohrn
120 Adrian Boot/LFI (T)
121-3 Martin Dohrn
131 Matthew Turner (T), HH Electronics (BR), Deanvard (BC), Roland (UK) Ltd (BL)
132 SKR Photos/LFI
134 Matthew Turner
135 HH Electronics
140 Roland (UK) Ltd (L), Matthew Turner (R)
146 AKG
147 Abbey Road Studios
148-9 Sequential Circuits
Front Cover Trevor Melton
Back cover Arnold Williams/LFI (L), Roland (UK) Ltd (TR), Martin Dohrn (BR)